5-5-85

60

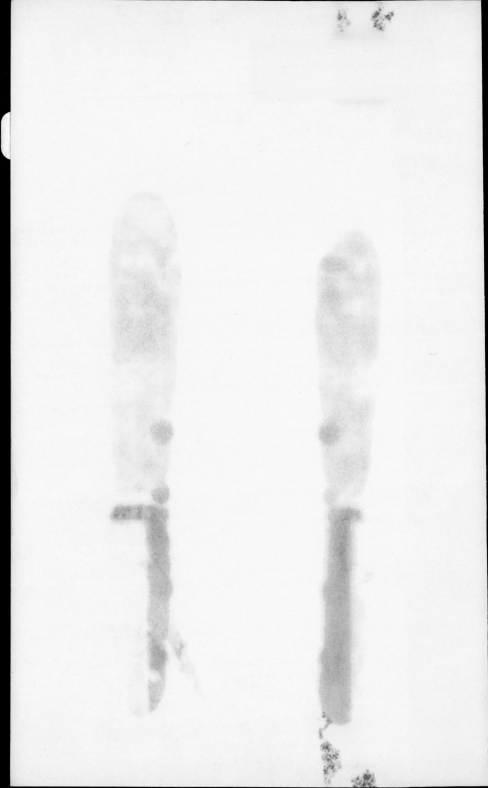

Direct Decision Therapy

Other books by the author:

THE ELEGANT PROSTITUTE (formerly THE CALL
 GIRL)
THE SEX-LIFE LETTERS (co-editor)
ACTIVE PSYCHOTHERAPY
GREAT CASES IN PSYCHOANALYSIS
THE PROSTITUTE IN LITERATURE (co-editor with
 A. Krich)
EMOTIONAL MATURITY IN LOVE AND
 MARRIAGE (with Lucy Freeman)

Direct Decision Therapy

by

HAROLD GREENWALD

EdITS, *Publisher*
San Diego, California 92107

Direct Decision Therapy

LIBRARY OF CONGRESS CATALOG CARD NUMBER: 73-75565
MANUFACTURED IN THE UNITED STATES OF AMERICA

CONTENTS

To Robert and Nancy,
David and Wendy

A man's character is formed by his decisions.

—Sartre

Section I

For in every act of love and will—and in the long run.they are both present in each genuine act—we both mold ourself and our world simultaneously.

—Rollo May

What I have attempted to do in this book is write about an approach to psychotherapy which is also a philosophy of life. Many of us are probably dubious about books on psychotherapy or philosophy because of the cumbersome style in which many such books are written.

Since one of my goals in writing this book has been the demystification of psychotherapy, I have chosen to write it in the same intimate personal style which I try to use in communicating with my students and clients.

CHAPTER 1

WHAT DIRECT DECISION THERAPY IS

THIS book is about the role of decision in psychotherapy and in life in general. When I first started working with the ideas in this book, I thought I had found an effective approach to psychotherapy. As I continued to work with these ideas and to speak about them to various groups of professionals and nonprofessionals, I became aware that I was also dealing with a philosophy of living, with a way of being in the world. The name I have chosen for this approach is Direct Decision Therapy.

I was close to forty when I discovered I was a failure. I had a job working at a resort hotel, and was supposedly in charge of building a golf course. I was supervising a group of partially dried-out alcoholics. A man I knew came up to me. I don't know what his real name was, but everyone called him "Mike the Plumber." Mike and I had been talking for a while when he asked: "How old are you?" I said I was in my late thirties and he demanded, "When are you going to do something, when will you get yours?"

At that point I realized that in many ways I was a failure. I was aware that I had many abilities and a high I. Q.; I was married to a remarkable wife, and had two great children. Many things were O.K. Except that I had had so many awful jobs—more than sixty of them —that some of the anger and annoyance and disgust with myself about my jobs had spilled over and affected my family feelings.

Then and there, speaking to Mike the Plumber, I had a moment of realization. I said to myself, "I'm going to do something."

Within one month, I had the best job I'd ever had: I had become an executive in a good-sized manufacturing company, and within two years as a result of reading a book by Theodor Reik about his being a psychoanalyst and not being a physician—I had also decided to become a psychologist. That was the big decision I made.

The payoff has been quite remarkable. A few years after that conversation with Mike the Plumber, I found myself with a Ph.D. and a full psychoanalytic practice. I wrote a book, based in part on my doctoral dissertation, which sold about a million copies and was made into a movie. I was being invited to speak about my work, and I had a very different feeling about myself. My modicum of success, having come so late in life, has been all the sweeter. So that for me the payoff of decisions is neither an abstract idea or something I use only for patients, but something I know very well from my own experience, my own life.

I would like to tell you how I came to formulate

Direct Decision Therapy. After having been a therapist for about twenty years, I was invited to Norway as a Guest Professor for a year. While I was in Norway, I was asked to prepare a seminar for psychologists and psychiatrists from various parts of the country. During the seminar I covered various therapies now being practiced: active psychoanalytic psychotherapy, hypnotherapy, behavior modification, and rational-emotive therapy. At the end of two days of lecturing, I was supposed to present a summary of the whole thing. During the seminar I also did demonstrations with different persons to illustrate the four techniques I had covered. When I came to summarize, it suddenly became clear to me that everything I had been doing in all those cases with people I had been treating could be explained in one way: I was helping these people to *make a decision to change.* That's how I presented the summary. That is, I expressed the view that the only thing that happens in therapy—regardless of the methods or techniques used—is that the person you're working with is helped to make a *decision to change,* and then is helped to carry out the decision. As will be seen later in this book, even the most difficult problems— homosexuality, addiction to drugs, and various forms of compulsive or destructive behavior—respond remarkably favorably to this kind of therapy, once a *wish* to change has led to a *decision* to change.

I had been teaching therapists and lecturing about psychotherapy for at least eighteen years, and every once in a great while someone would come up and say, "You know, I once heard you explain something that I found helpful with one of my patients. After I got through with the seminar and my summary on decision in Norway, I had a whole new experience. Eight out of the forty people attending came up to me and remarked, "What you said about decisions helped me with my *personal* problem." These were all people who had had psychoanalysis or psychotherapy, people who had already had a therapeutic experience. Obviously, with that kind of feedback, I wasn't going to let the idea go, so I began to develop the entire area of personal decision-making. Since then, I have had similar experiences in various parts of the world whenever I have spoken on the subject.

While I am organizing it as therapy, I'm really talking about more than therapy as practiced in an office, because this is something that many people can apply for themselves, and I think that people reading this book will have a chance to *use* some of the insights I will share here. You might consider yourself the patient as I describe the method. Whether you're a professional or not, the best way to learn therapy is to go through the therapeutic experience yourself. The most valuable part of my training was my own psychoanalysis. If you want to use Direct Decision Therapy, it would be useful to apply it to yourself as you read about it.

One of the steps I took in developing Direct Decision Therapy was to review my experiences with patients, and I saw how many times the crucial event that had happened was that they had made a decision. Then I came across a book called *Decision Making*, which really deals with decision-making as applied to economics. This was also helpful in my thinking.

I don't think anybody's theory can be fully appreciated without seeing a relationship to his personal life. If you cannot apply it to your own life, what good is it? Obviously, a lot of my own experiences influenced my theory and I am therefore including an autobiographical section which may help explain why Decision Theory is so compatible and so sympathetic to me. This is not to say that I am so good at decisions. If I were, I probably would never have thought of the entire theory.

In any therapeutic approach, I try to remember certain things. One, which has almost been talked to death, is to be authentic, to be myself. I would like to define this a little more operationally than it usually is: that is, as a therapist, I should try to be the same as I am in my nonprofessional life. I'll tell you a story about how I did that in one aspect of my life and how that has been very useful to me ever since. I've been a public speaker since I was four years old, when I was pushed onto a soap box in Brooklyn and made a speech before an adult audience all about World War I. Later I won medals for public speaking in elementary school, high school and community centers. At college I was on the debating team. One of the ways that helped me to make the transition to becoming a psychologist was a job I had lecturing about psychology to the guests at the same hotel (the Concord in Kiamesha Lake, N.Y.) where I had formerly worked on the golf course.

One time, after I had finished speaking at the hotel, and was on my way home, a friend who was driving back with me asked me some questions about my lecture, and when I got through answering them, he said, "Why don't you talk as simply as this when you talk to an audience?"

I said, "It has to be larger than life; you have to get their attention." But then I thought about it and made

a decision to try it: I would speak to any audience the
way I speak to anybody else in ordinary conversation.
I really had to work at it. It was much easier to go off
into oratory.

Well, it's hard work, if you are a therapist, to speak
in an informal way. You have the mantle on you, and
you think you have to carry a lot of things with you, but
authenticity pays off. For me, that is one of the most
important preconditions to successful therapy.

The other one is empathy. Achieving empathy takes
a certain amount of effort. When I first meet a person
who has come to me for help, I try to forget everything
I know about psychology. That was very difficult at the
beginning, when I didn't know very much. It's much
easier now, when I think I know a lot. I try to look at
the person, try to look at the problem, in a completely
new and different way. I try to forget everything I
know about neurosis, psychosis, transference and dynamics. I ask myself, "What's this person telling me?"
As far as possible, I try to see what he is telling me
through his own eyes; I try to put myself in his place.

If a therapist doesn't like people and doesn't have
some feeling about them, no matter how awful they
seem to be, he is not in the right field. There's not
enough money in psychotherapy to make it worthwhile
unless he can get gratification from it. Maybe it's a wish
for power, maybe it's compassion. Whatever it is, if one
is not really committed to the people one works with,
if one doesn't get a good feeling out of doing something
helpful for them, it's better not to be a therapist, because it can become too difficult, too painful and boring.

The first question I ask a person who comes to see me
is, "What's your problem?" You can ask yourself right
now—"What problem do I have?"

Get that stated as clearly as possible. One of the problems today is that people don't describe a problem as they experience it, but rather as it has been defined *for* them. "I am very self-destructive; I can't find meaning in life; I want to actualize myself; I want to be more authentic."

I remember asking a young woman who told me all these things, "What do you really mean? What do you really want?"

She answered, "I'd like to find a husband." She had explained her inability to find one when she used those general terms, but it's necessary to define the problem as specifically as possible in order to find out what kind of help is wanted.

There are, in a sense, two kinds of problems. Of course there are many more, but let's divide them into two simple categories. One is a very specific situational problem : "I have an unhappy marriage." "I have a fear of heights." "I am anxious when I speak in public." These are very specific problems. More frequently, a professional therapist sees people whose problems have been called "characterological:" "I am unhappy." "I can't be assertive." "I am very passive in many situations." Their problems become, not specific symptoms, but their whole way of being in the world.

One of the most common problems I get is the one Thoreau described so perceptively when he said, "The mass of men lead lives of quiet desperation." A lot of the people I work with are trapped in unhappy, bitter marriages; terrible jobs they hate; wearing themselves out with imaginary illnesses which are not experienced as imaginary—these kinds of long-continuing problems. The insight that I have found extremely valuable is to look upon all of these problems as choices and to ask myself, "Is this the person's choice?" To me, it is extremely important not to start with a prejudgment of the situation.

If a person is depressed or angry all the time, this is either the way he chooses to be or is the result of decisions he has made. And so after he presents the problem, I search for the past decision which is behind the present problem.

Let me give you some examples of what I call "life choices" or "life decisions." There are many people whose decision at some point was that they were going to be perfect; that they would do everything in such a way as to be absolutely perfect without any errors. Others have made the decision to be so accommodating, so kind, so good, so non-threatening, so agreeable, that the whole world will love them. I have a friend who, every time I wanted to have lunch with her or talk with her, told me, "I can't. I gotta go visit Joe in the hospital," or, "I gotta buy a present for Lee," or, "I gotta run an errand for Fred." She was always so busy doing things for people that a friend, a comedienne, once said to her, "Listen, one more present and you're going to get it right in the teeth. I'm sick and tired of your presents." This woman had made a decision to be loved by everybody.

Then there are those who make the decision to be "different." They study how the rest of the world is, and act in the opposite way. If everyone has short hair, they have long hair; and if everyone has long hair, they have short hair. I had an uncle like that. In the labor unions in the 1920's there was a fierce struggle between the right wing and the left wing. While the right wing was in power, he was an ardent leftist. Then the left wing took control of his particular union and he became a rightist. He joined a temple in order to fight against the administration there, even though he didn't believe in religion. As soon as he led a group out of that place, he immediately went on the outs with his followers. His decision was to be different, to be in constant and total rebellion. Many people make that kind of choice—to be different, to call attention to themselves, to be conspicuous.

Then there are people who have made the decision to suffer. They have the capacity, like many mothers, to snatch disaster out of every victory. Every event can be turned into a catastrophe, and they know how.

Another type (I owe this term to someone at a seminar where I was working) I call the "silent gotchas." These are people whom professionals call "passive-aggressive." They try to do everything pleasantly and never disagree until they've "gotcha." Maybe that sounds a little implausible, so I'll give an example. I was working with one of the brightest psychologists I've ever known. He was in graduate school, and he was at the difficult stage of having completed all his degree work except for writing his dissertation. Several years had passed, and we talked about the way he was putting off this final task. He explained that his father and mother wanted him to get his Ph.D., his wife wanted him to get it and even his girl friend would sometimes ask, "When am I going to be able to call you doctor?"

Then he got me involved, too. At first I would respond with, "Well, it's up to you." But then he started bringing in his research proposals to me. I would make some suggestions, and then he would make it all more complicated. Months passed and he couldn't get his proposal accepted by his faculty committee. One day he came to me and said, "Well, I'll never be able to get a doctorate at this university. If I want one, I'll have to start all over again." And then, to my astonishment, he smiled triumphantly, because he had "got" me. He was willing to sacrifice everything to "get" everybody through his failure, his defeat. This is the kind of self-defeating behavior to which a lot of people dedicate their lives.

What I'm describing are different kinds of life decisions that people make, different ways of operating. These are some of the ones that cause problems. There are, of course, other decisions which are valuable, like the decision a person makes to be assertive; to be kind; to be cooperative; to improve the world.

I was talking to a young man recently whom I have known for many years. It used to be very difficult to speak with him because whatever the subject of the discussion, he would smile in a superior way and nod his head and tell you how much more he knew about it than you did. Recently I discovered I could talk to him. Now he is interested, asks me questions and wants to know my opinion. The change was so noticeable that I commented on it, and asked him, "How did it happen?" And he remembered making the decision when he was working on a project with his wife. No matter what he said, she wouldn't listen to him. She knew another way to do it, or she knew why it wouldn't work. At that point he realized how similar this was to the way he had been operating. Once he realized that, he said to himself, "That's stupid," and he started to listen to others. The result was that a number of very nice things began to happen to him; the payoff was favorable.

One of the most important things in working with people is to find out the context in which the former decision was made—the decision that is now causing trouble, the one that is no longer functional. I have found that if I really understand the context in which that decision was made, no decision is completely stupid or irrational. That's why it's very helpful for me to get into the mind of the other person, so I can figure it out, how he made his decision, no matter how bizarre it may appear to me.

Let me give you an example. A young man refuses to do any work. He goes to school, but doesn't do any of the necessary work. He drops out and gets a job. When someone tells him to do something, he says, "You can take this job and shove it." He absolutely refuses to do anything.

This is obviously not a functional decision. It's not helpful to him. I try to find out the context. I'll ask him, "When did you start doing this?" I'll try to find out how he got into this pattern of behavior; how did he come to make the decision to refuse to do what is expected of him? I discover that when he was a child and was asked to do anything, he used to be eager to comply and was happy to be given a chore to do, but he remembers that he never could do it right. Whatever he did, it seemed to him that all he got was criticism, and—what's even harder for a child to take—he was made fun of, laughed at: "Look how he brings that milk bottle. Did you ever see anyone bringing the milk bottle that way? He's a real loser."

Remarks of this kind and sometimes anger and punishment followed his acts. When he would undertake something, he found he could never carry it through as well as his perfectionist parents and the rest of his family demanded. Well—sensibly enough, given that context—he made the decision never to attempt anything. Because if he didn't do anything, he couldn't be criticized or laughed at. Within the context of his life, that seemed like a rational decision, an appropriate response.

A man comes to me and complains that he cannot be close to anyone. He feels that there's a wall, or, as he sometimes describes it, he feels there is a "pane of glass between me and other people, and I can see them but I can't feel any direct contact." He tells me that he finds this very painful. So I ask, "Is it possible that this is your choice?" He thinks about it and says, "Yes, I was very close to my mother. I loved her. I had a wonderful time. When I was four years old, she left. Somebody said, 'Oh, she went out for a walk.' But she never came back. She had gone to the hospital and died. And then there was a whole series of relatives I was farmed out to. I made up my mind. No more: I'll never be close again." At that early age he could remember making up his mind, "No more, never again will I let myself get so close to somebody and experience that pain again." That's not an unusual cause with people who have problems with closeness.

Another way I find out the context of a decision is to ask when somebody complains about something, "What's the advantage; what's the payoff?" For instance, a woman complains that she's very depressed. Here the therapist must probe gently, because if he questions the person in a disapproving way, what he's saying is, "You're a faker."

That is not so. She is really suffering. So say, "Look,

I know you're suffering, but is it possible that there's some payoff for this suffering, some advantage? Have you ever thought of the possible advantage?" After discussion, this woman was able to see that her depression was a self-defeating expression of a loneliness she was able to take decisive measures to correct.

Frequently the depression will lift immediately if I have simply asked the proper question, and the patient will tell me the payoffs. Not all the time, of course, and only when I can question the patient in such a way that I am not experienced as being judgmental. That would kill it. If I ask my questions in such a way as to give the feeling that I am saying, "I think you're a faker; you don't have to suffer," I am in trouble and they're in trouble. I must explore whether there is any possible advantage to this behavior, and yet continue to show I am sympathetic. That's what I mean about being able to get into the person's head and show him that I am there. Then he will be able to tell me, rather than feel I am doing this only to collect evidence against him.

Some therapists are always playing Mr. District Attorney: "Why are you doing a thing like that?," trying to "get" the patient. Such therapists ought to display a sign warning, "Everything you say will be used against you." That's not a productive attitude. The attitude has to be very much of trying to understand the payoffs for past decisions. And this can take a long time or it can take a very short time. The ways of getting this information can be as varied as the schools of therapy. One can use an encounter group, Gestalt therapy, the free association of psychoanalysis, or a completely nondirective way. Whatever the method, "Tell me about yourself" is a good way to start.

Then, after the person has described how he has lived, what the choices were which caused him to live this way and what the payoffs were for these choices within the context in which they were made, I ask, "Well, would you like to change?"

Many people don't necessarily want to change. It's not up to me to decide that they should change. Many times people are not ready to change. I try not to push them, because that would just make it more difficult for them to change when they are ready. If I push, I would just postpone the moment of decision, postpone their moment of change. I don't push them because most people have been pushed enough in life. So I just ask, "Do you want to change?"

You can ask yourself, if you find that you are doing something that displeases you, "Do I want to change this? There are payoffs to my procrastinating, to my depression, to my overeating, to my drinking too much, to my just hanging around." There are a lot of payoffs to all this and you have to ask yourself, "Do I want to give this up?" It's essential to find this out.

Now, one of the ways you can decide whether you want to change is to ask a very important question: "What are the alternatives to my present behavior?" There are always alternatives. One of the problems that most people I see have is that they don't recognize the alternatives or they see only two choices. We have a great tendency to perceive everything as either-or; either black or white; either yes or no. Many of us look at life only with such limited alternatives.

I remember a woman who came to see me saying, "What shall I do—continue to live with this horrible monster who's making life so impossible for me, or shall

I commit suicide?" Obviously there were other alternatives, but she couldn't see any at the time.

Sometimes people see no alternative at all to the way they are. "I'm stuck with a husband I hate. I feel myself falling apart, the work is just too much; I can't stand it; I have to take care of the children and I get no help from him, only difficulties which he puts in my way, but what can I do? I have no alternative." They never even think of looking for alternatives.

It's very important to ask people whether there are any alternatives to the way they are living. Once in a while they are so stuck and have such blind spots about their lives, that they can't see any alternative, any other way of living. Sometimes it's important to start exploring the other possibilities. I tend to believe that the greatest growth in an individiual, the best development and the best chance of his not having these kinds of problems again come if I let him find the other choices rather than try to sell him on another choice. It is very easy to become an evangelist for another choice. I might, for example, say that a person should be monogamous or I might say he shouldn't be. Either way, I'd be pushing him. The decison he arrives at *himself* is the most valuable for the individual, because one of the things I'm trying to help people learn is not just how to deal with their immediate problems, but a whole way of dealing with life in general. That's the difference between psychoanalysis and behavior modification. Psychoanalysis has as its goal a way of dealing with problems in general, whereas behavior modification aims only to teach one how to deal with a specific problem. What I am trying to do is develop a method of dealing with problems in general; that's why selling people on a solution or alternative is not helpful, but having them get the practice of looking for a variety of solutions *is* helpful

Suppose after you've allowed yourself enough time for examining possible alternatives, you choose one. At this point, again, it becomes important to examine the possible payoffs and consequences of the one you've chosen and how they compare with the payoffs and consequences of the previous choice. This is the essence of the decision process. All systems of decision-making deal in terms of what the payoffs are. How does this one compare with the other one? Most people can project a little into the future, and see what is the advantage of the payoff.

Well, suppose a person finally decides. I try not to be in a hurry to be a cheerleader, not to say "good work," not to play coach. It's more important that he arrive by his own determination. Because he is going to have to do the work, not I. I can't be with him all the time. I can't lend him my ego, so it's *his* decision and he's approaching it completely from his own point of view.

A person says, for example, "Well, I want to give up dope." I ask, "Well, why?" It's a good question. "Why do you want to give it up? After all, with dope you have a tremendous way of dealing with anxiety." No method we know will get rid of anxiety as quickly as taking heroin—unfortunately. It's not that it doesn't work. It works very well. I make sure to present the advantages which I have got from listening to him, from his previous way of being. "Why do you want to give up suffering? As long as you're suffering you can control your whole family. You can tell your wife and she will do everything that needs to be done, if you suffer enough.

Don't forget, cry and the world cries with you. Laugh and you laugh alone."

Many people really don't believe they have any alternative. Now, what we could say (and what many therapists have been saying for many years) when a patient says "I can't do this" is, "You don't *want* to do it." When someone says "I can't do that," I try to look at it from the context of his life; not from an "outside" attitude of "he doesn't want to do it." He wants to do it, some part of him wants to do it, but at this point the payoffs for the present behavior are greater than the payoffs for a changed behavior, or the fear of change is too great.

Now, one very important payoff for the present behavior may be reduction of anxiety. Suppose somebody is suffering because he can never assert himself. Everybody walks all over him. He feels like a "dish-rag, like a doormat, like shit." And he says he can't change, no way he can change. "Well," I say, "this is your choice." But to just put it that way is not enough. If I start with "What are the advantages to that? What are the payoffs to that?," if I really study with them what the payoffs are, there are still people who will say that they can't change. Therefore I try not to put the emphasis on their changing. To me, this is not manipulation because I believe with my value system that the emphasis should be on awareness. All I ask is that people be aware of their choices. They don't *have* to change. Once I insist on change, I am back in the same kind of relationship they have had in the past, which often led to the trouble to begin with. Because usually if I study the context of their lives, it seems to me someone wanted them to act in a certain way and they wanted to act in a different way. That's why they had to develop all kinds of methods of opposition which we label neurotic.

Let's look at some of the kinds of problems people come to me with. When a person comes in with something that appears to be completely outside his choice, say a very painful tic, I could certainly use behavior modification or one of the learning-theory techniques to deal with that, but before using anything I would ask, "Are you sure you want to get rid of it?" What are the advantages? Does it attract attention to him, set him apart? Even though I'm eventually going to use some other technique, I still deal first with having him study the payoff, because too often when I have used techniques that have been very effective in other cases, they weren't helpful because I had skipped a step, hadn't dealt first with the payoffs.

Now, when somebody has made a decision, the next job is to help him carry it through. For one thing, many people think that once they've made the decision, that's it. Unfortunately, it's not so. In many cases much more than one decision is required because some decisions deal with long-ingrained habits. Somebody who makes a decision to stop smoking still needs a lot of help in stopping because that is a habit with rewards of its own, principally the relief of tension. So he has to make his decision every time he is faced with the thought of picking up a cigarette. When I decide to lose weight, I can't just decide it once. I have to decide it every time I sit down to eat. I have to ask, "Do I want this food or do I want to be slim and beautiful?" "Do I want to eat the steak with the baked potato, the sour cream and the chives, the salad with roquefort dressing, apple pie with ice cream and the cocktails beforehand, and the wine with it and the brandy afterwards? Or do I want to be slim and beautiful?" In my case I decide that I'm not going to be narcissistic so I eat the potato and the pie and the ice cream. You really have to decide many of these things over and over again.

Let's use the example of the diet again. Very often, like many people who diet all the time, I go out and have a big meal and say to myself, "There goes the diet," and I forget all about dieting. Well, that's not necessary. It's too bad I had the big meal, but I can go back to carrying out the decision the next day. Since I know this, I break my diet rules all the time.

Say a man makes the decision not to be homosexual any more—and then he meets a very groovy young lad with a very round ass, and loses himself. He doesn't have to continue to be homosexual just because he did that once. So in this case the therapist has to remind him that 1) the decision has to made constantly; and 2) just because he slipped, it doesn't mean that it's all over. Another consideration to keep in mind is that even when someone doesn't carry through a decision, the very making of it can be a valuable experience. It's helpful for any person to guide him into a "no lose" situation. Many people have been in "no win" situations all their lives. So I try to help them into a "no lose" situation.

One man I had been working with made a decision to stop drinking. Months went by and he didn't take a drink, and then one night he got drunk. But when he got drunk this time he knew he was doing it as a conscious choice. He didn't claim "I was led to drink by evil companions" any more, or some other excuse. He knew he had made the choice, and because he knew this, he

was able to tell me the context within which he had
made the choice. He had trained himself always to examine the context in which he made a choice, so he
knew the payoffs. What he recognized was that whenever he was out with a very attractive woman, he would
get drunk. And he had been out with such an attractive
woman. He then remembered all the feelings of anxiety he experienced when other men looked enviously
at him for having this attractive woman—his fear that
she would leave him, his fear that he would be made a
fool of in that situation. He realized that he chose drink
as a way of dealing with those fears. It seemed to me
that in that one session when we discussed this incident
he got a great deal more insight than we would have
had in many months of traditional, free-associational,
uncovering therapy. I have found that focusing on what
happens when people do not carry out a decision can
be very productive in arriving at understanding. I deal
with the question of payoffs; that is, I stick over and
over with the payoffs for which they decided not to
stick with their decisions. This particular drinker, while
he had not managed to stick to his decision, had nevertheless discovered that he had the guts to make it, and
to make it again.

This is a simplified description of my method, and I
will go into greater detail in Section III. But one of the
hopeful things about this approach is that it sees human
beings as having some control over what they are,
rather than to see them as victims of their biology or
their history or their learning or their glands. Yet I
don't believe that we have complete and total choice
over our lives. Obviously, we don't.

A young man tells me the story about the time he

wanted to kill himself. He is driving his car and comes to a bridge, and he figures, "Here's my perfect chance. There's a curve in the bridge and if I don't make that curve, I go off the bridge." So he rolls down the windows and steps on the gas and goes zooming up the bridge, and he runs out of gas. No gas, no suicide. Fortunately, this young man had a sense of humor, which should not be underestimated as a therapeutic tool.

Obviously, there are situations in which we don't have choices: our biology, our body, whether we'll be tall or short. We don't have a choice about the kind of world we're born into or about many of the experiences we have. We accept those limitations. But we do have a certain amount of choice. I remember listening to Konrad Lorenz, the eminent biologist and ethnologist, speaking about this matter. He was asked: "Do you believe in causality or in choice?" And he answered: "As a scientist speaking objectively, of course everything is causal. But as a human being, my experience tells me that I make decisions all day long." It is the area of choice which I think is the proper area for psychotherapy to concern itself with; that's the area where you can make the greatest amount of improvement.

Sometimes you have to change the milieu, that's true. That's another approach. Sometimes you have to change the chemical composition of a disturbed person with drugs or diet; that's another approach. But for a psychotherapist, somebody who has an interest in an individual's growth, his capacity to deal with life, it is helpful to deal with the matter of choice. Both from my clinical experience and from reading biography, I see over and over the crucial role played by the choices people make.

One of the most important partial techniques that I use frequently when somebody says he's unhappy and depressed, and makes a decision that he doesn't want to be depressed any more, is to say, "Then, act as if you're happy"—using the James-Lange theory that we are happy because we laugh, and not that we laugh because we're happy. I suggest to a person that he act as if he *is* the way he wants to be. If he is not assertive, I suggest he act as if he *were* assertive. I give him homework and say, "Okay, you want to be assertive. What are some special places where you can act as if you're an assertive person?" And if he can't think of any, I have a whole bunch. Very simple things like having someone walk into a restaurant and not order food and just use the bathroom. Ask for matches without buying cigarettes; or ask a very handsome man you're interested in how to get someplace. Or I tell someone who can't speak in class, "The next time you go to class, prepare three questions you're going to ask." I work out with him things he can do to "act as if" he were the way he wants to be—the chosen desired behavior—and then I say, "Okay, let's see if you can be that way." In addition to acting "as if," I also ask people to imagine themselves the way they would like to be. If a woman is overweight I might ask her to imagine herself slim and attractive in a lovely bikini.

One of the problems in dealing with decisions is finding out which one is operative. Usually there is a whole hierarchy of decisions and every decision you have made influences every future decision. So it is important to find out which decision is dominant. A woman gets up at a meeting where I am speaking. She says she wants help in carrying through a decision not to see a young man any more. When we speak longer, we find out why she is seeing him. It becomes clear that the reason she continues to see him and says "yes" is that she doesn't know any one else who can give her such a hard time. Her choice, as it turns out, is to suffer. He is only an instrument in this decision to suffer. So it is often important to get behind a decision. In this case the decision in front was not to see the man. The crucial one was whether she wished to suffer.

I decided to write this book, or thought I had decided to write this book, two years ago, but I hadn't been able to carry it out. So the other day I finally had the good sense to say to myself, "Now, let's see, what are the decisions that are interfering with this?" And I came up with some interesting ones. One decision I had made a long time ago was that everything should be easy for me. I was defined at the age of three as a genius, and therefore I decided that everything I do should be easy. When I sit down to write, I can't sit still and struggle with an outline because that would cast doubt upon my status of genius. I should be able to sit down and write, and all my thoughts should spring full-blown out of my brow, like Minerva out of the brow of Jupiter. So that was one crazy decision I had made, not to work like a mere mortal! Once I realized that this was one of my problems, I sat down and, for the first time, prepared a detailed outline, which I am now working from. It was necessary to become aware of a decision I had made. Actually, there was a whole series of decisions that I had to examine—not just the decision to write the book, but all the decisions which were interfering with this one.

If you learn to do this kind of self-questioning some of you will be able to apply it much better than I can,

because it's notorious that everyone picks up a theory
in the area where he has trouble. Many therapists who
call themselves existential and talk about closeness and
intimacy are among the coldest herrings you ever met.
These are people who are incapable of live interactions
for the most part. Obviously, if I chose to write a book
about decisions, this is where I have had the greatest
problem. And problems we have solved for ourselves
are often the ones we can best solve for others.

The process of helping people with decisions starts
the first moment I see them. One of the first things I ask
is, "How long do you want to come for therapy?" We
agree on the length of time it should take, with, of
course, the provision that we not be inflexibly bound to
a timetable. Very often in my experience, because a lot
of my patients have come looking for classical psychoanalysis, the problem was to convince them that they
didn't have to come for so long.

CHAPTER 2

IT CAN WORK
VERY QUICKLY

ONE of the most practical applications of
Direct Decision Therapy has been in the realm of brief
psychotherapy. A number of investigators have found
that there is very little relationship between the length
of therapy and the results—very little difference between the briefest of therapies and the longest, most
intensive therapies. The problem is that the patient
who insists on extended therapy will not permit himself
to improve without a long, continuing relationship.

Since I am convinced from my own experience that
this is so because of many conditions and situations, I
have been pleased to see how frequently the application of Direct Decision Therapy makes a very brief
therapeutic relationship successful. When at the very
first session, I ask the patient, in order to give him
training in decision-making, how long he wants the
therapy to last, those whose friends have had a lot of
therapy or those who have had previous therapy themselves usually respond by saying, "About two years."

When I asked one woman that question, she said,

"Two and a half years." I asked her why, and she said, "That's what it took all my friends." I asked her how she would feel about a shorter term and she said, "I don't think it can work."

In another case a man who had no experience in therapy and knew nothing about me, but had received my name from one of the national organizations with which I am affiliated, came to see me. He was a man in his middle sixties; he had been a carpenter until he injured one hand, and had retired. He had bought a small apartment house which he was managing. With this, supplemented by his Social Security, he was getting along all right financially. When I asked Harry how long he wanted therapy, he said, "Oh, about three sessions." He then described his present situation, the kind of situation that in my earlier psychoanalytic days I would have thought impossible to cure not only in three sessions but in three years. Nevertheless, I went to work and applied Direct Decision Therapy. First we worked out what his problem was. He was retired and felt there was nothing in life left for him to enjoy; he had given up sex five years before and told me that it had never been really pleasurable for him in the twenty-five years of his marriage. He described an early childhood in which he had been called godless and lazy until he had decided, as a result of an early and unfortunate marriage, to live the "good life," which, to him, meant working very hard. It soon became clear that he had made a basic decision, many years before, that he would be a hard, scrupulous worker and that pleasure was not for him. Pleasure was something that was sinful, wrong, against his entire ethical belief. I asked him what the payoff to this decision was, and he explained that by living in his way he had earned the respect of his parents and their support in many of the activities that he wanted to undertake. He had also earned the respect of his friends and relatives and was thought of by everyone as a "good" person. "Well," I said, "what would you like to do now? Is there any way that you can get more satisfaction out of life without sacrificing this respect, which is apparently so important to you?"

He said, "No, as I'm sitting here talking to you I realize how silly it was, how many of my friends and relatives who pretended to be so insistent on a strict morality were hypocrites and having affairs while I kept my nose to the buzz saw."

"What would you like to do?" I asked.

"Well," he said, "I'd like to have some fun now."

We then discussed the various ways he could have fun. The first thing he decided was that he would no longer think he was evil if he looked at another woman besides his wife with enjoyment, and he would no longer think he was evil if he fantasized having relations with another woman. He also spoke about how he would take more time to read and to enjoy reading, going to movies and to restaurants with his wife. How he would make an effort to accept the possibility of pleasure.

When he came back for the second session, he was remarkably changed. He walked differently, he spoke differently, and he launched into an excited story about how, shortly after he left the first session, his wife had looked at him and said, "This is crazy, Harry, but you look different somehow."

During that week he had had intercourse with his wife twice for the first time in five years. Not only had he had intercourse, but he found it particularly pleasurable, more pleasurable than he remembered it from the years before. He then told me about books he had read, about programs he had watched on television and how life had begun to have a new meaning for him. He discharged himself at the end of two sessions. He called me back three months later and again six months later, and each time he reported continued progress toward his goal of having a better time.

This story is so incredible that each time he called me, I carefully questioned him to find out how accurate this picture was. He assured me that it was all true, and that he had never before recognized that the whole matter had been a choice he had made and that therefore he could make an opposite choice.

In another case, a man who was a hard-working executive, head of a small radio manufacturing firm, came to me, not so much because he wanted to, but because his wife and family insisted that he needed therapy. He described the typical life of a hard-driven executive, getting up early in the morning, rushing to work, spending long hours at his desk, visiting customers, coming home with a brief case full of papers and books all connected with his work, working on them at home until he dropped off to sleep at midnight, with very little communication with his family and very little time for pleasure and enjoyment.

In his case I did not make any suggestions at all, but asked him why this was so. He told me that he had to do this, that he had been very poor as a young man and had made the decision that he would never be as poor as his family, so he worked his way up the ladder until he owned his company. He felt that he had to continue to implement this decision, working this hard in order to keep himself solvent financially. What choice did he have? How else could he live?

When I pointed out to him that this was a decision he had made, a decision which was quite understandable considering his early poverty and his resentment of that poverty, but still his decision, he stopped, thought for a while and said, "I understand."

As an executive, he was used to making decisions, so when he came back the next week he told me that the first thing he had done when he got back to his office was to reorganize his entire routine. He gave a large portion of his responsibility to a junior member of his staff and asked his secretary to route many of the telephone calls that he used to take himself to other members of the company. In a short time he found that he had more time for his family and more time to enjoy himself. Obviously, as an executive, he knew about decisions, and all he needed was to recognize that his previous hard work had been a decision of his own, and therefore he was able to change it.

In another case, I was conducting a workshop on Direct Decision Therapy at a psychological convention, and at this workshop a now-distinguished psychiatrist, who had been a patient of mine several years before with mixed success, attended the first session. When the question of choices came up, she pointed out how hard she had been working, how she felt driven and was concerned about her health, but that there was no choice for her. We discussed this a little further, explored whether there was no choice, until finally she said, "By God, you're right, I can have fun." She walked out of the session and did not come back to any further sessions. When I met her a few days later, I said, "Where have you been?"

She said, "I made a decision to have fun and I started right at once. I've been having fun these last few days instead of sitting in any dreary workshop."

One of the important things I had to do in order to make brief therapy possible was, first of all, to decide for myself that it could be done. Unfortunately, when a therapist believes strongly that it is impossible for any therapy to take place except in a long, extended relationship, he communicates this to the patient. Then, of course, therapy takes a long, long time.

It is interesting that most psychoanalysts believe that a thorough analysis, or even help with what is called psychoanalytically-oriented psychotherapy, requires several years, forgetting that most of the leaders and founders of the American Psychoanalytic Association themselves were originally trained in one-month analyses in Vienna during their vacations. With the great need of so many people nowadays to have the benefit of therapy, it becomes a social necessity to work further in developing briefer and more effective means of working with troubled people.

CHAPTER 3

MAKING DECISIONS
FOR GROWTH

VERY often, extended therapy is a way to avoid reaching any kind of decision that you have to act on. I constantly try to use the therapeutic situation to help people learn how to make decisions. I will ask, "How much longer do you want to continue?" or "What else do you want to work on?" I will constantly try to give people the opportunity to make decisions and help make them aware that they *are* making decisions. A lot of people are not aware they are making decisions; that's why they need the awareness. That's why I call it *"Direct* Decision Therapy," because I would say all therapy is decision therapy. And I make my patients aware of that. Many people will tell you that they can't make decisions. These are the people who have made a decision not to make any decision.

There are people who never make a decision and tell you that they can't. If they go to a store to buy a dress, they can't figure out which dress to buy. When they get up in the morning, they don't know what clothes to put on. If they go to a restaurant, they can't make up their minds what to order. If they are in school, they don't know what courses to take. They spend their entire lives unable to make decisions.

Often you find in such cases that in the past they were very strongly criticized for decisions they made, and they therefore now criticize themselves for any decision they make. This is one of the best ways to arrive at a condition of low self-esteem. Some studies have shown that people who have low self-esteem have trouble making decisions. I believe it's the other way around. Once they have had the experience of having all their decisions rejected, obviously they are going to have a low estimate of themselves and will give up making decisions. Many of these people try to get everybody around them to make decisions for them. They don't have to take responsibility this way; they don't have to take the blame for failure.

When I was young and women were supposed to be chaste and pure, they would sometimes explain how somebody seduced them by saying that the first thing they knew, somebody had their clothes off, or had got them to take one drink too many. It was never anything *they* did; it just happened to them. Now I have men who tell me the same story. It shows you how things have changed. They want to avoid the responsiblity for their behavior, but I doubt they fool anybody but themselves.

Then you have people who make decisions, but always the wrong ones; or they look upon them as the wrong ones. They're similar to the nondeciders in that they say, "Whatever I do, I make the wrong choice. I pick the wrong woman, I buy the wrong car. I made decisions, but always the wrong ones."

I associate them with the first group because they are blaming themselves before anyone else can blame them. They make decisions in line with some secret pursuit, which may be to suffer, or may be to be different from everybody else. You always have to find out what's behind making the wrong decision, because the people who make them are not necessarily stupid. People can make wrong decisions, of course, if they don't have the information about human behavior on which to base enlightened decisions. Sometimes the therapist has to supply data, give them some understanding on which to base decisions—alternatives of which they have previously been unaware. But when someone constantly, consistently chooses the wrong ones, there's *some* decision operating, however misdirected it may be. The girl who says, "Every man I've ever gone out with in my life has been the wrong man for me" is telling the truth, because a long time ago she chose to see men as no good, rotten, brutal, exploitative. And she very carefully chooses men who will meet those criteria. She's not aware of this exactly, but her relationships work out that way. And if you ask her, "What about nice guys? Do you ever meet any nice guys?" she says, "Yes, they bore me. I'm not interested in them." This girl, if she is to find a happy relationship with a man, will have to make a decision to jettison the preconception of men that has brought her so much injury. She must decide to "unblock" her receptivity to "nice guys." If, that is, she really *wants* to change.

The majority of us make very fine decisions, but we can't carry them out. Every New Year's we make great resolutions, but we can't carry them out. Or rather, we have *chosen to believe* that we cannot carry them out.

We avoid that critical judge that we carry around in our heads by trying to take credit for our great decisions and avoid the disappointment of such decisions' not working out as well as we would like them to.

To illustrate this, I will tell you something about my own life and the role that decision played in it.

Section II

Freedom is the recognition of necessity.

—*Spinoza*

CHAPTER 4

MY DECISIONS,
MY LIFE,
MY PATIENTS

As I look back at my life, particularly those aspects which impelled me to become a psychotherapist, I am struck by the role which decisions played in it, although with 20–20 hindsight I now see that sometimes it was the lack of a decision.

Obviously it is possible to organize the experiences of one's life in a variety of ways. I have chosen to organize them in terms of choices in behavior and in ways of looking at the different things that happened to me, or that I caused to happen. I would like, too, to discuss how some cases which I treated in other ways now look to me from the point of view of my theory about decision.

My earliest memories are of living in a three-room apartment on the poverty-laden Lower East Side of New York City. The toilets were in the hall, and for bathing we used the gray slate washtub in the kitchen. In addition to my father and mother, my aunt and uncle came to live with us and so did my grandfather. Obviously we were not exactly wealthy. But in one way I was fortunate: I was an only child surrounded by a large number of admiring adults. So that by the time I was three, my name in the family was "Little Genius." I decided early that I was very intelligent, and very little that has happened since ever caused me to change that decision. It was this belief in my brightness which was probably at least partly responsible for another incident and another decision. My aunt, who had come over from Europe at the age of twelve, was attending a small school on the Lower East Side, and I went to her graduation ceremony. For a child of four it was long, boring and difficult to take, so I squirmed, talked out loud, asked questions and in general made a nuisance of myself, until the principal, exasperated by my interruptions, pointed his finger at me and said, "Keep Quiet, you!"

Not at all taken aback, since the adults of my experience had been so accepting of my comments, I shouted back, "You'd better not point your finger at me like that or I'll bite it off!" When I was removed from the hall, kicking, screaming and protesting violently, I saw that both my parents were laughing. For several years thereafter, this incident was retold as a sign of my freshness, but in a tone of admiration for my outspoken intransigence. The payoff there for me was the admiration of my elders, so one of the things that I apparently decided then and there was to talk back in an impudent manner. This is the way I have reacted to authorities ever since.

Since I believed myself to be bright, and since I had chosen to be impudent, when I entered public school it was such torture that when I think of it now I still feel depressed, angry and bitter. One of the problems I shared with my fellow students was that here we were, living in an overcrowded ghetto, and we were taught by middle-class teachers. My teachers demanded discipline and cleanliness and ways of behaving which were very difficult for many of us to follow. The chief offense that I seemed guilty of was talking out in class. Frequently I was kept after school, often I was punished. I still remember a hard-bitten teacher (we called her "Murder Sackerman"), who instituted the practice of having me come up every morning at the beginning of class, hauled out my knuckles and struck them with a thick "Board of Education" ruler as a warning to me to behave the rest of the day. It was not a successful tactic for insuring my control, and I continued to present many difficulties. In addition, I found the work terribly tedious and boring. Reading had come very easily to me, but not to some of my fellow students, and I used to have to sit in class hearing them repeat over and over again, in slow, dragging tones, a few words from the very dull readers that we used.

Things didn't get better in the higher grades, because when I would get my textbooks the first day of school I would go home and read them all in one or two days, and the rest of the term was then, again, terribly boring. I found it difficult to pay attention; I would speak to my fellow students and indulge in constant daydreaming.

My mother had had two more children after I entered school; the aunt and uncle were still living with us in the small apartment. My father worked very late hours and my mother was tense and nervous from overwork and was very disappointed that my early promise had not been realized when I went to school. Among the Jewish immigrants on the Lower East Side, ability in school was a highly prized achievement. Before I entered school, all the relatives had predicted how brilliant my educational experience would be. Instead, I brought home miserable report cards, and my father was often summoned to see either my teacher or the principal about my misconduct. My father came to school so often that some of the other students thought he was the district superintendent. All of this combined to make my teachers angry at me, and to make me feel the desire to escape.

The library was my greatest escape. Reading and books became a passion. From the age of eight on, I was an addict. I waded through book after book; I would go on binges of reading books about engineering, books about reporters, as well as books about athletics. In addition to the library books, there was a whole other area of books that I read. Books about the exploits of Frank Merriwell, Horatio Alger's books about boys who rose from rags to riches, and Nick Carter's detective stories.

There was one problem, however. The library was about six blocks from school, and there were other schools closer to it so that very often by the time I reached there, the best new books were gone. I remember running all the way from my school to the library in order to get the choice books. By the time I was in the seventh grade, there were very few books that were interesting to me so that I was very short of material and in desperation, I started to read what we called "girl's books," which included books of fairy tales and other fanciful matters.

When I got to the eighth grade, a wonderful thing happened. When I entered the eighth grade and brought proof to the library, my seventh-grade promotion card, I was given the right to use the adult reading room. The card was stamped, "For Adult Reading." The second time I used the adult department, I thought a catastrophe had happened to me, which actually was to influence me greatly. With a friend, I was in a dim, distant corner of the library, far from the librarian's desk, when I found a book that had in print things about sex. This was the year 1920. The present frankness in literature had not yet begun, certainly not in the books to be found in the East Broadway Library. When I found books that mentioned this taboo subject, I was fascinated.

One afternoon a friend and I were standing looking through one of these books, *Adolescence*, by G. Stanley Hall. G. Stanley Hall at that time was the president of Clark University in Worcester, Massachusetts, and was responsible for introducing psychoanalysis to the United States by inviting Freud and Jung for the first American series of lectures on the subject. As I was reading this book about the stirrings of sexual feeling in adolescents, I was highly gratified to see written in a book what I knew so well from my own experience. The librarian came over and said, "The library is closing. May I have the book you are reading?" I thought, "This is it, no more library." She held her hand out and there was no way I could refuse, so in fear and embarrassment, I handed it to her.

Fortunately, she was a very understanding woman, and I am still grateful to Miss Waterman for what she said. She blushed slightly when she looked at the page

I was reading, and said, "We have more books on this subject, and next time you come in, if you ask me, I will be glad to point them out to you." Of course, I could no more ask her for these books than walk in the air. She was to be a central character in my erotic fantasies for the next five years. Thank you, Miss Waterman, wherever you are.

However, from that book I discovered the wonderful world of psychoanalysis. I began to read omnivorously in that subject as once I had read about engineering, newspaper reporting and college athletics. Many of the books that I read at that time were popularizations of psychoanalysis, and I found them fascinating. In addition, I also felt a sense of power which these books gave me because I thought I could understand many of the feelings and attitudes of my friends. When they talked about their mothers, I knew every Oedipal conflict that was burning within them; I treasured every slip of the tongue, and encouraged them to tell me their incest-laden dreams (my interpretation). These things made me feel so powerful that I hesitated to tell any of my friends about these books because I didn't want them to share in my secret power. Years later, when I attended a psychoanalytic institute, I often felt that some of my teachers followed the same practice of withholding information, because they made it so difficult for me to understand psychoanalysis when they lectured about it. It took me a long time to realize that they were just incapable of speaking about it in a clear way. It was then that I appreciated my friend Dr. Toby Bieber's remark: "If I don't understand what someone is saying, it's because they don't know what they're talking about."

Naturally, I thought of becoming a psychoanalyst. I dreamed of unraveling difficult, complicated cases, of returning people to sanity from the depths of madness. But there was a problem. In most of the books I read, it said that psychoanalysts had to be physicians (the official line of the American psychoanalytic movement). And while I conceived of myself as bright, I also had decided that I was incapable of controlling myself —since I had misbehaved so much in class—and that I was incapable of doing the kind of rote studying I knew was required for medical school. In addition, there was a very real problem of money in my family and the doubt that they could afford to send me to medical school. At that time we used to believe that you had to study Latin in school in order to go to medical school and I was having so much trouble with French, failing it every other term (the only subject I ever failed in high school), that I thought I could never learn Latin.

Meanwhile, I continued to drift through high school and college. In both, I managed to drift through because, convinced of my intelligence, I decided not to be one of the hard-working, studious types. I was firmly convinced that the fact that they worked so hard was an indication of their general lack of intelligence and that for me to do so would be an admission that I wasn't so bright. It would also have been a retreat from my general rebellious attitude. I managed, because of high test scores, to get into the City College of New York, then at its intellectual zenith. I left college for a year to work in the theatrical office of Al Woods, then an important Broadway producer. During that time I had the opportunity to get rid of one of my earlier ambitions. Since I had had the leading role in a high school play,

I was interested in acting and often thought of it. Unfortunately, as with many of my ambitions at that time, I never thought I could achieve it.

If I had any remnants of that ambition, they were dissipated by the experience of sitting behind the desk in the office, saying to all the anxious young people, "Sorry, no casting today." Some of the people I turned away later went on to become important in the theatre or movies, but all I remembered was the look of hope quickly dashed by my words, "No casting." I gave up, at that point, the ambition to become an actor and went back to college. I was graduated from City College in 1933, in the height of the Depression. There didn't seem to be any jobs around, and I took anything I could get my hands on. My first job was working for a Broadway press agent, Mac Millar. Together with two others I sat in a small room, grinding out paragraphs about Jack Benny not working this week because he was trying to decide between radio, the movies, and vaudeville—which, translated, meant he didn't have any bookings. However, though the job only paid about three dollars a week, I felt important being close to the famous personalities of the theatre.

That job didn't last very long, and then I went on to work for a not very successful attorney, for the munificent salary of five dollars per week. During this time I wrote press releases for him, answered questions about liquor law and helped organize and work for a liquor trade bureau. Meaningless, poorly-paid job followed job until I reached a pinnacle of what was then success. I got a job on the WPA—Works Progress Administration. First I was a teacher of remedial reading. It was while teaching remedial reading that I again became interested in psychology. A psychologist with a masters degree came around and tested my pupils and I was impressed by his air of omniscience. But the thought of going back to school hadn't entered my mind.

It was, however, in this job that I made my first therapeutic discovery, perhaps my first success. In my remedial reading course the students were taken out of the classroom and I would work with them in very small groups. In one group of four children about the age of eight, there was one very shy, retiring child. Too often such children are labeled hopeless, and teachers do not pay much more attention to them. At that time this sort of neglect was not in style, and I was given the task of teaching the boy how to read. One of the problems in attempting to reach him was that he had great difficulty speaking. If I asked him a question, he couldn't answer. I would ask him his name, and he remained mute. In my ignorance, I decided that his problem was inhibition, so I undertook to uninhibit him.

The other children in the class were able to speak, at least, so I put them all together and said, "When I say, 'What is your name?' all of you will say, 'My name is Edward'—the name of the withdrawn boy. I asked them, "What is your name?" and they said, in unison, "My name is Edward." I said, "Louder," and they said, "My name is Edward." Pretty soon, Edward joined in and was yelling as loud as the others "My name is Edward!" Since I didn't have a regular classroom, I was using the school auditorium, and I decided to get him even looser, so I said, "All of you march around the stage, put your books on your head, take out your rulers, hit the books in rhythm and as you march, yell 'My name is Edward.' " (Now we would call this an Encounter Group.)

Just as I had the four of them marching around the stage of the auditorium, yelling "My name is Edward" at the top of their lungs, hitting their books with the rulers, the plump, middle-aged Acting Principal walked in, stared in shock and disbelief and said, "Mr. Greenwald, what is going on around here?" Luckily, I knew how to answer. This lady had achieved her eminence as Acting Principal not because she had passed any examination or had any remarkable educational knowledge, but because of her activity in the local political club. In those days, a term which was later to become anathema to many conservatives in the educational system was "progressive education." So I said to her, "This is progressive education." She nodded very sagely and said, "Oh," and walked out.

We continued. By now the kids were walking and dancing, and finally, at the ultimate moment, I had Edward stand alone in front of the auditorium, yelling as loud as he could, "My name is Edward." I was so engrossed in my work that I didn't pay any attention to the bells that were ringing until I turned around and saw that the principal had summoned all the teachers of the first floor to watch this example of "progressive education."

Fortunately, Edward's teacher was a good one, very understanding. Some time later she came to me and said, "Edward is making great progress. He is becoming a conduct problem!" Considering that he had been so withdrawn, I believed she correctly assessed his behavior. In my language now, I would say that Edward saw that there were payoffs for deciding to express himself, and therefore decided to take the risk of challenging the anxiety he experienced by speaking out loud.

After the experience of being a remedial reading teacher, I got myself transferred to a project which involved working with young people on the Lower East Side, organizing "cellar clubs." In many of the poor neighborhoods, young men of eighteen or twenty would get together, rent a cellar or basement apartment, furnish it with discarded couches and chairs and start a club. The cellars were usually dimly lit, with an incongruous array of furniture. The boys used the club to play cards, and once a week they would have dances. The back room of the club was used as a place to make out with the girls. I think I know a lot of girls who would still be virgins if it hadn't been for the cellar clubs in those days.

The head of the project, Frank Kaplan, was an unusual man. He had this excellent idea, but at the time it seemed to me that he was an ineffective administrator. Apparently I was mistaken, because later on he was to organize and develop a multimillion dollar corporation, Educational Playthings, which was later sold to the Columbia Broadcasting System.

Our job, when working with the cellar clubs, was to try to develop a program that had more content and was more educational for the young people in the neighborhood. I would take them to ball games, plays that the Federal Theater was putting on, and in addition, I tried to generally enrich their cultural perspective. It was an exciting challenge and we had many interesting sessions in which we trained and studied in a variety of ways how to lead a group. For me it was a valuable experience.

In the neighborhood, existence was tough. Some of the boys later grew up to be in the rackets; one became an outstandingly successful prize-fighter, Rocky Graziano. But there was one thing about them. They understood payoffs. They were not interested in an activity just because it was labeled "cultural"; it had to sell itself to them in terms of pleasure. They taught me how important it was to be straight, to keep my language free of jargon, and in general, to deal with the kinds of people that many therapists feel incapable of working with—such as drug addicts and delinquents.

They didn't have to accept me into their club. I found that I had to win my way in because I had something to offer them. In a short time I became a specialist in sex education, not only for my club but for a number of other clubs. I went around to various clubs, lecturing on sexual matters. Some of their questions were quite naive, but I learned then, as I have since in working with my patients, how many people have strange, mistaken notions about sex. For example, one young man told me that he had "intercoursed" a girl and she told him that if he used an orange after intercourse, it would prevent pregnancy. I asked him if she meant eating it, because that would probably be as certain a method of birth control as anything else. It turned out she meant squeezing orange juice onto her crotch.

While working for Youth Services, I was asked to speak at an adult summer camp. Since they offered a free weekend and an opportunity to address a large audience, I accepted happily. My talk on Friday evening seemed to go over quite well.

The next morning I was walking around the camp grounds when I spotted an extraordinarily attractive young woman sitting and talking with an acquaintance of mine. I went over to him and struck up a conversation until he introduced me to the girl—Ruth Palley.

At that time I was still self-conscious about my short stature, and while I found Ruth attractive, I was concerned that she would think me too short. But when she stood up, I was delighted to find that she was a good five inches shorter than I. The more I looked at her, the more I liked what I saw. I have always been attracted to women with high cheekbones and good mouths. She had both to a superlative degree. We played handball and she beat me, because I am not a particularly good player, and she, being ambidextrous and very graceful, was an excellent player. Despite that, I was very happy when I ran into her in the city. (I had lost her phone number, which I had scribbled on a matchbook cover). We began to see each other frequently and eventually decided to marry.

Now, thirty-five years later, I still consider this the best single decision I have ever made.

Not only do I continue to find Ruth exciting and attractive, but she is the one person in the world whom I always have things to talk to about; to argue with, and to work with. Her constant faith in me has been a source of strength and an important drive to make me try to live up to the opinion she has of me.

Our two sons, Robert, now a theatrical director, and David, a clinical psychologist, have been two additional reasons for my deep satisfaction in the decision to marry Ruth. During many of the years when our sons were growing up, I was too busy trying to establish myself in the profession to be able to give them the time and attention they wanted. Fortunately for all of us, Ruth, with her unusual energy and understanding, seems to have more than made up for this deprivation. This is one reason I have always believed that the mother's role cannot be overestimated in the raising of children.

From the Youth Services project I went on to another WPA-funded project, serving as a lecturer for the Mayor's Committee on City Planning. This was another opportunity for me to develop my career as a public speaker. I was usually scheduled to speak in school auditoriums during the assembly period, sometime between the Pledge of Allegiance and the Star-Spangled Banner. Sometimes I did not have the chance to speak before the whole large auditorium, but before a small class. I remember one time being asked to speak to a class out in Queens that was meeting in the homemaking room. Walking in, to my amazement, I found myself staring at twenty-two giggling teen-age girls, each one of them sitting on a bed that was used in practicing homemaking. I had many experiences like that, and these experiences speaking before large as well as small groups helped immeasurably in making me feel comfortable in speaking before an audience.

Finally, I was able to leave WPA and get a Civil Service job. During the Depression, anybody in my circle of friends who managed to get a job on Civil Service was truly considered a success. For a while I was an interviewer for the United States Employment Service. Then I took an examination and became what was then called a Social Investigator; now they are called Caseworkers. But instead of being assigned to the Department of Welfare, now Social Services, I was assigned to the Bureau of Child Welfare, with a caseload almost entirely of unmarried mothers who were supporting their children.

At the time I didn't recognize it, but later I realized that many of these women supplemented their slim welfare incomes by working as prostitutes. Among the staff of the Bureau of Child Welfare at that time, there was a sharp division. Many of us who were young and who had just come from the recent Civil Service examination for Social Investigator were interested in seeing if we could help rehabilitate these women and find some way in which they could earn a living and restore their feelings of self-confidence and worth. On the other hand, there were many older workers who saw their job as a kind of detective job. Often they tried to trap the woman into compromising situations with men. It's an interesting thing that, while these older workers were trying to entrap their clients and had a social point of view that I couldn't agree with, they were in general friendlier, heartier, and easier to talk to than the dedicated, up-tight young people.

At that time, this job seemed like a dead-end job, but as I look back at it, all these WPA jobs have been extremely useful in my present work. The knowledge of how to deal with such varied kinds of people—cellar club boys, unmarried mothers—plus the opportunity of speaking in public, has helped me in my career as a psychologist.

So much nonsense has been written about the difficulty of middle-class therapists and social workers speaking to lower-class patients and clients. This never seemed a special problem to me. Because of my education and present income I'm definitely middle-class, but it is still difficult for me to identify myself as such.

At the moment I am a Professor of Clinical Psychology and Chairman of the Program of Humanistic Clinical Psychology at the United States International University at San Diego, but in a lecture last week, when a student raised an objection to certain academic requirements, I said, "You'll have to take this up with the administration."

Then I stopped and said, with considerable surprise at this moment of self-revelation, "But I'm part of the administration too!" I don't think of myself as middle-class, even though I am. An interesting problem is that many of the therapists who talk so eloquently about the difficulty of middle-class therapists working with lower-class clients, come themselves from very simple and humble beginnings. It is fascinating that nobody ever complains about the difficulty of working with upper-class clients. We all think that we can manage that. Of course, the reasons for this are not too hard to see. It is financially so much more rewarding for a therapist to treat an upper-class client.

After my stint with the Bureau of Child Welfare, I went to work for the Department of Welfare and the New York City Housing Authority. One of the things I recognized along the line was that whenever I had a job working with people, I enjoyed it. When I had to work with papers and fill out multitudinous forms, frequently incorrectly (and I would have to do them over many times), I was very unhappy and bored with the work.

The war came along and I became an instructor in the United States Army Air Forces. In the Air Force, I witnessed a fascinating example of how decision operates in changing the entire system. The Air Force assigned me to be an instructor because in my educational record, (which I filled out in a rush as I hated forms), I put down my college degree, B.S. (Bachelor of Social Science), and for my major I put down Eng. (English), which they thought meant Engineering. So I was sent to the Aircraft Engineering School. It was necessary for those of us chosen to be instructors to go through the entire course of training. At the time I entered it, the schooling consisted of the instructor standing up before the class, lecturing for eight hours a day.

Suddenly, the brass decided that this was not the way to train aircraft engineers and aircraft mechanics. A general appeared one day, entered the school at one end and left at the other, and with him went all the chairs, and from then on, we were supposed to learn by doing. There was no preparation for this, yet I realized that if they had tried to institute such a change in plan gradually, it would have been much more difficult. In its own drastic way, the Air Force succeeded in a re- markably short time in transforming the school and the student body from passive listeners to a situation in which people actually learned by operating tools and equipment. In my present therapeutic approach, this is similar to what I describe as behaving the way you want to be. In other words, instead of trying to work out all the kinks, the Air Force at one point said, "Behave as if you are learning by doing," and in a short time we *were* learning by doing. Now, when I am working with a depressed person who wants to be happy, I suggest, "Behave as if you were happy," and in a remarkably short time, some people become happy.

After leaving the Air Force, since I was living on the Gulf Coast of Mississippi in a very pleasant home on the peninsula called Henderson Point, close to Pass Christian, I thought it would be nice to stay there for a while. I got a job at Higgins Aircraft. Higgins had been a tremendously successful builder of small military ships. Now he had established an aircraft plant which was, at the time, the largest single factory in the United States under one roof.

As a boat builder, Higgins ranked with Kaiser as one of the two great glamour manufacturers of the war. Particularly, the Higgins PT boats played crucial roles in the invasion of many Pacific islands. However, as an aircraft manufacturer, he was still an unknown quantity. Since I had been teaching electrical systems in the Air Force, I went down and applied for a job as an electrical engineer, still using my college B.S. and my Eng., knowing that it would be thought to mean Engineering. There was no opening in the electrical engineering department but the personnel man told me that there was an opening for an industrial engineer. Quickly I assured him that industrial engineering was my real interest and training but that I hadn't known that there were any vacancies. He sent me to the Chief Industrial Engineer for an interview.

At this point, my entire knowledge of industrial engineering had been gained by listening to a union organizer telling a story about how he had succeeded in unionizing employees at a General Electric plant. The industrial engineers came around and took movies of their work, and the employees organized, saying they weren't getting paid enough to be movie actors. So when the Chief Industrial Engineer asked me what kind of work I had done, I said I had used some very advanced methods including the use of movie cameras, but that we had some difficulty with employees who didn't want to be movie actors for the price of assemblers. The Chief became interested in the project and started to explain how it might be possible to hide the cameras so that the employees wouldn't know that they were being photographed. He enthusiastically hired me.

I was hired on a Friday, and I was supposed to report to work on Monday. I went to the library, took out a book on industrial engineering, read it over the weekend and reported to work Monday, with some anxiety about what I would be able to do. Fortunately, I was assigned to a humorous, friendly Irishman called Mickey Finn. He and I got along very well, and soon began to play "big business." We didn't take it seriously, but engaged in it as a joke.

One time I came up to the office from the factory floor, where I had been tracing a part, carrying a scrap of newspaper on which I had written the part number. Finn stood up from his desk and said in mock-seriousness, "What have you got there, H.G.?"

Proudly I held up my scrap of paper and said, "Here you are, M.F."

Finn studied the scrap with the scribble on it and then stuck out his hand and said, "H.G., you've done it again. You're the kind of man I like to have on my team."

At that point I looked up and saw that the Chief Engineer of the entire plant had stopped and was looking on. For a moment I was concerned that this kind of foolery would not go well with our Chief Engineer, who seemed committed to playing the game of Big Business humorlessly. But the next day he summoned me into his office, looked up and said, "H.G., you mind if I call you that?"

Cautiously, I replied, "Not at all, R.H."

Then he went on with this little speech: "H.G., I've been keeping my eye on you and you look like the kind of man I like to have on my team. You look like the kind of man we can give the ball to and you'll take it right over the goal line."

The upshot was that I was promoted to group leader. Now I had twelve people under my supervision in charge of preparing reports to top management. Unfortunately, while I then recognized the importance of playing the game, I made the mistake of applying my newly-found enthusiasm for the efficiency methods of the industrial engineer to my own department. I reorganized the department so that six people could do the work more efficiently that the twelve who were previously employed. After a few weeks had passed and I had not received the salary increase I had expected because of my promotion, I went to the Chief Engineer and said, "I was wondering about an increase, R.H., since I understand the job carries such and such a salary."

He leaned back and said, "Yes, you've done a very nice job, but unfortunately we can't pay you as much for supervising six people as the former man in the slot who supervised twelve."

Perhaps it was this kind of efficiency that caused Higgins to be so fantastically unsuccessful as an aircraft manufacturer. As far as I know, it was the only plant in the United States that succeeded in building minus one airplane. We never seemed, during all the time I was there, to produce a plane or even parts of a plane that could pass inspection. The Air Force did send us a plane to take apart to use as a model, but we were never able to put it together again.

I eventually left Higgins to the bats and the owls and went back to New York to work for a number of research and engineering firms, writing technical manuals. This was the best-paid occupation I had ever had, but one which convinced me increasingly that my interest was not with machines but with people. I did not act on this realization, however, and just drifted from one opening to another until one of the firms I was working for went bankrupt. Shortly after the bankruptcy, a friend of mine recommended me for a job as a kind of public relations fund raiser. It was while I held this job that I became ever more interested in psychoanalysis. One of my duties was as executive secretary of a committee for mental health in Palestine, now Israel. I got in touch with a great number of psychiatrists who were members of the committee for mental health. I was struck by their poise, their overall intelligence and their ability to speak in a direct way to me. But, I was not a very good fund raiser and did not fit in with my colleagues. I was fired, probably because I was more involved with the volunteers—the people who contributed money and served on committees—than with my colleagues.

Then I got a job with a small airfield and airline in Monticello, New York, and after that, Ray Parker, then the general manager of the Concord Hotel in the Catskills, hired me for the job of constructing a golf course. This was the point at which I realized that I had spent my life getting nowhere. Then Jules Winerick, the son of the Concord owner, suggested to a guest who was bemoaning his inability to get intelligent, able help, that I be considered for a position. He hired me for a vague job as Assistant to the President.

The company I went to work for, which manufactured shoes, was housed in a complex of old factory buildings about fifty miles from New York City and yet it could have been a thousand miles away. It was situated in a part of New Jersey from which you could see the Empire State Building on a clear day, and yet many of the employees never went to New York except on some very important occasion such as a saint's day or the wedding of a relative. It was an isolated community and the people working in the factory were a compact group. My interview with the employer was a little unusual in that he did not ask that I have any experience in his business or any other business; all he was interested in was my I.Q. He was convinced that an intelligent person could learn the business and help him. He gave me a very simple assignment. "All I want," he told me, "is for you to show me how to make more money and do less work."

At the beginning I had no defined duties but was expected to go around and familiarize myself with the company. There were about five to six hundred employees, all of whom called the president by his first name and who had a special relationship with him. This was fostered by a series of events such as softball games, bowling leagues, Christmas parties and Thanksgiving turkeys and other means whereby the President tried to maintain a personal relationship with his employees. As a matter of fact, the relationship was quite good, so that at a time when other companies in the neighborhood were suffering from severe labor shortage, we never had any trouble getting help.

Since he was interested in employee relationships, I found myself drifting into a position I created for myself which was roughly that of a personnel director or director of industrial relations. I founded a house organ with news of the latest happenings in the different departments. I also instituted a policy of interviewing employees who were applying for jobs. It was then that our president, Sidney, had a great idea. He was trying to figure out some way in which I could take charge without having to fire anybody else. Since he spent a lot of his time outside the company and since he was concerned about what would happen to it after he left, he thought up a plan. He had me prepare a series of standard operating procedures which would cover every possible contingency. The procedures were supposed to describe every step of hiring, every step of employee relationships, all the steps in the planning of the manufacture and practically everything else connected with the company. Sidney hoped to reduce everything to paper, and then it would be my job to see that the procedures were enforced. However, the procedure for making the procedures was a rather cumbersome one.

The first job was for me to prepare a draft of the procedures which I would then send to Sidney. He would read the procedure draft, dictate suggestions and corrections, and then a typist would type them up on a special memo sheet that could be detached at any length, so that you could have five, six, up to fifteen memos on one long 'bedsheet' as we called them. There would be six copies of these. I'd get one, Sidney would get one, and the secretary would get one, and others were placed on file. There was supposed to be an elaborate follow-up to make sure that the memo was answered.

It was very difficult indeed to satisfy Sidney with any of the procedures. He was a strange combination. Sometimes he was fun-loving. For example, one time he was making a speech to the employees, standing on a tall packing box in the shipping room, and he stopped at a dramatic moment, and unfurled his necktie, which turned out to be some eight feet long. Another time, he called in the men's softball team and said to them, "You know, because you guys were so discourteous to the women's softball team and wouldn't let them practice when they were supposed to, look what they did to me," and he opened his jacket. To the stupefaction of the softball team, he was wearing a pair of rubber falsies.

When it came to the procedures, though, all sense of humor departed from Sidney. He was trying to make each one of them absolutely perfect. After an exchange of memos back and forth, I would finally get the procedure to the point where Sidney would okay it and then I was supposed to circulate it to each of the foremen. Many of the foremen had only a fifth- or sixth-grade education and they had difficulty just reading the procedures. They were very worried about signing them, and certainly about making any written comments. In a few cases they called me over and asked me to explain procedures to them, and made their suggestions orally.

After all the foremen and the other executives had passed on the procedure, I was supposed to incorporate their suggestions and send the procedure as corrected back to Sidney. Generally it did not meet all his perfectionist requirements even then, and there would be another exchange of five or six memos until we could consider a procedure complete and put it into the Book of Procedures. Here is an example of one of the procedures:

It was a tradition of the company to give candy to the employees on their birthdays. I therefore had to write a procedure explaining that it was the timekeeper's duty to make a record of each employee's birthday as soon as he was hired and keep it on a special file. The timekeeper was to obtain a box of candy from the purchasing agent on the proper date and send it to the employee. That seemed like a simple enough procedure, but we went through the usual number of changes and the circulation through all the foremen and executives, and finally when I thought the procedure was complete, I sent it to Sidney for his final okay. He sent back a long, indignant memo demanding to know why nobody noticed things and complaining that he alone had to find all the flaws in the procedure.

What was the big flaw? I hadn't said what to do with employees whose birthday fell on the twenty-ninth of February on non-leap-year years. When would they get their box of candy, on February twenty-eighth or on March first? It happened that we had no employees who gave their birthdays as February twenty-ninth, and as a matter of fact, after considerable research, I found that most people born on February twenty-ninth fix their birth date on the twenty-eighth of February or the first of March. But Sidney wasn't satisfied with that simple explanation. He insisted that we include in the procedure the point that if anybody was born on February twenty-ninth, he would be asked at the time he was hired whether he would prefer to have his birthday celebrated on the twenty-eighth of February or the first of March, in years when it wasn't a leap year. If I had had any doubts about the absurdity of big business, my experiences with Sidney removed them.

Yet I am grateful to Sidney for having given me the opportunity to carry out a series of interesting experiments. One of my duties was to read a variety of business publications to which the company subscribed, and since Sidney did not like to read very much, he wanted me to give him short summaries of them. As I read the literature, I came across the famous Hawthorne experiment. The Hawthorne experiment was a test of the effect of changes in lighting on the productivity of employees in a particular department of the Hawthorne plant of General Electric. It was found, as might be expected, that as the lighting was improved, productivity improved. But then when the light was decreased the experimenters found to their amazement that productivity still improved. Fortunately this material was analyzed by a very bright management consultant who realized that the factor that was important was not the lighting, but the fact that someone was paying attention to the employees.

With this in mind, I decided to try a similar experiment. Instead of introducing the extraneous factor—the lighting—I picked ten employees, and went around to their place of work once a day and asked them how they were getting along. When I started, they made complaints about the work—that the parts weren't coming well prepared from the other departments or that the employee next to them had body odor which made life unpleasant, or that there was too much noise, or that they didn't like the music playing over the P.A. system. But as I continued to visit them every day, they began to tell me more and more personal problems. At the end of two weeks, the employees, all of whom were supposedly at maximum economic incentive because our plant was on piecework (pay according to the amount of work turned out), increased their productivity by an average of twenty-five percent.

After I had done this experiment with the first ten employees, I discussed my results with the plant superintendent and others. They thought that my results were due to the fact that these were all low producers and that my paying attention to them had frightened them. In the second batch of ten, I included a number of high producers, and this time the percentage of improvement ran just about the same. If anything, the higher producers improved even more. I repeated this experiment with four other groups and in each case, the increase in productivity ran about twenty-five percent.

Another strange thing happened. As I spoke to the employees about their work, they became more and more involved in telling me about their personal problems and asking for advice. In my psychoanalytic days, I would have said that they developed a transference. It seemed to me that the reason for the increase in productivity was clear. Someone was showing interest in the workers. But the fact that they came to me with so many of their personal problems was a little surprising.

When I showed Sidney the results, he was very impressed, and in fact consented to constructing a private office that I could use for interviewing applicants and, in addition, for seeing people who had problems. As the workers began to come to me more and more with their personal problems, I recognized the need for further training. First I tried to go to New York University, and visited the department of psychology one evening to inquire about graduate courses. The young faculty member there told me that I'd have to come in the daytime. I explained that I worked in the daytime, and he launched into a long analysis of my motivation: if I was truly motivated, I would manage to come during the daytime no matter where I was. So I never went to New York University.

Fortunately, at just about that time, I came across a book by Theodor Reik. I was excited by the frankness and openness with which he described some of his own personal problems. Today it is not unusual for a therapist to talk about his problems; in fact, some are so involved in discussing their own personal problems that they rarely give their patients a chance to talk. But in that day it was rather an unusual thing, and I had never come across it before in any of the psychoanalytic books I had read. I was very impressed.

I was also interested to learn that Theodor Reik was not a physician but a psychologist. On an impulse, I wrote him a letter, asking if there was anyplace in the United States where an individual who was not a physician could be trained in psychoanalysis. By return mail and in his own handwriting, Reik informed me about the National Psychological Association for Psychoanalysis, which was then in the process of formation and would begin formal classes in New York in September. I wrote immediately and received an application. I was very excited and could not wait the four months to September, when I would start my training.

Sidney was helpful. The company had a policy of paying for courses taken by employees to better themselves, so they paid for my first two years of training at the Psychoanalytic Institute of NPAP. A number of employees of the shoe factory made appointments and came to see me privately to discuss their problems. Probably my first formal patient was a woman about twenty-one years old who told me that she had trouble working because she suffered from nightmares, severe anxiety and a whole series of symptoms that impaired her functioning. I began to see her on a regular basis, twice a week. She would come and talk to me about her problems, which were remarkably classic.

At that time I had not yet taken any formal courses in psychoanalysis, but it didn't require much training to understand a dream which she recounted about being chased by her father with a tool in his hand. I didn't make the interpretation for her, but asked her what she thought that could mean. She blushed and said, "I guess I was attracted to my father." Several other similar dreams came up. We discussed them, and I was able to explain that this was not really as unusual as she thought. Some time after we started to talk, she told me that she had been in her dentist's office and come across an article in a magazine about a man who did work "just like mine," and she called the author "Frood" because she had never heard of Freud.

Sometimes I wish that many of my patients had shared her ignorance, because this girl made remarkable progress and within a few weeks the night sweats had disappeared, her anxiety had lessened, and she was able to work. Once she had got her problem out into the open, she was able to discuss it, comprehend it, and, in effect, conquer it by dismissing it as not abnormal

and, therefore, not frightening. She started to enjoy
going out with young men her own age for the first time
in her life. After she had reported this improvement, I
asked her, "What do you think did it?" She said, "Oh,
I know. I made a novena and I asked God to help me."

I was a little disappointed that He was getting the
credit for the work I had done, but I knew enough to
keep my mouth shut, and then she added something
which was an inspiration to me then, and that I have
often thought of when things were not going so well
with a patient and I needed a little encouragement. She
said, "I know how God helped me. He gave you the
knowledge so that you could guide me."

One of the requirements at the National Psychological Institute for Psychoanalysis, as of most psychological
institutes, was that I undergo my own analysis. At first
I was troubled by the prospect, but after a while I realized that a great part of my interest in psychoanalysis
stemmed from my wish to solve my own problems. So
I studied the analytic society's referral list, and, picking
the therapist whose office was closest to me, called to
make an appointment with Mr. A.

I was quite nervous and excited at the thought of
going to see him. I try to remember that nervousness
and excitement when I see a new patient now, try to
"relive" the heightened sensations he is experiencing
on his first session.

When I rang the bell and was ushered into Mr. A's
unpretentious office, I sat down in a chair facing him.
He looked at me and said, "How can I help you?"

My answer was, "I need to be analyzed because I
want to be a psychoanalyst. I'm a student."

He smiled and said, "But I can't analyze you unless you have some problem. Don't you have any problems?"

So I searched around and found a problem. One of the things I was supposed to do for Sidney was make a weekly report of all my activities. Now, that wasn't really a difficult thing to do. I could have just kept a sheet of paper at my desk and written down what I did each time I did something. It was usually twenty percent interviewing applicants for jobs, ten percent preparing the company newspaper, ten percent representing the company at local meetings of the industrial relations association comprising representatives from other industries in the neighborhood, and the rest devoted to writing and working on the procedures.

It was very difficult for me to write up these procedures, and I was always behind schedule. Procrastination has been a habit of mine for a long time, and not one that I am now completely without. So I presented this as my problem, and Mr. A. and I spent a long time analyzing it, what it meant and how it was part of my general rebelliousness, what Sidney represented to me, and a host of other analytic attempts. Yet I continued to procrastinate.

After I had completed a certain amount of work with my own analysis and taken a number of courses, I went into supervision analysis with a wonderful woman psychiatrist. One day I brought the matter of my procrastination up to Dr. B., and instead of trying to analyze it, she said in her charming southern accent, "Harold, you're just going to have to do it." At that point, I *decided* I would just have to do it. It was one of the first times I became aware of the power and meaningfulness of decision. Then and there I realized that I had to make a decision and carry it out. My report writing improved, and within a short time I was doing better at my job than I ever had before. Of course, this is not to say that my other analytic experience was not also helpful to me.

Many times I have wondered, What in my analysis was most helpful? Frequently I did not have a very high opinion of Mr. A.'s intelligence or perceptiveness. I found his habit of reassuring me particularly annoying because I didn't feel I needed this kind of reassurance. Also it seemed to me that often he was posing as the Great Therapist rather than listening to me completely. And yet after my analysis, when I was freed of many inhibiting pressures, I was able to do a number of things I couldn't do before.

For example, I got a job lecturing on psychology at the Concord Hotel. It was kind of an accident. I was speaking at a place in New Jersey, and Dave Patsiner, who was the assistant to Arthur Winarick, the president of the Concord Hotel, heard my lecture and said, "Why don't you come and speak at the Concord sometime?" It was interesting that it was he who suggested it. Perhaps it was because he was not related to me—unlike the Winarick family, who were cousins, and my brother Phil, who was director of entertainment then, as he still is.

The first time I spoke was on a hot summer day and I was speaking right next to the swimming pool. I had a good-sized crowd and I was very fortunate that two of the outstanding guests at the hotel that summer, Sam Levinson, the humorist, and Irving Mansfield, then a television producer who is now the husband of the popular novelist Jacqueline Susann, went to the management and said, "If you can get somebody like this to speak to the guests it would be a very good thing if they could come regularly." So I was asked to come back the next week, and for about six years I returned periodically to speak.

It was a valuable experience, learning how to speak to a wide variety of people about psychological problems. It was also experience in learning how to get them to speak to me, because after a while I tired of lecturing and would get these large audiences involved in discussions about personal problems. Sometimes the problems were too personal to come up before such a large group. For example, one time a man got up and said in front of an audience of about three hundred people, "What should I do, Mr. Psychologist? I have a loss of manhood."

Because I didn't want to explore this in front of an audience, then being committed to secrecy and privacy in all communication, I tried to change the subject by asking, "What's your occupation?" He answered, "I raise breeding bulls." It was a wonderful example of compensation.

I began to get a number of private clients, so I rented an office and in addition to my full-time job with Sidney and courses at the NPAP, began to see patients for therapy. As I became more and more involved with the work, I asked Sidney if I could switch to a part-time basis. He was reluctant but said, "I guess that's the only basis on which you'll work."

My practice increased until I was ready to leave Sidney altogether, because my interest was overwhelmingly in psychoanalysis and very little in the manufacturing of shoes.

When I finally left the job, I was approaching the completion of my course work at the Psychoanalytic Institute and thought that I should get a doctorate. One of the problems of working as an analyst was that my patients insisted on calling me "Doctor." So did the guests at the Concord Hotel. I would correct them, but they continued to call me Doctor and this made me feel like a kind of fraud. In addition, I knew that sooner or later a licensing law for psychologists would be passed and so it would be useful to get a doctoral degree.

Now I was no longer fearful of going to graduate school. Something that had happened as a result of my therapy made it possible for me. I think it was chiefly that I had decided that I didn't have to be so perfect, didn't have to be so brilliant, and that I could even work hard if I went to graduate school. The result was that with the exception of statistics, (where I just didn't have the time to put in the work required to overcome the poor teaching of this subject), I completed my graduate work at Columbia with an "A" in every course for which a grade was given. I wrote a doctoral dissertation about call girls which, as I have mentioned before, attained considerable attention.

This was not to say that my path through the Institute of the National Psychological Association was an easy one. Far from it. First one had to be admitted to matriculation, which required an interview. After admission to matriculation and the completion of a certain number of courses, there was another interview before a committee on readiness for control. At this interview I was supposed to prepare a case and present it. By this time I had had a number of cases that were quite successful. In my naiveté I thought that all I had to do was present one of these cases, until I discovered to my amazement that I did not pass the interview. The members of the committee thought I had such serious problems that I should be discouraged from continuing in the field of psychoanalysis.

I learned that one of the "problems" I had was that my analyst happened to be on the wrong side of one of the quarrels that was raging within the ranks of the NPAP, as they do in the ranks of most professional psychoanalytic institutes. It's a contentious profession, and it is my guess that one of the reasons is that psychoanalysts sit it their offices all day saying very little and when they do say anything, the patient listens to their words with great attentiveness, eagerness and concern. This makes it difficult for psychoanalysts to function in a democratic organization where other members do not listen with the same eagerness and concern. Many of the splits and schisms which have taken place in various psychoanalytic organizations are due not so much to the theoretical differences, which generally appear after the split, but to these clashes of personality.

One of the easiest ways of expressing anger or hostility toward a member of the institute either for heresy or for personal reasons is to refuse to pass his candidates. Perhaps I did have some problems which I wasn't aware of, but I don't think that's what they were complaining about. At the time, I was not aware of experiencing any anxiety. I actually had less anxiety than the average candidate who goes before a committee. I had been speaking constantly in front of audiences. A committee of only three members was not nearly as difficult as the two, three and sometimes as many as five hundred people whom I would speak to weekly at the Concord Hotel, many of whom were hostile to the ideas of psychoanalysis and psychotherapy. Of course, this hostility has recently changed dramatically, so that when I now visit the hotel or speak at a convention I find that a large number of people in the audience are in therapy and frequently come over to talk to me.

There probably was an unrecognized anxiety during my interview, and it took me all the time I was at the institute to realize that what is required is not to show control, an ability to handle a case well, but to be able to recognize one's own problems and express them clearly. But I remember my fury at the members of the committee who did not pass me. One of the reasons I believe that I worked so hard was that then and there I decided that some day I would show them.

And so it has come to pass. It is a rather strange situation. Now, membership in the NPAP really means very little to me professionally in terms of practice, but at the time it seemed like almost a life-and-death situation. I have actually known at least two candidates in psychoanalytic institutes who committed suicide when they could not pass one of the hurdles. It took me years to get the full satisfaction, but one of the women who found me most wanting came to consult me years later about a difficult case. Another member who had been, I felt, particularly unfair and hostile asked me to refer patients to her if I could, because she was having difficulty filling her practice. It is hard for me even at this time, so many years later, not to enjoy these two little triumphs.

I have often wondered about the factors that went into my decision to become a psychologist and psychoanalyst. Many of them, of course, came out of certain associations. When I was working for Sidney, for example, he once decided to have all of his employees tested. He had a consulting psychologist give us intelligence tests and a number of personality tests. The one I especially remember is the Thematic Apperception Test, in which the subject is asked to look at pictures and make up a story about them. I did very well on the intelligence test, so well that the psychologist questioned the results, and in fact seemed angry at me for having achieved a high score. Naturally, I found that very gratifying. But even more exciting was the TAT. So interesting was this to me that I made up my own test by cutting out pictures from magazines and newspapers, assembling them, and, as a parlor game, gave them to people who would visit my wife and me, and ask them to make up a story. It was a kind of group therapy because everybody joined in analyzing the productions.

One obvious reason for my interest in the field was simple curiosity. It has always seemed to me that curiosity is one of the most undervalued and underestimated of human drives. In fact, it is more than a human drive; there are many other animals who are obviously impelled by curiosity. When I was working for Sidney, he once came across an ad for a mousetrap. Since our factory was a very old one, it was overrun by mice. This trap worked in the following way. There was no bait, just a large black box with a hole. The theory was that if a mouse came to that hole, it would poke its nose inside, out of curiosity, and would activate a mechanism which smacked the mouse on its backside and thrust it into the box. When we looked at the ad in the office, everyone laughed and thought it was a most absurd device. However, Sidney ordered it, and installed it in the factory. Every morning it was packed full of mice.

Curiosity about people was one of the most impelling things that lead me to my decision to become a psychoanalyst. Also, I cannot neglect the fact that at various times I was dimly aware of my problems, like the one I mentioned in connection with writing the reports for Sidney. I had difficulty in carrying out certain things that I was assigned to, particularly those that involved writing. Many times as I sat at my desk, struggling to put down the details of the procedures, I would be furious with myself at resigning myself to such idiocy, the work being so meaningless. I knew that few people would follow the procedures, and even if they did, what great difference would it make? And yet there I was, at my desk. I was convinced then that one of the reasons I was operating at such a low level was that I didn't have the self-discipline to do the kinds of things I needed to in order to get out of the situation. I did not feel enough in control of myself to be able to handle it.

I would get great satisfaction from people who would say, when I told them one of my ideas, "That's wonderful. You should really write a book." Having achieved this gratification, I didn't go any further with it. I left it there, and again and again I was angry with myself. How well I remember going past bookstores, looking at books in the window, and feeling how much I wanted a book with my name on it to appear in the window. It was easy to escape into fantasy and see myself a famous author. It was much harder to sit down and discipline myself to the task of writing.

I experience difficulty even at this very moment writing this book. The difference is that now I am doing it. One of my problems, of course, was the enormous demands I made on myself in my fantasies, the goals I wanted to attain and the belief that I couldn't do it. Here, too, was a vital reason for my interest in studying psychology. It was difficult for me to admit that I needed therapy for my own problems. It was much easier to use the excuse that, since I wanted to become a therapist, I had to have analysis.

At the Psychoanalytic Institute I was disappointed in the courses. Many of them were dull, but this time, instead of escaping into fantasies as I had in my earlier school experiences, I decided to force myself to pay attention. Sometimes it was extremely difficult. One of our instructors, for example, gave a course on the general theories of neurosis. His idea was to completely avoid any concrete example and put his lectures on the level of abstraction, which made the material almost meaningless. He delivered all this in a flat monotone and did not encourage any class participation. Despite the fact that he had a Ph.D. in psychology and should have known something about teaching methods, he, like many psychologists, used the worst methods of teaching in trying to convey some of the fundamentals of such problems as learning.

Theodor Reik, a far more eminent psychologist, made his classes at the institute almost the polar opposite of this dull professor's. In most of Reik's sessions, he presented his own cases, as well as many fascinating stories about his relationship with Freud. However, I was bored in many other classes, and I might have dropped out except for one line that my analyst used which kept reverberating in my mind. When I explained some of my plans for shortening the process of education to my analyst—the fantasies I had of getting a fast degree without any further training—he said, "You're trying to be a professor without going to school."

I decided after I heard this several times that my attempt at a magical short cut was an unrealistic demand that I was making on myself. So I went to classes and read many of the ponderous psychoanalytic tomes, which sometimes seemed to be written in double-talk, as though the purpose of these books were not to communicate information in usable form, but to demonstrate the writer's erudition.

That was one of the reasons I decided to write and speak as simply as I can, even though I know that I may sacrifice many potential admirers. For example, I wrote and published a paper on the treatment of the psychopath. It was a paper that was influential in obtaining important speaking assignments for me, and was fairly well received by members of the profession. It was also a paper that influenced many of my colleagues to send me psychopathic patients, because many of them had no idea what to do with psychopaths. Also, many psychologists who felt burdened by an excess of conscience came to me for their own analysis. When I asked them what they hoped to get out of analysis with me, they would say, "Could you teach me to be more of a psychopath?"

One day I was at the home of some friends, and a young woman there who was married to one of the most formidable psychopaths I have ever met, an extremely exploitative, conscienceless man, said to me, "I read your paper on psychopaths."

I asked her, "What did you think of it?"

"Not much," she said. "I understood every word, so what could I get out of it?"

So many people think that if they can understand something they read, it's not very worthwhile. This is one of the reasons, for example, why Alfred Adler has never got his just dues as an innovator, even though many of his ideas were adopted by so many of the Neo-Freudian schools that it would be more correct to call them Neo-Adlerian. Yet because he wrote so simply that anyone could understand him, he has never received the respect that Freud and Jung commanded, because they wrote in a much more complicated manner. In justice to Freud, I should add that some of the things he wrote about were, in the original German, written much more simply. For example, instead of using the word "Id" in his own language, he used "das Es" or "it"; instead of "Ego" he said, "ich," meaning "I." This also is true for a number of more complicated phrases, but in translating his works into English, physicians like A.A. Brill decided to make it more difficult and complicated and put the terms in Greek or Latin —the same as their prescriptions.

My passage through the analytic school was not an especially triumphant one. But finally, because they changed administration, I was made a member, the equivalent of graduation at that time. I was so angry with them that I only attended one meeting until years later, when I was elected president of the association.

Not satisfied with just being a psychoanalyst, I had also received, from Columbia, my doctorate in psychology. One of the things that puzzles me is why so many students complain that the material in graduate school

is meaningless as far as practicing psychotherapy is concerned. As it happened, because of my clinical experience (by now I had a full-time private practice), I did
not take my degree in clinical psychology, but in social
psychology. Theoretically, this field was even further
removed from psychotherapy, yet hardly a day passes
that some of the concepts of social psychology are not
useful to me, whether I'm doing therapy with an individual or a group, or trying to understand some complicated social phenomenon.

It was while at graduate school that I made another
important decision. I was taking a course in behavior
disorders at the time I was treating a woman who was
a call girl. She was the first one I had ever met, as far
as I knew. A friend of mine, Eddie Jaffee, a well-known
theatrical press agent and public relations consultant,
had called me and asked if I would take a call girl as a
patient. I answered that whether I accepted her as a
patient or not did not depend on her profession, but on
what her problems were.

Eddie Jaffee has been responsible for some of my
most fascinating patients. Once he referred to me a
patient who was a lady wrestler, and her problem was
that when she got amorous she would hug her boyfriend tightly and break some ribs. Another time he
sent me a famous Broadway personality who had been
one of Billy Rose's Long-Stemmed American Beauties,
a tall, statuesque, extremely witty young lady who was
painfully self-conscious about her height. Another time
it was a French *chanteuse* who was really of gypsy
origin; she assured me that she could read my entire
personality just by looking at me. When I asked her to
please do so, she refused. I often wonder what she saw.

But this time it was a call girl. I was so naive about the

subject that I wasn't even sure exactly what the term meant. I knew it was somebody who had something to do with men. So when she came, I thought it was a joke because she looked like one of the most demure girls I had ever seen. Today I would probably be able to recognize something in her looks which made her different from the art student or modern dance student she was dressed like. But at the time I was not aware of it, so I asked her what she did, and she said very simply, "I have sexual intercourse with men and they pay me for it."

Years later she told me that she thought I was joking when I asked. She was very proper in her speech; in fact it took her about three years before she would use the word "fuck" in my presence, very much unlike some of my more "respectable" clients who came from Park Avenue or Westchester and knew that you use dirty words when you talk to your analyst.

After listening to the girl's story, I was fascinated. Many psychoanalysts believe that all curiosity is a derivative of voyeurism—of the wish to observe sexual intercourse. I would rather say that this is just one form of curiosity. One of my fantasies about how great it would be to become a psychoanalyst was that I would sit there and beautiful women would come in and tell me about their sex lives.

With Sandra, the call girl, this was certainly true. So, for my class in behavioral disorders that I was taking at the time, I prepared a paper on prostitution. When I got through delivering it, the professor, who was a rather proper gentleman, and shy, came over to me and said, blushing: "You know, this might make a good subject for your dissertation." That sounded like a good idea to me, and I eventually presented the idea to the committee in charge of our program. Several of the committee members felt that Professor Lorge, a famous experimental psychologist, would never permit such a dissertation subject. I decided to go directly to him.

I told him that I was planning to do a study of call girls, but that everyone had told me that he would be opposed to it. From my experience in therapy I knew how many people respond to the negative, and despite his eminence as a psychologist, Dr. Lorge was no exception. He drew himself up indignantly and said, "Who said I would be opposed to it? Just because I wouldn't let Albert Ellis do his dissertation on a sexual subject, they think I'm opposed to it. My previous objection was that his dissertation was not educational in nature and he should have done an educational dissertation because he was at Teachers College. Since you're at Columbia, I think it's a very good subject."

He then made a very important methodological suggestion—that I train some of the call girls to do the interviewing of other call girls, to see the difference in the results. He hypothesized that such a group outside society would respond differently to each other than they would to me, a professional and therefore a representative of the Establishment.

Of course, since it was an academic dissertation, I had to find a title for my study that would be properly academic. I chose: "A Study of Deviant Sexual Occupational Choice of a Group of Twenty New York Women."

Through my friends and through some of the women I had in treatment, I found a number of women who were willing to be interviewed. To me, the interviews were fascinating. Very often they were conducted late at night, after the girl's work was over, and I found myself having pleasant, informal, friendly relationships with the girls. Some of the interviews I conducted with a tape recorder, or wrote down verbatim. This created a problem for me because one of the members of the committee, the eminent social psychologist Professor Otto Klineberg, who after retirement became a professor at the Sorbonne and a consultant to UNESCO, called me in and said, "Harold, you know that within the tradition of psychoanalysis one uses all kinds of language, but in the social science tradition, that kind of language is not generally used. I suggest you make some changes, so that where in your dissertation the girl says, 'Why should I suck his cock?' couldn't you say, 'Why should I perform fellatio?' "

I explained to him that his modification didn't sound like a call girl speaking, and he said, "Well, maybe you could use blanks." So I took out all the direct terms and substituted blanks, counting them out very carefully so that instead of using the word "fuck" I would put, "_ _ _ _." I later learned that one of the more popular pastimes at Columbia, when my dissertation got into the library, was for the students to try to figure out what letters fit into the blanks.

When it came time to write my dissertation, I again had my old problem with getting things down on paper. I delayed a few months before I could get started. One of the ways I got started was to lie down on a couch, put on the tape recorder and try self-analysis. What I did was to allow myself to free-associate until I realized what held me back.

It was fear.

My associations were the remembrance of an incident that occurred when I was in the fourth grade. I had written a composition which the teacher had liked very much, but unfortunately my handwriting was very poor. It used to be the custom in our school to send some of our compositions to the principal's office. Since the teacher liked my composition so much, she wanted to put it on the top, but she couldn't put it there because it looked so sloppy. In this school, as in so many other schools, the form and neatness was counted for more than the content. So she asked me to recopy the composition. For two days I sat in the back of the room, sweating over the work. It was sheer torture. I never did succeed in making it neat enough, and the best I was able to do was second or third down from the top.

After this discovery, I decided to challenge the fear. But like all other decisions, it was one that I have to make *over and over again.* Since then I have come to other conclusions about my difficulty in writing. As part of my training I had to have what we call "control analysis." That was, I went to two experienced psychoanalysts for a period of one hundred hours at least, to discuss my cases. They would not only supervise me, make suggestions about technique, but would frequently discuss some of my problems in handling the patients. The first of these supervisors was a wonderful woman named Ruth Berkley. She was extremely helpful. There was no use analyzing why I had such difficulty writing; I just had to do it. She was also very helpful in building up my self-confidence.

When I first started seeing patients on an individual basis, I was apparently so anxious that they left after only one session. My analyst pointed this out to me, but what could I do with the knowledge that I was anxious? When I first came in, Dr. Berkley apparently recognized my anxieties, and spent some time feeding my ego in a wonderful way. She told me to realize how intuitive I was, and since she had been a student of Theodor Reik she frequently compared me to him, which was very high praise. She helped me realize that one of the reasons I sometimes put such enormous demands on myself was that often I felt so inadequate.

Or as Theodor Reik once said to a patient, "Don't make yourself so big; you're not so small."

When I went to see Reik, he had written thirty-nine books, and if he had ten minutes between patients he would work at his table, writing additional material. I took up the question of writer's block with him. I couldn't present it as my own problem, because I didn't want to admit it to him, but I did have a number of author patients at the time, so I presented it as their problem. He gave me an interesting idea on the subject.

Reik often spoke in parables, and when I asked about writer's block, he quoted Thomas Mann, who had said, "A professional writer is a person who doesn't like to write." Although that made me feel better, it didn't enlighten me very much. He then said (and this is the parable), "Did you ever think of God working? In the Bible it says that for six days and six nights He made the earth, and on the seventh day He had to rest."

That was all he said, but I recognized, after thinking about it, that that is a very useful thing in any kind of therapy, to let the patient draw his own conclusions. What Reik was getting at was that for most of us, certainly for me, the exciting and interesting part of writing was thinking up the idea. This was Godlike. I had a wonderful, magnificent idea—but then I had to work. Like most people, I did not see myself as Godlike when it came down to the boring, arduous, demanding task of actually writing. Naturally, with my demands on myself, it never came out as well as I had imagined it, and still doesn't. If this book were only as good in reading as it was in my mind, it would be tremendous. However, I had to learn that I was not God or even Godlike. I had to learn to sit down and transcribe.

A few years later, when Reik met me in the street, he kept after me to write because he thought I had ability as a writer. I asked him how he did it, those thirty-nine books. He didn't give me the psychoanalytic business about God or creative ideas, but said simply, "I force myself."

In other words, he had made a decision to force himself to do it. He did explain that the more he forced himself, the easier it became, the same as I find in going on with this book. The more I force myself, the more I challenge the fear of committing myself to paper, the fear of criticism of the way I write and what I say. There is plenty of that; I can see many of my colleagues laughing at this material, finding holes and faults in it, but probably not as great as the ones I find. Yet I have to decide that, bad as it may be, I have to put it down. When I read it after it is transcribed (I use a tape recorder to overcome the anxieties of writing or typing it out) it all seems like a horrible mélange. I have to decide over and over again that I will go through with it.

Reik also used some other devices to force me to write—devices that would make him non-Freudian in the eyes of the psychoanalytic heresy hunters. For example, he would consciously stir up my competitive feelings toward him by saying, "When are you going to get started? After all, I have written thirty-nine books." Or when he met my wife, he said to her, "You will have to be a Lady Macbeth, driving him on with your ambition!"

He was rather surprised when my wife, Ruth, said, "I think he works too hard already, Dr. Reik." For me, that was probably more helpful than if she had tried to drive me on, because then my early decision to be rebellious would probably have made it impossible for me to write at all.

In my career, two things that my wife has said stand out. Her response to Reik was one of them; the other came when I told her, "I'm thinking of going back to school to study psychoanalysis and get a degree in psychology." She was most enthusiastic and supportive, saying, "That's great!"

Years later, when I had achieved a degree of recognition in the field and had an exciting and interesting life and practice, I remember one of her friends saying enviously, "You're so lucky to have an ambitious husband who was willing to go back to school and study."

I stopped this friend and said, "What would you have done if your husband had wanted to quit the best job he ever had, a job that was paying in the neighborhood of $25,000 per year?—which was a much larger sum of money then than it is now. What would you have done?"

She answered promptly, "I never would have stood for it."

In making the decision to become a psychologist, and

in making the decision to write, I have found Ruth's support enormously helpful.

I worked nights, occasionally taking amphetamines to drive myself on, to finish my dissertation. Then the great day came when I had to present it before the committee and defend it. I was fortunate in my committee. There were three of the most eminent people in the field. Goodwin Watson, then head of the social psychology program at Columbia University, was chairman of my committee; Otto Klineberg was the second; Dr. Nathan Ackerman, the psychiatrist-psychoanalyst who was later to play a seminal role in the development of family therapy, was the third. In addition, three other people had been called in: Dr. Herbert Hyman, sociologist; Dr. "Lank" Osborn, head of the Marriage and Family Life department; and someone from the Department of Clinical Psychology whose name, for obvious reasons, I cannot remember. He was the only one who gave me trouble, asking questions about the size of my sample and other minute details, but eventually I passed.

I had been looking forward to that moment with great expectation, but I was not really prepared for the results. The committee came out of the room (I had been outside, sweating, awaiting their decision) and said, "Congratulations, Doctor," and instead of the elation I expected to experience, my heart sank. The sun wasn't any brighter, the grass wasn't any greener, and the sky wasn't any bluer. Somehow instead of the joy that I had expected, there was a feeling of concern, dissatisfaction and disturbance. It took me several months before I really appreciated my new status as Doctor.

It took several positive incidents for me to enjoy it. One such incident came when I visited a psychiatrist friend of mine. There were several people there and he carefully introduced me as Doctor Greenwald. It was obvious that to him as a physician, the status and title of Doctor was quite meaningful. And later, at a meeting of the American Psychological Association, when I raised my hand to participate in the discussion, the chairman recognized me as Doctor Greenwald and I had a real feeling of acceptance that was quite enjoyable. Now, years later, the title of Doctor is not nearly so meaningful to me as it was in those days, but I must admit that I still like it.

At the time I studied at the Analytic Institute of the NPAP, most of the training was rather rigidly psychoanalytic. We had only a few instructors who did not follow the orthodox Freudian model. In fact, the staff was so Freudian and so orthodox that when I reported, as I had been assigned to, on the work of Franz Alexander, then head of the Chicago Institute of Psychoanalysis, my instructor was annoyed because I did not attack Alexander's mild deviation from Freudian orthodoxy. My own analyst had been trained in a Sullivanian institute and was less rigid, which was one of the reasons I was suspect at the Institute.

However, the formal part of my training had been rather orthodox, and now I had the task of coping with patients who did not present the standard neuroses that were common in Freud's day.

One of the first patients I worked with was a twenty-five-year-old secretary named Madeline. The first time she came to see me, she looked rather strangely at me, looked at the couch in my office, and said, "You only have a couch. What do you want to do with me?" Soon she forgot about the danger and began to rehearse a tale of sad deprivation. For a few weeks I went along sympathetically listening to her troubles, and the more I listened, and the more sympathetic I was, the more her troubles increased. In addition to her twice-weekly sessions, she started to telephone me several times a day.

Even in those early days, when I felt eager to be of service to my patients, when I felt in a sense that it was important to be needed, it soon became impossible for me to meet all of Madeline's demands. She had no qualms about discussing her problems with anybody, and if I wasn't available when she called, she would pour out her troubles to the answering-service operators. They got to know her quite well, and whenever they called to say that she had phoned, it was always, "Oh, poor Miss Madeline is in real trouble. Do you know what happened? She used her father's favorite razor to shave her legs and after she got through she forgot to change the blade and her father tried to shave and cut himself and he said to Miss Madeline, 'What are you trying to do, kill me?' Can you imagine what that poor girl is going through? Please call her as soon as you can."

Madeline had been a beauty contest winner at the age of six. It is interesting what that kind of experience does to a girl. Apparently she had decided then and there that she was beautiful, and no amount of contrary evidence, as she grew older and lost her youthful good looks, had any effect on her self-image. One Sunday I got a desperate call from her. She said that she must see me at once. Now, I know that to respond to these "emergency" calls simply rewards the depressive behavior of the patient and tends to fortify it. Unfortunately, some well-meaning therapists feel that they must respond to every such call, and the result is that they carry on long relationships with patients who only get more depressed. In those days it was not so clear to me as it is now, and I dealt with it by rushing down to the office, on Sunday.

After telling me how desperate it was for her to see me, when she came in, she said nothing and just sat. All she would do was sob. When I asked her what the trouble was, she shook her head and said nothing. Finally she looked up at me and slyly said, "Do you have a knife?" Obviously she was intent on giving me the message that she wanted a knife in order to commit suicide.

I said, "No. I'm sorry. I don't have a knife here."

She was quiet for a while, thought it over and then said. "But I know you do have a pair of scissors."

So I asked, "What do you want the scissors for?"

She replied, as if she wanted me to know that she was lying, "I want to cut the hem of my dress." She picked up her dress and showed me that the hem was slightly frayed, and continued, "You don't trust me, do you? You don't trust me with the scissors!"

One of the reasons for my keen awareness of the power of negative suggestion today is that I know it has worked on me in the past, as it did this time. I gave her the scissors, and she took them and cut a little piece of the hem. Then she said, "I can't do it here. Will you let me take the scissors into the bathroom. Do you trust me?"

So I said, "Surely, I trust you. I know you won't do anything wrong with them."

She went into the bathroom and then opened the door, stuck out her head and said, "You won't let me lock the door, will you?"

I answered, "You can lock the door if you're afraid I'll come in."

She locked the door and remained in the bathroom for twenty minutes. I sat in my office and felt the gray hairs sprouting on my head as I wondered whether or not my risk was justified. Finally, she came out, threw the scissors on the floor and said, "You son of a bitch, you hate me, don't you? You don't care what I do to myself, you know I was going to use the scissors to commit suicide, you really hate me!" Then she picked up the cord of the telephone and wound it around her neck, threatening to strangle herself. When I didn't panic, she stopped.

It is obviously pointless to ask such a patient to lie down on the couch and free-associate. I had to find a different method to use when working with Miss Madeline. Finally I realized that I had to enforce a certain amount of discipline and could not be as nondirective as a psychoanalyst ideally should be, so I insisted that she call only at stated times. I insisted that she stick to a subject she was discussing instead of screaming and yelling without any content. As I continued to insist, she did begin to function a little better. It was one of the times when I saw how even someone who has been judged "psychotic," as she had been in previous therapy, can decide to behave differently.

At the time Madeline and I were beginning to make progress, I got a call from her sister. She demanded, "Why are you taking Madeline's money? You know there's nothing wrong with her."

"What makes you think I even know Madeline?" I asked, since Madeline had told me that no one in her family knew she was coming to see me.

The sister answered, "You see, I'm studying to be a policewoman, and for practice I was shadowing my sister. I shadowed her to your office; then I cross-examined her and she broke down and told me the whole truth. You know there is nothing the least bit wrong with her, so why do you keep taking her money?"

I was willing to continue to treat Madeline, whom I was seeing for a nominal fee; but now that her sister had found out through her clever police work, the father and another sister joined in and were constantly after Madeline to stop wasting her money on a psycho-analyst. So when they all started to call me, I suggested to them, "Why don't you pick a psychiatrist"—one of the things they upbraided me for was that I wasn't even a psychiatrist—"and if you find one who agrees with you that she does not need treatment, I'll be very happy to refund all the money that Madeline has paid me."

So the family went to a psychiatrist—who recommended immediate hospitalization. The same thing happened with two other psychiatrists they consulted. None of them wanted to treat her. As one of them explained to me over the telephone, "Obviously for technical reasons we cannot treat her in the office." Translated, this meant that she could not afford their fees, and that they were reluctant to handle a patient who acted in such bizarre ways.

Finally one of the psychiatrists had her hospitalized at Hillside Hospital, and while I was unhappy because I thought she could have been helped on the outside,

I must admit to feeling relieved that I didn't have the daily calls and demands from Madeline. The relief was short-lived, however, because soon various staff members of Hillside Hospital began to call me and say, "Would you please speak to Miss Madeline and tell her to talk to us? She says she will only talk to you."

When I did speak to her, all she wanted was for me to get her out of there. Since the matter was not in my hands, as I had not recommended the hospitalization, there was nothing I could do, and when she refused to talk I guess the staff at the hospital administered shock therapy out of sheer frustration. It has often seemed to me (and some research bears me out) that shock treatment is used frequently by hospital staffs, not so much because they expect it to cure the patient but because they feel angry and annoyed with him for frustrating all their therapeutic efforts.

When Madeline came out of Hillside, many pounds heavier because of the insulin shock treatments, which caused compulsive eating, she told me that she would never act as crazy again because it had been such a horrible experience. Hillside was then, and is today, one of the best psychiatric hospitals in the country. But Madeline had found her stay there such a traumatic experience, and had hated the shocks so much that she *made up her mind* never again to act in such a bizarre manner.

Unfortunately, I didn't understand the full implications of her reaction until quite recently. Because here was an obvious decision, based on the understanding of the consequences of being crazy, not to be crazy any more. Eventually she moved some distance away, and I recommended another therapist to her. Once she had decided not to be psychotic, she proceeded to improve. Soon she married, and the last I heard, she was reasonably happy in her marriage and had given up much of her suffering.

Madeline was only one example of the kind of patient I had early in my practice, many of whom were difficult and obviously "unsuitable" for Freudian classical psychoanalysis. In fact, it was ten years before I found a patient who was suitable! Because I was in practice for ten years before people started coming to me for their training analyses. They were, of course, people very suitable for orthodox psychoanalysis. As a matter of fact, I believe that this is one group for whom a lengthy analysis is useful. For one thing, most people who want to go into the profession have the discipline to have gone through graduate school or medical school, generally have reasonably strong egos and comparatively mild neurotic complaints, tend to be on the obsessive-compulsive side, and so can happily lie on the couch and free-associate.

Seriously, though, it is useful for any practitioner to have long therapeutic experience so that he has enough understanding of his own problems and difficulties not to put them off on unsuspecting patients. I must admit that it is difficult for me, as an active person, to sit back and listen and say nothing. It took years of practice before I could keep quiet while a patient was talking.

I remember one psychiatrist patient who spent two years speaking at great length every session, three times a week, and seldom gave me the opportunity to say a word. Occasionally I would try to interfere, and he would ask me to shut up because he had lots of other things to say. At the end of two years, he looked up

triumphantly and said, "Some resistance, hey?" His entire goal in the therapy was to talk and talk and talk, so
that I couldn't lead him into a painful confrontation
with his problems. Another patient whom I saw when
I was trying to do orthodox analysis came, lay on the
couch and didn't say a thing for the first two sessions.
At that time I was trying to see desperately if I could
wait out my patients, and for two sessions I sat there
without saying anything. At the third session I questioned the man and asked him why he didn't talk. He
said, "Am I supposed to?"

I said, "Yes, that is what is generally done in analysis."
So he started to talk, and at the end of nine months he
had improved considerably. I asked him, as I generally
do in order to learn when I do something right, "What
helped you?"

His answer was, "Having somebody present whom I
could talk to, and have a reason to look at myself, and
a time and place where I could come and examine what
I was doing, why I was doing it and how I could change.
But the most important sessions were those first two
sessions when I didn't say a word and just merely
looked at myself." There are some people who do not
need any further help than to be given this opportunity
to discuss their problems; and then they are capable of
reaching an awareness of what they are doing, and an
awareness of the choices they have made in the past
and their ability to make new choices.

The fact that I had been given the unearned title of
"genius" at the age of three was one of the problems I
had to overcome. Frequently I preferred to take no

action but remain secure in the conviction of my genius. However, a fortunate result of my experiences as a psychoanalytic neophyte and a student at the NPAP was that for once I was defined as not being quite good enough. This motivated me to demonstrate to my detractors that I was not only as capable as they were, but that I could be even more capable.

In studying many successful men, I have been impressed how frequently the decision to become successful was based on anger and on a decision "to show them." One of my relatives managed to work his way up from poverty to being a multimillionaire and an owner of the famous Concord resort hotel. As a young man, he and my father had been partners. My father dissolved the partnership because he felt that cousin Arthur was not a good businessman. Years later, when my father was a guest at Arthur's, surrounded by many people who were fawning on Arthur, as people are apt to do with a successful, self-made man, Arthur jumped up, rushed over to my father and said, "You see this man? He said I wasn't a good businessman, and that's why he didn't want to be my partner!" Apparently this criticism of my father's had goaded Arthur along his path to success. This was at least one of the factors that made him decide to strive so hard to achieve eminence in his field.

Often I was able to use this knowledge in working with my patients. For example, I had as a patient an extremely intelligent man, a psychologist who, like so many others, had completed all his studies except his dissertation. He came to me to discuss a number of problems, and among them was his inability to write the dissertation. One time, as he was discussing his wife and how bad she felt that he had never completed his doctorate, I said, "You know, she would hate it if you ever did write your dissertation and get the Ph.D."

He said, "You're wrong. She's always after me. She keeps nagging me to sit down and write. She keeps saying, 'When are you going to get started?' "

I answered, "Oh, come on, now. By now she knows perfectly well that the fact that she keeps after you prevents you from ever writing it. She's too jealous of you to want you to have that success."

He leaned back, thought for a moment and said, "Son of a bitch. You're right!"

As he started to work on his dissertation, he brought in considerable evidence to support my theory. Every time he started to work, his wife would nag him and say things like, "Today is Sunday. Why are you working? Why don't you spend more time with your family? Is that dissertation more important to you than any of us?" Each time she urged him to stop writing, he took it as an added spur. He was able to finish his study quite brilliantly, and has since gone on to be successful and nationally known in his area. He also has a different wife.

Let me add another example. At one time I was seeing a husband and wife together. Helen and Stan made the play *Who's Afraid of Virginia Woolf?* seem like a drawing-room comedy. Helen's attacks on Stan were constant and expressed with great anger and viciousness. So much so that some other members of the therapy group they were in fled in terror before Helen's attacks. She would say things to Stan like, "My husband has not yet awakened to the fact that a man knows how to make love to a woman. Sometimes I wonder if he has all the equipment a man is supposed to have. How would I know, since he never gets to the point of trying to use it? Once a month he deigns to make his own kind of ineffectual love to me."

Another thing she would attack him for was his inability to earn a good living. "He never could make a living. He's no man. What do I need him for? I earn more than he can." She was a semi-successful television actress and was in demand for character parts in which she played the sweet, gentle, kind and forgiving woman.

In a group, one has the opportunities of using different members of the group to illustrate situations. There was one woman in the group, a startlingly attractive woman who was very angry at her husband and was always denouncing him. One time some members of the group asked her, "How was your marriage at the beginning?"

Margaret, the unhappy, beautiful wife, replied, "The first two years were nice. He was nothing and I was queen in the house. I ruled him with an iron fist. Then he started to make money and became successful. Since then, life has been hell for me."

Armed with this information from Margaret, I turned to Stan and said, "You think you are revenging yourself on your wife with your passivity, your inability to earn a living. Here is an example of what happens."

Stan decided to change his passive mode, and—partly because he believed me, partly because at some level he wanted to make his wife happy, and partly for his own satisfaction—he began to work with new energy, new determination. He was an appliance salesman, and soon was the star salesman of the firm in which he was employed. As many of these large appliance firms do, this one held monthly sales contests. In one year, Stan won eleven out of the twelve contests. He won a trip to Hawaii, a new automobile, a complete outfit of clothes, and a set of golf clubs. Along with success in business, he also became a more successful lover. Not only was he more successful with his wife, but he managed for the first time in his life to have an extra-marital affair, in which he was assured by his girlfriend that he was one of the most tender and at the same time most assertive lovers she had ever come across.

What was Helen's response? One would have thought that she would be happy, she who had insisted on his entering therapy and who demanded that he become more assertive and more of a man. But when he reached these two goals, when he was able to assert himself in business and in discussions with her instead of retreating behind a newspaper, and was able to assert himself sexually, it was then that she decided to leave him. All the years of suffering and all the years which she had described so bitterly had not caused her to leave. But now Stan had achieved the goals which she originally set up for him, and she found the marriage impossible.

The irony of the situation is that they are now both happier and more fulfilled. It is several years after the divorce now; and they are both doing much better. Their son, who had previously presented serious learning problems at school and was considered an unmanageable child and a behavior problem, has become much more peaceful and productive in his school work.

When I have described such cases, I have frequently

been taunted by colleagues who thought my treatment was manipulative, even though they admitted the success of my work. Many fellow therapists sometimes seemed to me to believe that it is better to fail with correct procedure than to help a patient with a procedure that is not orthodox. What I was actually doing was helping these patients channel their aggressiveness, which was resulting in neurotic passivity, into activity. This is one example of the many ways of utilizing the neurotic decision, in this case to be hostile, for the purpose of arriving at a new way of life. It would be nice to move directly to an understanding of the individual's wish to realize himself rather than to have him do it for such so-called neurotic reasons. At a later stage, both Stan and Helen were able, when separated from each other, to drop the need for this kind of hostile interchange, and were able to act in a different way with their new mates.

I recognize that I myself have frequently been able to work much harder when there was a challenge involved. One of the things that helped me get through my first book was this: I was at a party, and there was a discussion of the book. One man turned to me and said, "Look, Harold, you're a nice guy, but anybody looking at you could tell that you're not the kind of person who could ever settle down and write a complete book."

This has sometimes also worked for me when I was doing therapy. While I learned a great deal from Theodor Reik, he was frequently less sanguine about the prospects for some of my patients than I was. For example, one of the more passive men referred to me was a fifty-year-old professor of geology. This was at the time

I was seeing Reik, and I presented to him this case of a man who was impotent and whose wife had left him, and who was now having an affair with another woman who was furious with him for his impotence. Reik was quite fatalistic and said, "Well there's not much you can do. I remember I once saw a man about the same age in Vienna who was very upset because he used to have erections when attractive women would come into his office. I discussed this case with Freud, and Freud said, 'There's nothing much you can do about it. These erections are just a dying flutter.'" Reik added, "That's what you have. This man's interest in becoming potent is the same kind of thing."

But I worked very hard with my professor, and in about six months he had not only regained his potency but was truly potent for the first time in his life. A year later he was not only potent with his girlfriend but with other women as well, so much so that the girlfriend called me up and said, "You know, I was the one who suggested that Fred come to you for therapy, but I didn't expect you to make him so potent that he would run around and sleep with my friends, too! I consider your behavior unethical."

I pointed out to her that potency, like dynamite, can be hazardous.

When I first discussed the case of a call girl patient with Reik, he was not very helpful. When I told him how depressed she was, he just recommended that I ask her to speak about her childhood, when she was happier. But as so many depressed people do, she insisted that she had never had one happy moment in her life. As I recognize that these comments indicate my competitiveness, I must admit that there were times when

Reik was extremely perceptive and helpful. When it came to discussing the problems of creative people with rich imaginations, he was able to make fantastic leaps of intuition, and it was from him that I learned to take chances and make these kinds of leaps.

Usually these leaps were based on his many years of experience. For example, I was treating a young man who had a great deal of trouble achieving anything in his school work. He presented a dream once in which he was playing baseball. He hit the ball into the outfield and thought it would be a home run, but the right fielder, after a long run, caught the ball, and he was out. I wasn't even sure that Reik understood the game of baseball, but his response was immediate.

"Ah," he said, "he has a brother." I was surprised, and questioned Reik, and he told me a long story about a diplomat he was treating in Holland who had dreams that he was playing tennis and that he was losing. This man also had a brother, and his problem was the fraternal competition. This was one way in which I learned to understand people when they presented dream situations that were similar to previous cases.

One of the things that has been helpful to me has been a feeling of tremendous optimism. It is my conviction that almost every patient I have ever seen could be helped if I had enough time and energy. That doesn't mean that I've succeeded with everyone, but when I didn't it seemed that if I had had more time or had been more skillful or another kind of person, I would have been able to help. This feeling is based on my conviction that there is considerable potential in almost everybody I have ever met or worked with. This does not mean that many of the people who presented themselves for therapy did not have serious and difficult problems with living. Even though I now believe these problems are based on decisions and choices that are no longer functional, that doesn't mean that the patients didn't experience them as painful and difficult.

I remember the first time I visited a state hospital. At that time I was an undergraduate taking a course in Abnormal Psychology. As part of the course, the class went to Manhattan State Hospital and the staff members at the hospital interviewed several patients for us to demonstrate their pathologies. While they described the pathology in very serious technical terms, it often seemed to me and to some of my classmates that there but for the grace of God, go I! They didn't seem as different from other people as the instructor was trying to make us believe. I remember that one of the older patients who was brought in was described as suffering from senile dementia, and the instructor commented on her deterioration. To show us how deteriorated she was, he asked her to repeat after him some very complicated phrases, like "Massachusetts State Artillery," and when she couldn't pronounce these words clearly, he called this evidence of her deterioration.

One of the members of the class had a different idea, and said, "Doctor, perhaps it's a problem with the English language. This lady is a Jewish lady who obviously speaks little English. May I try her with some Jewish phrases?" He did, and the poor old lady had no trouble at all repeating phrases in Jewish. It was at that very moment that I decided that if I ever worked in this field, I would take it for granted that people are not as disturbed as they are made out to be. It is difficult to maintain this attitude sometimes, because one is frequently persuaded by one's teachers of the necessity for detecting pathology. My feelings have always been that if we could become as sensitive in detecting strength in the people we work with as we are in detecting their pathology, we could be a lot more helpful.

One of the fringe benefits being a psychologist has given me is the opportunity to teach. In a way, I've been teaching since I was in high school, when I got a part-time job teaching English to foreigners. It is one of the things I enjoy doing most. Even when I had to do practice teaching for an education course at college, I found the challenge of being in front of a class, of getting the students interested and attempting to get my ideas across, a most pleasurable experience. Shortly after completing my work at the Institute of the NPAP, I was appointed to the faculty and started to teach a course on the basic writings of Sigmund Freud. I have always had difficulty in following rigidly the teachings of any one prophet, but I did find my application to the early writings of Freud quite rewarding.

In my mind I was able to divide Freud into two parts. One was the clinician taking painstaking notes and making observations on the people he was working with. To me, this part was fascinating. It was almost as if I could experience him as a therapist working with his patients. Later on I was to amplify this impression by many of the stories that Theodor Reik and other patients of Freud were able to tell me. It became clear that if Freud had been attending the Institute at the same time I was, he never would have been permitted to become a member because his techniques and attitudes varied so much from that required by every Freudian institute operating at that time. In fact, I feel quite convinced that if Freud had been working with the kind of people I was working with, he would have changed his technique even as he described it, much further. He was, after all, the foremost revisionist in the whole field of psychoanalysis. Apparently psychoanalysis is a very good technique for people who happened to have been born in Vienna before 1890. However, it was a useful experience for me to study Freud's clinical experience, and to separate it from some of his more fanciful leaps and his effort to establish a broad philosophical base for psychoanalysis.

Shortly after my book, *The Call Girls*, was published, I was invited to take part in a course given at Columbia University's Teachers College on the Psychology of Family Relations. It was exciting to go back to Columbia and stand up in front as a lecturer rather than to listen from the audience. The first full class I got to teach, however, was at Pratt Institute in Brooklyn. For the most part, my students at Pratt were people interested in the arts—industrial designers, interior decorators, and people interested in teaching art or illustration. The students tended to be much more articulate with their charcoal than with their words.

At the end of the course I gave them a simple examination, asking them to write down what they had found to be most valuable in the course. One of the students whose intellectual attitudes were fantastic had great difficulty writing the simplest English. At the same time, he had contempt for people whom he considered to be in the lower levels, describing them as illiterate, but spelling it "eliterate," and he thought very little of plumbers, but he spelled this word "plummers." I was interested in reading his paper, in which he said that the thing which interested him the most was Freud's psycho-sexual theory of development. However, he spelled psycho "syko" and he wrote: First there was the oral stage, when the child was interested in the things that he put in his mouth; then there was the anal stage, when the child becomes interested in the area around the waste products of his body; and lastly there is what he called the phallic stage, when the child becomes interested in the "gentile" area. When I read his answer to the class, I explained that the author of this paper was actually a "genital."

Each of these teaching assignments was just for one semester or year and my title was then Lecturer. A few years later I was still teaching at the NPAP when I received a call which was, to me, one of the most exciting and pleasurable honors I have had. The chairman of the Psychology Department of the Graduate Faculties of the New School for Social Research called me and asked if I could take over a class in Theories of Psychoanalysis, which had formerly been taught by Dr. Ruth Monroe, an extremely well-known and knowledgeable psychologist who had written a book on the subject. One of the reasons they asked me to do it was that I had, shortly before then, edited a book called *Great Cases in Psychoanalysis.* The most exciting thing to me was that my title—on my first regular appointment—would be Professor.

The graduate courses at the New School were very interesting. My class was very large, but I found one aspect of teaching there frustrating. At that time they had about two hundred people with masters degrees working for Ph.D.s and the school was graduating only one a year for the Ph.D. There were constant changes in the faculty and there was an emphasis on academic psychology despite the fact that most of the students were interested in doing clinical work or therapy. The remark of the chairman of the department still remains in my head, and I've never really been able to understand it. He said to me, "We don't want to teach them anything that they can use." Theory, yes; its application, no.

Several times I was tempted to warn my students that they were not supposed to find anything I taught them in class useful, or I would be fired. This attitude is, unfortunately, not unusual in psychology, and it is part of a continuing battle within the field between those who would make it a professional discipline (like medicine, in which people are taught how to do therapy or diagnostic work) and those who would try to make it a pure science, in which people would learn how to conduct research and make discoveries—preferably about rats and pigeons. This conflict has never seemed a real one to me because I believe some of the most profound insights about human beings have not been achieved in the laboratory, where so many academic psychologists think of themselves as imitation physicists of the nineteenth century (physics of the twentieth century being much less rigid). The discoveries and hypotheses about human beings that have had the widest influence have been those that have emerged from the clinical practice. However, the struggle continues on many college campuses, and absurd efforts are made by the two different sides to prove themselves right.

I have had as patients a number of experimental psychologists who came to me with great contempt and even disgust for the unproven hypotheses, as they called them, of clinical psychology, and, after their clinical experience in therapy and in groups, decided to become clinicians themselves. Another ironic response I got at the New School was that my lectures were "too popular." Years later, when I gave my first lecture at the United States International University in San Diego, the institution I am presently connected with, I remembered this comment with some concern, and told the dean who had sat in on my first lecture that I had been accused of being "too popular." His reaction was very different from that of the faculty at the New School.

"In order to be a good teacher," he said, "you have to be a good showman."

Unlike the academic psychologists who were then in charge at the New School, Dean Rucker had a doctorate in education from Harvard and had a better understanding of what it requires to teach than the more academic people, who frequently took the attitude that the duller and more difficult it is to follow the material, the more scientific and worthwhile it is. A friend of mine was once involved with a senior colleague of his in preparing a paper for presentation before the American Psychological Association. When the senior colleague was unable to make the presentation, he asked my friend to deliver the paper, and, beforehand, to read it aloud to him. His comment at the end of the reading was: "You are reading it with too much expression, too interestingly, and people won't consider it scholarly."

It is fascinating that this attitude remains despite the fact that most of the outstanding psychologists I have heard speak have been entertaining and charming. This included B. F. Skinner, the darling of the behavior modifiers, who is a humorous, warm, friendly speaker —more "human" than many of those who consider themselves "humanistic."

Years ago I had the opportunity to hear Alfred Adler, one of the pioneers in the field, and A. A. Brill, Freud's first translator into English. Both of these men were quite interesting, humorous and popular speakers. So were Fritz Perls, the founder of the Gestalt Therapy movement; Eric Berne, the author of *Games People Play*, who founded Transactional Analysis; and Albert Ellis, whose Rational-Emotive Therapy has had an important influence on my own development. I have had the opportunity of being on programs with all of these men, and they were attention-compelling speakers.

All my previous teaching assignments were carried out on a part-time basis in addition to my full-time practice. One of the most difficult things for me has been to confine all my activities to the office, so even my teaching at NPAP and, later, for the American Institute of Psychoanalysis and Psychotherapy and two or three other institutes, was conducted in my office. I was pleased when I received an offer to do some work outside the office, as a consultant at a treatment center for children and their families in Brooklyn called Pride of Judea.

It was a challenging situation, because by this time I was seriously modifying my psychoanalytic positions, and most of the staff members were still wedded to the psychoanalytic model, even though they hired me as a consultant in group therapy—which some of the orthodox analysts considered the work of the devil. At the

"Pride," too, I had the opportunity of working in a truly interdisciplinary situation. There were psychologists, psychiatrists and social workers on the staff and it was fascinating to see how all three disciplines could work together without any one of them fighting for a particular position. One of the members of the staff was a social worker from Norway, Tikkon Christenson, and when I discovered that she was Norwegian I asked a friend of mine, the Swedish actress Viveca Lindfors, to teach me how to say a few words in Norwegian. So one day when I was at the "Pride" I said to her, in what I thought was Norwegian, "How are you? How do you feel?" She didn't understand me. This was to be my experience with Scandinavian languages many times thereafter.

I repeated it again and she said, "Oh, no, you're not speaking Norwegian, you're speaking Danish." However, my gesture led to an increased friendliness between us. She invited me to her home for dinner, and I met her husband, Bjørn Christenson, who was then about to assume the position of head of the Department of Psychology at the University of Bergen in Norway. We had a wonderful evening, with many exciting discussions, helped along by the excellent wine they served. At the end of the evening, Bjørn asked me if I would be interested in going to Norway, if the opportunity presented itself.

My wife, Ruth, and I had been discussing for some time how nice it would be to take a sabbatical leave from my practice. I had been working for about twenty years as a psychologist, and so I thought it would be great. But Bjørn's question seemed like one of those casual invitations that are made at the end of a pleasant evening, and I forgot about it until about a year later, when I received a letter from Bjørn asking me if I was still interested in coming to Norway, and if so, could I help start the clinical program at the University of Bergen.

Ruth and I discussed this back and forth. On one side there was the practice, and all the people who felt dependent on me—and, of course, the sizable income that I was earning, compared to the modest sum which the University of Bergen could offer to pay. So we put the decision on the back burner. In effect, we decided, for the time being, not to decide. (It is interesting that while I am writing this entire book on decision and choice, in my own case one of the methods I have used in making a decision is to think about it a little while and then stop thinking about it so consciously and wait for the decision to pop out of my head). One evening, when Ruth and I were having dinner, I suddenly said to her, "Do you see any reason why we shouldn't go to Norway?"

She said, "No." Before she could say another word, I went to the telephone and sent a cable to Bjørn, accepting.

It was one of the best decisions I have ever made. In the few months before our departure for Norway, I made a great discovery. I told all the people I was working with that they had three months in which to complete their therapy with me. Many of them had settled in for the long-term, drifting kind of therapy that they had expected it to be. But once I told them they had a comparatively short time to complete it, most of them showed an amazingly rapid improvement, so that several of them terminated therapy before I left for Norway. This is one of the reasons that

I now try to set a time limit with everyone who comes to me for help.

There were many details to take care of. Ruth took care of most of the practical ones, such as subletting our apartment and packing for the trip, and finally the Great Day arrived. My brother, Phil, had arranged for a private room at the airport, where we had a little party. Then we took off for Scandinavia.

When the plane landed at the tiny airport in Bergen, it was hard for me to believe that this was a city large enough to have a university. The Bergen airport, while it is an international airport and gets flights direct from the United States, looked more like the kind of place you would expect to be used for flying a private plane around. But it is one of the best-run airports I have ever been in, and I used it many times while we were in Norway.

Bjørn met us at the airport and took us to a lovely nineteenth-century home which we were subletting from Arild Haaland, one of Norway's most prolific writers and critics. It had a magnificent fireplace in the study, a huge living room, a huge dining room, paintings of the Battle of Copenhagen and real chandeliers holding many candles, the only way the dining room could be lighted after dark. We didn't believe it; we felt as if we had been ushered onto the set of an Ibsen play. In addition, our landlord had furnished the house with a fine collection of Scandinavian paintings and sculpture. We felt as if we were living in a museum.

By now I felt reasonably confident of my ability to deal with audiences, but I was unprepared for the special kind of audience that my Norwegian classes presented. Fortunately, the graduate students' knowledge of English is remarkable. Many of them not only speak English well but very idiomatically, their discourse filled with allusions to modern American and British literature. While I do not believe strongly in national differences—and I was soon to find that the differences between the kinds of problems that Norwegian and American patients presented were very superficial and unimportant—there are differences in behavior within certain situations. For example, the Norwegian student has been conditioned throughout his school life not to speak unless spoken to, and tends to sit back and listen very attentively to a teacher, and, unlike American students, does not volunteer questions or interrupt and is loath to engage in spontaneous interaction.

There *is* some language problem. In Norway there are two major languages and many dialects. One language is Riksmål (also called Bokmål), which was until recently the official written language. There was a movement to develop a language that was more Norwegian, Riksmål being too influenced by Danish in the opinion of the growing nationalist movement, and so a collection was made of the dialects of the different fjords and this was standardized as Nynorsk. So now there are two official languages in Norway and the students are expected to know both, and write examinations in either.

In one of the Norwegian journals there was a discussion whether or not it is correct to end a word with "e" or with "i" under certain circumstances. This became a matter of great importance in this comparatively small country of fewer than four million people. But then there was a movement for unification and a third language was added, Samnorsk, which is supposed to combine Riksmål and Nynorsk. In addition, there are many local dialects, and, as frequently happens in a country as dominated by its capital as Norway is by Oslo, people speaking dialects from smaller places are inhibited about speaking freely in the presence of those who speak the more-or-less accepted and official dialects. Perhaps the only exceptions are the people of Bergen, who are so proud of their city that it is common to hear a Bergenser say, when somebody asks him where he is from, "Excuse me for boasting, but I am from Bergen."

There was a great consciousness of pronunication, which leads many of the people, when they speak English, to feel self-conscious about their pronunciation of English. Since my English pronunciation was formed on the Lower East Side of New York and resembles that used by actors playing the parts of gangsters, I assured my Norwegian students that their English was much better than mine. In fact, while I didn't learn as much Norwegian as I would have liked to, I feel that the best thing that ever happened to my English was being exposed to the British English spoken by my Norwegian students and colleagues.

I remember the first day, and seeing before me a wall of impassive faces. The impression was illusory, and after several months I found not only that were they able to drop this reserve when they got to know me better but that the friendships and relationships I formed with students and colleagues in Norway were in many ways deeper and richer than many of the friendships we have formed in the United States. It was easier to form relationships in Norway.

The people of Norway are extraordinarily polite. It

seemed to me that even the patients in the psychiatric
hospital where my office and classroom were located
were more polite than their American counterparts.
Psychotics, people who had been diagnosed as paranoid
schizophrenics, behaved with greater considerateness
then mildly neurotic patients do in the United States.

In addition to teaching university classes, I also conducted two post-doctoral seminars for psychiatrists and
psychologists in the Bergen area. One of them was for
the staff of the psychiatric institute where my office was
located. At the beginning this was attended only by
psychiatrists and psychologists, and our small group
met in the library. I had been in Norway only a few
weeks when I decided to lecture in double-talk Norwegian. I didn't know any Norwegian, but if you listen
closely to any language it is possible to do a pretty fair
double-talk imitation of it; and so, as they were sitting
around in their white coats in the library, I launched
into a completely nonsensical talk. I had mentioned my
plan to only one of the psychiatrists on the staff, and
after about fifteen minutes I turned to the others and
said, "Are there any questions?" One of them said, very
politely, "I beg your pardon, sir, but I am having difficulty understanding your Danish accent." The friend
whom I had informed of my intended speech, generally
a very serious and sedate fellow, dissolved in laughter
so strenuously that he almost fell off his chair.

The most important influence on me, in dealing with
my students and patients, was psychological. They pro-
foundly altered my entire approach to the problem of
dealing with people. As my students pointed out toward the end of my stay in Norway, I had started out
by explaining the necessity of using manipulation and

maneuvering techniques to help patients. However, little by little I became more and more convinced, apparently not consciously at first, that I was moving in quite another direction. The culmination of my change came when I formulated my ideas about Direct Decision Therapy.

Now, I do not believe that this idea contains all of the revealed truth. But there is within it a basic attitude of respect for the individual and a belief in his capacity to deal with his problems with guidance rather than manipulation. I moved from a position in which I felt I had to manipulate my patients to one in which I gave them the opportunity of choosing more successful functioning.

When I first formulated my theory, I thought it was based completely on my clinical experience; but I couldn't help but be impressed when one of my best students in Norway, Erik Larson, pointed out this change, and also the similarities in what I was stating and what Ibsen had written about in *The Lady from the Sea,* and Kierkegaard had written in *Moment of Decision.* Apparently without my overt knowledge, the Scandinavian experience was influencing my thinking considerably.

One of the most exciting things about being in Norway was the chance to work in a hospital, but also, since I was officially a Fulbright professor, it meant that my name was circulated to various universities in Europe. What happened was that after I conducted my first workshop in Norway for a group of psychiatrists and psychologists invited from all over the country, I started to receive invitations to other places. After four months I never was to spend a full week in Bergen. I spoke about Direct Decision Therapy and demonstrated it in such places as Jyvaskala in north-central Finland, at the Catholic University of the Sacred Heart in Rome, in Spain, in Berlin, as well as in various parts of Norway, several of the important hospitals in Oslo, and finally at the Norwegian Psychoanalytic Association in Oslo. While European audiences are more cordial than American ones, I did find their questions searching and relevant. European professionals, it seems to me, are better trained in philosophy (perhaps less so in practical matters) than their American counterparts, and they followed with great interest what I had to say, thereby helping me clarify my thinking with the serious questions they asked.

With my students at the University of Bergen there was a constant dialogue on the subject, and there was a similar dialogue with the students at the University of Oslo, but perhaps the most exacting demands on me were made when I spoke before the Norwegian Psychoanalytic Association. The problem there was one that came up again and again when I spoke to groups in the United States. At first they attacked me for doing symptom treatment, on the supposition that if I helped the patient get rid of his symptoms, they would pop out in some other form because I had not dealt with the underlying pathology. When I was able to answer many of their criticisms with quotes from Freud, a member of the Norwegian Association said, almost in despair, "You present yourself as an innovator in the psychoanalytic tradition, and yet you are able to quote Freud better than any of us."

While there seemed to be a certain rigidity in the Norwegians' character on the surface, I certainly found the head of the psychology program, Bjørn Christens—son, remarkably flexible in the opportunities he gave me to discuss my theory and present it in different situations and to engage in arguments.

Part of the reaction to me, of course, was based on the ambivalence toward Americans in general. In 1969, progressive people throughout Europe were becoming increasingly disenchanted with the American adventure in Vietnam. At the same time, many of the people in the field of psychology were interested in learning from American colleagues, who, they felt, had developed further than they had. Even though I had to bear their displeasure at America's increasing participation in Vietnam, I shared the glory of the American advancements in the field of mental health. There were two groups I had difficulty making any impression on: the people so committed to psychoanalysis that they thought any deviation was an act of heresy, and some of the Maoist Communists, who were sure that since I was an American I had to be a reactionary capitalist representing intellectual colonialism. When, on a more recent visit to Norway, in a discussion on the image of man, I criticized the Marxist "economic image of man," I probably caused more resentment of my position than by anything I had said up to then.

It was difficult for us to leave Norway. We had formed so many close friends in the ten months we were there, and had developed so much in our learning. Ruth had started to work in the hospitals, where the patients are not nearly so fluent in the English language as my colleagues in the field, and so, combining her background as a dancer with her training as a social worker, she developed a nonverbal approach which was very popular and she was very much in demand to demonstrate her technique of movement therapy. Though it was difficult for us, I made the decision to come back to the United States. For one thing, I wanted an opportunity to test my new theory on the American scene and perhaps to get a wider audience for it.

In any foreign country, no matter how cordially one is received, there is some alienation because of the language problem, and my experience with Norwegian was characteristic. In high school and college I had been a very poor language student. The one subject I failed with remarkable consistency was French. As it was taught at the time, it required endless memorizing of verb endings and conjugations and rules of grammar, and in high school, particularly, I thought it was beneath me to sit down and study such things. In college, where I took another year of French, it was a little easier because it was mostly translation and my vocabulary and ability to read French were not so bad. However, on several trips to Europe I found that I could speak the languages much better than many of my friends who had studied much harder, because I had long ago given up any effort to speak English perfectly and with it the effort to speak any other language grammatically correctly, so I was less inhibited in my attempts to speak German or French or Spanish or even some Italian. It may sound a bit simplistic, but I think I made the *decision* to speak all these languages, and by making that decision I was able to communicate. Sometimes I had difficulty understanding, but in every one of those languages I got to the point where I could express myself, so that I had confidence that I would be able to learn Norwegian.

I was not prepared for their great feuds about proper pronunciation, and when I finally learned a few words in Bergen and went to Oslo and used these words, I was criticized for my accent. This constant accent correction made it almost impossible to communicate in Norwegian. A young woman we met, Martha, who had come from the United States, had managed to learn Norwegian perfectly. She explained that the way she had done it was to speak only to children, who were not so critical. However, when the daughter of a friend of mine tried to help us with our Norwegian, and we didn't pronounce a word correctly, she immediately called us idiots. She was six years old.

I recognized that part of the correction was called for, for there are nuances to pronunciation which alter the meaning of words. However, I find that if I speak Norwegian in Sweden, I am understood. In Denmark they can't understand me because they don't want to, because the Danes have considerable antagonism against the Swedes and they think that anybody speaking a Scandinavian language that isn't Danish must be Swedish, so they have a tendency to be critical.

We came back to the United States, and as we got off the plane, I must admit that I did not find the prospect of returning to New York City a very pleasant one. New York has always been my home; I have lived there most of my life, except for a brief stay in Mississippi and Louisiana during the War. I always felt that I knew New York better than most natives; I knew the restaurants, the neighborhoods and the people. While I was living there, I was able to take the changes and the harassment that ordinary life in New York produces. Just to go from my office on West 81st Street to any place within the city would become an exercise in frustration tolerance. I couldn't drive in my own car because I wouldn't find a place to park it. It is difficult to get a taxi, and at four P.M. or during a rain it is almost impossible. Public transportation is awful. Just getting around became a problem. Of course, it was easier for me than for most people who work there, since my home and office were just around the corner from each other, and if I didn't want to get out of that area, I was O.K.

There was also the problem of danger. My wife was mugged twice within six months, both times in broad daylight. When I parked my car at the garage two blocks from my home, I had to be aware of the fact that a number of people were mugged daily in the neighborhood and that 82nd Street had for a time been referred to as "the death block." Also the weather, the hot and humid summers and the cold, bitter winters—all these things combined to make me think about moving to a pleasanter place. However, I recognize that intellectually my home will probably always be New York, no matter where I wander to.

I was finding it difficult to re-establish myself, and to set about building up a practice again. Not that it was difficult in terms of opportunities, because by now there were quite a number of people who wanted to come and see me, but I tried to restrict my practice while I thought of what I wanted to do next. In September of 1970, during the first convention of the American Psychological Association that I attended after articulating my new theory, I presented a full workshop for the first time on Direct Decision Therapy, at the meeting of the Association for Humanistic Psychology in Miami. After presenting the theory, I asked for a volunteer, and, strangely enough, the volunteer who came up to discuss her problem was trying to decide whether to continue to work in New York or to go to California. We soon came to the conclusion that the decision she was trying to make was not just between living in New York or in California, but depended on what these places represented to her. New York represented hard work and a conscientious striving for success and achievement; California represented fun and pleasure. Since I had at least intellectually decided some time before to do only things I enjoy and like, because these are things I am usually more successful at, I found this discussion very helpful.

Shortly after the discussion with this woman (when I met her a year later she was a California resident), Everett Shostrom, who was a professor at the United States International University and whom I knew from previous conventions where we had often shared the platform, asked me if I would be interested in teaching in San Diego. Of course I was interested, and told him so. Then I went back to New York again, and I wasn't sure whether anything would come of this. I sent in my *curriculum vita*, as requested, to the Dean of the Graduate School of Human Behavior, and a few months later I got a letter saying that if I was ever in the San Diego area, I should get in touch. So some months later, when I was in California, I called the University and went out to visit it. I was impressed with the campus, with the leisurely, country-like atmosphere and with the friendliness and general openness of the faculty members I met. I was invited to speak in front of a class. The response of the students was quite stimulating, and I felt that the United States International University might be a nice place to be. I was invited to come out to teach for the summer, and I accepted. With the help of some friends, I found a little house in La Jolla, and began the life of a full-time academic professor.

This was really my first appointment as a professor; all previous appointments had been as visiting professor. At first I thought of playing the professor game. It meant wearing clothes that were already considered old-fashioned in Norway. Some of my colleagues, no matter what the temperature, were still wearing the dark suits, the white shirts and narrow ties with clips which had disappeared from most of the rest of the academic United States three or four years before. The students, of course, presented a very different picture. Very few of them wore jackets, unless they were defending their dissertations for the doctorate in front of the committee. It wasn't just the generation gap, because many of the students were quite mature. For me, this was another plus. Perhaps because I was a mature student myself when I went to graduate school, I have always found that the mixture of ages is valuable; it is more stimulating for both students and faculty when the students vary in age from the twenties to the sixties. My first summer was quite an exciting one, because I had an opportunity to try my informal style with the students.

Not that the school is necessarily heaven on earth. Some time before, Carl Rogers, the founder of Client-Centered counseling, one of the leading schools of American psychotherapy, had resigned to protest some of the academic restrictions. There were a number of fascinating contradictions present. It was educationally rather free in form, yet there were "moral" restrictions on student behavior which had disappeared from most campuses ten years before. When I was questioned about what my attitude would be toward these restrictions, I explained that while I didn't agree with them, I also didn't think resigning would do any good, but that I would be interested in working to change what I didn't agree with if this was possible. The decision one has to make when he disagrees with an institution is always a problem. One approach is to withdraw. My tendency is to stay and try to introduce change. I'm not sure it is a better decision because as one stays one tends to find more and more justification for the institution. It is too easy, when one becomes a part of an institution, to start compromising and changing one's opinion to fit in with the attitude of the institution, so that instead of changing it, as may have been the original intention, the institution changes the individual to conform. This has not been my experience at United States International University.

I made a number of decisions. One was to stay as far away from academic politics as I could. Since I had comparatively little experience in the administration of universities, even though I may have had some great ideas about it, I didn't think that I could be very helpful in that area. In any event, I wanted to concentrate on my teaching and writing. The students are a very exciting group, with the openness and friendliness so characteristic of southern California. In the East I often felt my students were there to prove how wrong I was. My students at United States International University are more like the Norweigan students, with similar sincerity, dedication and interest. Of course, this isn't true of all. There are a number, as in any other place, who are thinking only in terms of professional monetary success, and they try to get a doctorate to earn more money, with little attention to learning anything but going through the ritual of getting the degree. Also there are many who seem interested in learning but unfortunately have got the notion that the only thing needed in order to become a good therapist is to be nice, to be sincere and honest. Now, while these are useful qualities for a therapist, I have always felt that a certain amount of hard knowledge is valuable and I try to supply some of it by direct teaching, some by lecturing, but chiefly by engaging in interchange with my students, with demonstrations in which I treat patients or volunteers from the class in front of the students. The response to this has been most rewarding.

Some of the most interesting students are the many priests and ministers who are students at the school. At one time, as one who had been raised as an atheist by a father who was one of the early members of the American Association for the Advancement of Atheism, I looked with suspicion on anybody who was connected in any official capacity with the Church. However, in my years of practice I have worked with a number of religious people and found them on the whole a group of dedicated, sincere people who have goals over and above the immediate goals of making as much money as possible. Many of them also have a greater social dedication and interest in improving the condition of their fellow men. So that, to my amazement, I find that some of the people I am most compatible with are people in the priesthood or in the ministry.

There is a kind of person I have found wherever I go that I believe the world needs more of. They seem not

Norwegian, not Italian, not German, not American, not Catholic, not Protestant, not Jewish, but world citizens. They are the people I immediately feel close to, and I know that we share a great many attitudes and feelings. One, for example, was a professor at the University of Madrid. Five minutes after we started talking, we knew that on all essentials we spoke a similar language. Others were: a student of mine at the University of Bergen; a woman I met in Stockholm; members of a group I worked with in Austin, Texas.

There are a number of such people at United States International University. These are people who tend to have a somewhat agnostic attitude toward authority. One of the reasons I find myself compatible with them is that no matter what they profess, they are never orthodox, they have a capacity for seeing things in a different way—outside the narrow rigidities of whatever place they happen to be in. Sometime I must study this phenomenon further and see what we can do to develop more people of this kind. Unfortunately, few such people are found in politics. Politics seems to require the capacity to draw on totally committed followers who never question the correctness of the leader's decisions.

In discussing the problems of Americans overseas in different parts of the world, I find that many are incapable of transcending their prejudices. There are always a few, however, like the people I am describing, who are able to transcend all prejudices, all differences of nationality, and get through to the essence of the people they are working with. This is one of my own goals —not only to be this way myself but to see if I can help other people reach that kind of attitude. I cannot see war and strife being supported by people who have such an attitude.

Being in San Diego has given me the opportunity to live in a different way. In California, despite some narrowness and provincialism, cut off from "civilization" as represented by cities like New York, London, Paris, Rome, Madrid, Stockholm, Oslo, and Copenhagen, there is an emphasis on pleasure. The ads in the California newspapers are full of camping equipment, swimming pool supplies, and for the most part people are dedicated to having a good time. Strangely enough, this feeling exists in the same place with some of the most reactionary individuals in the entire country; I have seen long letters in the newspapers attacking Nixon as a fellow-traveler and Kissinger as a member of the Communist international conspiracy. But when I go to a retail shop, a supermarket or a restaurant, there is a pleasantness and a friendliness which makes life much easier than it is amidst the tension and competitiveness of New York. Perhaps I needed both kinds of experiences.

Looking back, I would not give up my training in the tactics of survival on the Lower East Side of New York, or having to struggle in the highly competitive atmosphere at Columbia and City College, where every student thought of himself as the potential intellectual leader of the country, or the Psychoanalytic Institute. All these competitive places were important to my development. I realize sometimes that I still maintain a competitive stance when it is no longer necessary because of the openness of the people with whom I am now working.

One of the decisions I have made is not to commit

myself forever to any one place or activity. Recently I went to visit a colleague who bought a lovely and beautiful home in the mountains northeast of San Diego. As I complimented him on the magnificent view and the fine details of the house, he said, "We've decided that this is going to be our last home." Since he is twenty years younger than I am, I was a bit shocked and depressed at this kind of decision. For myself, my decision is never to make that kind of permanent home —even though, as I work at this moment in my study, I hear the noise of the people digging the swimming pool in our back yard, and even though we have bought the home we live in (which was difficult for me to decide, because I always thought that the ideal situation was only to have as many possessions as one can carry on one's back) and are experiencing the pleasure of having, for the first time in our lives, a home of our own that we can change in whatever way we like.

We have the home but we are both ready, if something new and different and more exciting comes along, to move on. I enjoy my practice immensely, but I keep it at a minimum and concentrate on teaching. If this doesn't work out, I will be happy to spend more time writing. I hope that after getting through this book, which contains so much of myself, I will find it easier to write the next one. But I know that hoping is not enough, that I will have to decide that I am probably not going to write the greatest book, but will put down whatever I know as well as I can, and as simply as I can.

Section III

An unexamined life is a life not worth living.

—Aristotle

Everything you do, you got to figure, what does it buy you.

—Prisoner in a Virginia Work Camp

CHAPTER 5

FINDING THE BASIC DECISIONS IN YOUR LIFE

As I use the term, a decision is a choice between alternatives of behavior; a choice of the way one organizes information, or the way one chooses to look at the world. I use the analogy of a map. We all have our own map of the world.

One of the reasons we want to have a way of looking at the world is that we want to be able to predict the future, and to choose a route. For example, if we decide that people are no damn good, that everyone is out to get us, this may influence us in a variety of ways. We may make it our business to avoid any action or not to trust people. Alternatively, if we decide that people are loving, warm human beings, then we may believe that people should be trusted and we will be nice to people, and open with them. The way we look at the world has a great influence on all our perceptions.

When I am working with people, I have to pay attention to the choices, or decisions, people have made about their behavior, how they have chosen to look at the world, what map they have constructed of the world. It is important to try to understand this map from their point of view.

All therapies start out studying behavior (what are the choices of behavior?) and the patient's way of looking at the world. In psychoanalysis, for example, the fundamental rule is: "Just say whatever comes into your head, no matter how embarrassing, how trivial, how difficult." What comes into your head is based on your choice. So when I listen carefully to the free associations of a patient in psychoanalysis, I am listening to how the patient chooses to see the world, how he chooses to behave, and about what he chooses to report. In behavior modification, where apparently the only interest is in modifying behavior by a series of objective tasks, one must first find out what the problem is. Since human beings have many problems, the patient makes a choice of the problem he presents. In reports on behavior modification, the therapist may talk about a patient coming in and discussing a fear of elevators, for instance, not including that she is also afraid to eat in public, because it didn't seem important for her to mention that. She is choosing what problem to report. She is choosing what she believes to be normal and abnormal. She is always exercising choice, particularly in what she talks about and how she deals with it.

One kind of therapy that might seem to be freer of this choice process is the study of dreams. We now know from the studies of rapid eye movement and other objective studies that most of us dream many times every night. The dream that the patient brings in, then, is the dream he chooses to bring in. This is communication, by way of a dream, in which the patient makes a choice. Choice is involved in the problems, complaints, and symptoms patients report. Someone comes in and says, "I have headaches." And after one works with him for six months, one finds out that he has headaches because he hears voices. He had never mentioned it before. In encounter groups the leader asks people to go through various exercises. Encounters, though they emphasize freedom, are probably the least free kind of therapeutic activity, because the therapist doesn't give the patients choices about what to talk about. He tells them what to do, he gives them a whole series of programed, carefully planned exercises in spontaneity. However, I find that group members, in the way they choose to carry through the encounter group activities, still exercise certain choices. If the leader is truly interested in the person, rather than in having his group carry through his exercises, he will be able to see and to study how patients choose to act in this comparatively structured situation. Even in therapy using hypnosis, when it seems as though the hypnotist is doing something to the subject, there is really a very complex interaction going on, because one can't hypnotize someone without his co-operation. Very often patients will tell the therapist exactly how they want him to behave. I will start to hypnotize someone, for example, and the patient will say, "Just a minute, speak a little lower. Don't speak so fast." So it's not a one-sided deal at all, but an interaction. No one gets hypnotized who doesn't choose to be hypnotized.

In almost any form of therapy, in any kind of discussion, in an employment interview, when you meet people at a party, you can think of it in terms of choice:

what they choose to talk about, how they choose to behave, how they choose to see the situation. A way of getting insight into what people are about is to consider that what they do and how they look at the world is their choice.

Given the total context of a person's life, all the decisions he makes can be looked at as rational—if you know the data, what he had to work with, and what the consequences of his behavior, the "payoffs," were. If I try to put myself into a situation when I am working with someone, in any kind of relationship, where every one of his choices makes sense, then I'm with him. Then I have joined his reality, instead of demanding that he join mine. Too often in therapy, therapists have specific expectations and demands of one kind or another and are deeply disappointed in the patient if he does not operate properly. Psychoanalysts may say that the patient "wasn't suited" for psychoanalysis, that he had too much resistance. I once worked with a woman who had difficulty expressing herself, and one of my colleagues in the audience said to me, "Why do you put up with this shit? She doesn't want to work." But if this person didn't have this kind of problem, she wouldn't have been up there with me in the first place.

My two sons, Robert and David, have taught me a lot about psychotherapy. When one was about four and the other was eight, I had my office in one room of our large apartment. They could hardly ever see me, and like every psychotherapist's children, their great ambition was to grow up to be patients, so they could see their father.

One time the younger one said, "Can I be a patient?"

So I said, sure, and I took him in, and he lay down on the couch and he didn't say anything, he just lay there.

My older son said, "What kind of patient are you—you're not saying anything!"

The younger one replied, "That's my problem—I can't say anything."

Very often the thing that is the person's problem is one that makes the therapist say, "I can't treat you, because you have this problem." He won't treat the alcoholic, the drug addict, the psychopath. This is obviously an absurdity. If I really understand the person, I can understand how his past choices made sense, and if I can't understand the sense they made to him, then I really don't understand the person.

I must try to understand the patient's decisions. If the person cannot speak when he comes to me for therapy, then I look at this as a choice on his part. But, to repeat, I try not to be judgmental; I try to understand what, in the context of his life, caused him to make such a choice.

A person who was always laughed at and ridiculed by his family while he was growing up is obviously not going to want to talk about the things that bother him, because his experience has been that to bring them up is only to invite ridicule. He made the decision a long time ago not to talk unless he is absolutely certain it is safe to do so. This makes good sense. If the therapist can understand the reasons for what is usually called "resistance," if he can figure out why the person makes such a decision, then he can help the patient by creating a situation in which his decision can work in a different way.

A woman came to see me and couldn't speak. I asked

her if she was ever able to speak, and I asked her if she had ever talked with her family. She said, "No."

I said, "Never?"

And she said that the only time she ever spoke was when the family was at dinner. She would get under the table and talk. I asked her to get under the big, long desk in my office, and talk. She said she couldn't do that, so I said, "Okay, I'll get under." So I got under my desk, and we spoke very nicely for the whole session.

When she came back the next session, she wasn't talking again. I got up from my chair and started to crawl under the desk, and she said, "I'll talk, I'll talk. Just don't get under that God-damn desk!"

What had happened was that I had created a situation in which she could make the decision to talk, in which the alternative to *not* talking was to see me under the desk. She didn't want me under that desk— possibly because this would have been an unacceptable reversal of roles. (Her husband called me a few weeks later and said, "You know what? My wife is beginning to hallucinate. Do you know what she told me happened in the office when she came in?").

One of the ways I try to help people reverse decisions which are not functional for them is not to meet them head on. In psychoanalytic terms, we call this "joining the resistance." The existential therapist Frankl calls it "paradoxical intention," and in learning theory it is referred to as "negative practice." When I use the negative, some patients say, "You're using psychology on me." Unfortunately, not enough psychologists understand the value of the negative. The depths of human negativity have not yet even begun to be plumbed. Most people are very negative, and for a good reason.

Let us approach this negativism from the point of

view of decision. The child becomes an individual the first day it says, "No." Until that time, it is an appendage of mother and father. It is acting almost as if it were only an arm or leg—some extra limb—of the parents. When it says, "No," that is when the effective separation takes place. That's when it becomes an individual with its own will, its own wishes.

While negativeness may be a pain in the ass to us, when we think of it as the development of the individual, when we recall its importance in our own development, we recognize that we did not become individuals until we first said no to an authority figure—to a parent, a husband, a wife, a lover. At that point we were being our*self.* When I understood that, I was no longer confused by negativism, or angry when I was confronted with it. There is little to be gained by getting locked into a power struggle. If someone comes in late and I say, "I want you to come on time next week," it's very difficult for him to come on time. If he does come on time, he feels defeated. He doesn't feel completely human; it won't be a growth experience.

But if I say to a negative person, "Come on time, or late, as you choose. It's your money," I am giving him a choice, freeing him. He is no longer stuck. We have stepped out of the power struggle.

At one time in my therapeutic endeavors, I started to use negativism as a therapeutic ploy, as a way of getting the patient over a problem. A patient would come late and say he was sorry, and I would say, "That's all right. You don't have to come on time—no reason to be compulsive about it."

I was doing it as a kind of ploy, because I knew it would stop him from being late. But I was more correct than I knew, because there *is* no reason why somebody has to come on time for a session. He's not hurting me, he's hurting himself; he has a right to make the choice to come late. Many people are not free to make an independent choice, unless we are ready to join them and to accept even their negativeness. It is important to try to understand the reasons for their choice, rather than criticizing. So much of the problem is that we don't try to understand the other person's reality, we don't try to understand where they're at, we just try to get them to act the way we think they should. And we do it in the most ineffective ways possible. Very often when we get into a patient's reality and see him acting in ways which we don't find acceptable, we think we have to do something about it.

Here we are involved in two different problems. One is that many people who are locked into an old struggle which they are replaying on the stage of the therapeutic situation, when we tell them what we want them to do or why we think they're wrong, aren't going to be able to listen. They won't be able to listen because all their lives somebody has said to them, "I don't want you to do that, for your own benefit," when it hasn't been for their own benefit at all. The second problem is that I'm not really sure what is "wrong" for that person. With age or greater tolerance and understanding, (or maybe I'm just lazier), I now find that some things aren't necessarily wrong, that for some people there may be very good reasons for doing "wrong" things. Take, for example, the question of young people dropping out of school. We give them long lectures on why they shouldn't drop out, but there are many who have very good reasons for dropping out. Who are we to say that somebody else should be in school, or shouldn't be, rather than giving him the choice? There is no comparison between what school will do for you when it's your choice and when it's something you're forced into.

It is important to establish a relationship with people one is working with in their own terms—to enter their reality. A hallucinating man comes to me and explains he's a sergeant in military intelligence. So I join him in that and ask him if he is writing any reports. And he looks at me significantly and nods. Here is a man who feels defeated by life, impotent. How can he deal with it? There is a rationality to his choice. He decides that he is a member of military intelligence; everything that happens to him (he has changed the map) is only proof of his importance, his value. He is no longer impotent, he's a powerful person, he is a man to be reckoned with because he is sending reports to people who are so important they can't be named.

The important thing about the work of people like Laing, or Cooper or Janov, is that in their approaches even the most extreme kind of psychotic behavior is acceptable. The biggest problem people have is not going crazy, but the fear of going crazy. Many of us lead very narrow, restricted, difficult, anxiety-laden lives because we're so afraid of going crazy. So a therapist says, "You want to go crazy? Groovy! Let it be a creative experience. This is a way of growth. This is a way of development, of getting in touch with yourself, of putting your shit together." As long as it is put in those terms, one takes away the fear.

Being a homosexual, for example, is not *per se* a problem—lots of people manage to be this way and have fun with it. They call themselves "gay." But the big problem is the fear that it is so terrible to do this. One of the

preconditions to good therapy is to establish an accepting atmosphere. I am trying to operationalize this and
show that the way to establish an atmosphere of acceptance, true acceptance, is not to say, when somebody is
spitting in your face or hitting you across the jaw, "I
love you," because that's bullshit and he won't believe
you, but to really try to understand what's going on, try
to see things from his vantage point. It's difficult if
you're being attacked, but you say, "You're hitting me
and I'm interested in what you're doing this for." Really
try to get at it, rather than to just call it names or to say
this person has a weak ego or is goofing off.

Human infants, when they enter this world, are
among the weakest animals on earth. Few other animals are so defenseless, so completely unprepared for
independent existence as the human infant. He has to
be taken care of by people around him. As he's growing
up, the memory of this basic inadequacy, anxiety,
rarely leaves. For a long period all our needs are met
and taken care of. Every one of us went through it. No
matter how deprived someone says he was in childhood, he really wasn't, because if he had been truly
deprived, he wouldn't be alive.

Children who are completely deprived, who are left
in a hospital with no attention paid to them, get
psychotic, or die. They actually die from lack of attention. Human infants are much too fragile to exist in an
atmosphere of complete deprivation. So that all of us
have had the experience of inadequacy, and of being
totally taken care of.

As infants, not only were we taken care of, but we

were often taken care of without having to ask for it. We're hungry, and the food appears, and it's in such a lovely container, too. Or we are wet, and magic hands appear, and they make us warm and dry, and we never have to ask for it. Then, it stops. And that's murder. Because we don't want to give it up. And we try to scheme and figure out how we're going to get back to that nice place, our own private Garden of Eden. We do this in a variety of ways. Some of us define love and love relationships as situations in which we will be treated as adults as we once were as infants, without ever having to ask for it.

When I work with couples, again and again they complain, "He never takes care of me or listens to me. He never meets my needs."

When I ask, "Did you ask him to?" the wife or girl-friend will often say, "If I have to ask him, it's no good, it's like asking for a birthday present."

Once you're an adult, you have to ask, but the problem is this terrible desire to get back to that time when we were completely taken care of, which we all have and work at in various ways. Some of us even go to the length of calling ourselves helpless nonentities, so that someone will come along and take care of us. Some of us decide to have all sorts of strange problems; we have illnesses and rejoice in them.

I was at a swimming pool recently and there was a big, husky man sitting next to me with tattoos on both of his massive biceps. He was having a conversation with two people, laughing and joking. I was curious to know what the conversation was about and overheard him saying, "There I was body surfing, and I look down and the sand is there and I fall down and five thousand pounds of water hits me on the back and ruptures my gall bladder. The pain went on for a few months but I finally went to the doctor and he says I've got to be operated on. Then I got blood poisoning . . ." and so on for forty-five minutes.

This big husky man is carrying on with all his ailments and this is supposedly the story we tell about aged women rocking in an old people's home! But he, in great detail and with gusto, described his helplessness. "Don't think I'm so strong because I have the muscles" is the message he was sending. "I, too, am a poor, weak person who needs to be taken care of."

Another way we try to return to the comfort and security of childhood is by trying to be smart and bright, as we were as little children, when we got a lot of attention for that. Or we try to be negative, or we try to be all the things that worked for us as little children, because we have a great wish to get back to that period. A lot of people think that this is characteristic of schizophrenics; I think it is characteristic of human beings. To some extent all of us occasionally try unfortunate methods of trying to get back.

Sometimes the decision is made to act difficult or to be different, to be intransigent at all times—whatever it is, you can understand that a decision to express helplessness is based on the wish to get back to the Garden of Eden. Because that's what the Garden of Eden was —the infancy of all of us; it was the land of milk and honey where all our needs were met, where we never had to work, everything was taken care of, as long as we didn't make the mistake of getting too intelligent, by eating the apple of knowledge. The Bible is a recapitulation of the history of the individual.

One way to be completely taken care of is to be incapable of doing things for oneself. All of us have been ill, and if we were lucky there was somebody around willing to nurse us and take care of us. It's a very nice feeling. Somebody comes and brings us all our meals. But we are idiots, and we get well, and so we have to take care of ourselves again. The crazy people aren't as stupid as we are. They decide that they can't take care of themselves and don't know how to deal with reality, so we take care of them, put them in a womb with a view, into a mental hospital, and we take care of them, as long as they are intelligent enough not to get sane. If they get sane, they're in trouble.

I've seen this over and over again, particularly in people who go into very fine mental hospitals. One, a private hospital in Connecticut, is a magnificent place. Each person has a private room in a beautiful dormitory. There is a little window that the guard—who isn't dressed like a guard but wears slacks and a sport shirt, and is called by his first name—can look into. The place is in very good taste, with nice modern furniture, tennis courts and a beautifully equipped theatre and bowling alley. But as I was going through it, I didn't see anybody around. So I asked, and I found out that they were all in the coffee shop. So I went to the coffee shop and got a contact high, so much marijuana was being smoked in that coffee shop. And they were having a great time.

I figured that anybody who gets well there is really crazy. As a matter of fact, I knew a person there and every time her doctor would say she was improving, her mother would be so happy because she'd be going up there to get little Gloria out of the hospital and home so she could go back to school and do all her course work and have to worry about dates and all the other things reality demands of us. Every time her mother went up there, Gloria would get really violently crazy, throw herself against the wall, start doing crazy things because she didn't want to get well, so the mother consulted me and asked what she should do. I said, "Put Gloria in a state hospital." The mother said, "How can you be so cruel to suggest such a thing?"

I said, "Put her in a state hospital and she'll get well in two weeks." Eventually they ran out of money and put Gloria into a state hospital, and in two weeks she was home. She didn't want that kind of nonsense. As long as she was in the pleasant hospital, the threat of having to go out and make it on her own was too much for her. She didn't want it. To me, it makes perfectly good sense to want to be in that lovely resort.

A great deal of so-called mental illness, neurosis or whatever, is basically a conspiracy between the patient and the therapist. It's to the advantages of both. If you didn't have a lot of crazy people, you wouldn't create hospitals for them or psychiatrists, psychologists, psychiatric nurses and the whole mental health superstructure. So it is in the interest of all of us mental health professionals to have a lot of "crazies" around. And what you get in these situations is a kind of conspiracy. A psychiatrist has to be really crazy to step out of that bind, because there are so many gratifications and advantages to getting along with psychotics, so many gratifications to being with them! I can be more honest, more direct, speak to them more openly about a fantasy than I can to "normals," because they don't have the hangups that the rest of us do, and they're willing to talk about it, and that gives me permission. In addition, they come in at the beginning of the session suffering, in pain and terrible agony, and we speak for an hour and they go out cheerful and happy. You never get that with neurotics. They won't give you that satisfaction. It's to my advantage for these people to be crazy!

I knew a fellow who used to come to every encounter group I ever ran, and in every encounter group he would be dramatically cured of his homosexuality. Can you imagine what would happen if he really got cured? I wouldn't have him to come to the group to show everybody what a great, magical job I was doing. So we were engaged in a kind of conspiracy. An unconscious wish on my part at the time was to keep him homosexual between sessions and cure him at the session. That made a great impact.

One gets into these long-range, ten-year therapeutic engagements in which the person is constantly involved with the analyst or therapist and the analyst is involved with the person, who tells everybody about the great progress they're making together, and everybody's having a good time.

It reminds me about the story of the two men in the jewelry business. One fellow bought a ring from someone for five dollars, and a friend looks at it and says, "I'll give you six dollars for the ring," and the first man sold it to him for the six dollars. Later the first man comes back and says he wants the ring back. "How much do you want for it?"

"Eight dollars."

So he buys it for eight dollars. The next day he sells it back for ten, and it goes up to twenty, thirty dollars and they keep selling it back and forth to each other until the price is one hundred dollars. A stranger comes and offers one hundred and twenty-five dollars and the man sells it to him. The next day the other man comes back and wants to buy the ring back again. The first man tells him that he sold it to someone else, and the second man says, "How could you do a thing like that when we're both making such a good living from that ring?"

As I said at the outset, a precondition to any kind of successful therapy is that the therapist get within the framework of the other person's world, suspend his own ideas, his own map before he moves in on the person. One of the preconditions of therapy, or any other kind of teaching or persuasion, is to see where the other person is at, and to try to see his problem from his perspective. I try to forget all the theories I know, and just try to see where the other person is at.

I try to see what my patients' decisions are like, because that's a good way of organizing the data I receive, but I don't let that interfere with what I see from the present. The other thing I try to do is be as natural as I can, not to be somebody different. I don't speak differently or pretend to different moral attitudes with my patients than I would with myself.

I know a woman psychiatrist who was married fifteen years to a man she didn't care for, and suddenly she met a man who attracted her, who happened to be married. So she walked off with him and married him. I met a patient of hers who was thirty-one years old and lonely. I asked her if she had ever thought of going out with married men, and she said, "Oh, I couldn't do that. My therapist showed me how self-destructive that is."

Such nonsense! When her therapist wanted a man (over the age of thirty five it's hard to find a good man who isn't married), she found a married man. When I pointed that out to the woman, she said, "Oh, no, my therapist would never . . . She always told me, whenever I was interested in a married man, what self-destructive behavior it was." That therapist had a very different set of morals and attitudes for her patients than for herself.

That is what we do, all too often. We say to children, you should be honest, truthful and loyal, and then we cheat the government on our income tax. When we don't tell them the truth, no wonder they don't trust us! A patient who is a little more mature is going to know what I am up to if I try to con him. So I might as well tell the truth about what I believe in. This doesn't mean that I insist on my way. For example, when a woman told me, some fifteen years ago, that she was going to an orgy, I thought that was terrible, and started to give her all the reasons why she shouldn't go, for her benefit. Of course, she didn't listen to me. But if I could have said, as I might now: "You know, I've been thinking about that and I'd love to go to one, but I'm scared"— or something like that—then we could have discussed it. We could have discussed the possible implications, the dangers, the possible advantages. We could then have discussed it more openly and honestly.

The same is true about feelings. I remember one time I was working with a paranoid patient and he said, "Oh boy, you're getting angry!"

I said, "Oh no. I'm not angry, I'm calm."

He said, "That's how I know you're angry, you're so calm!" He was right. Of course I was angry. Why try to deny it? But I thought I shouldn't admit it. I have a much better basis for an understanding, though, if I am able to say that I'm angry. When somebody is doing something I don't like, something I find morally reprehensible, I may say, "I personally find your kind of life very difficult." Or I say, "It's against my own code, but let's see what it's doing for you." All too often we translate what we don't like into some kind of scientific or psychological term. When I was more Freudian, and didn't like what a person was doing, I said, "You're acting out and indulging an infantile behavior." Humanistic therapists sometimes say, "You're being inauthentic, you're not actualizing." All they are really saying is, "I don't like what you're doing." Well, why not say it that way?

Every decision one makes in life in one sense or another influences all future decisions. When I am dealing with a person, I try to find out what his decisions have been and where I can make the most effective intervention. I have to discover the basic decision. A woman says she has trouble making a decision to go out with a particular man or not. When we discuss it a little longer, I find out that the real problem is that with this man she gets plenty of pain and suffering, and she can justify her view that men are no damn good. The real decision she has to make is whether she wants to continue to establish this point of view, or whether she wants to take a chance and move out of suffering. Once I put her on to that, she was no longer so blithe about it, and said, "I don't know. That's kind of frightening. All my life I have worked with suffering. I don't know if I am ready to give it up."

The problem is to get down to the basic decision. There are a number of basic decisions that people make. One of the major ones that few of us consciously make is whether to live or die. Because if we haven't decided to live, we are not fully alive. Camus, in *The Myth of Sisyphus*, said that one can't decide to live when one hasn't examined the question of suicide. Only then do we really decide to be fully alive.

Many people don't make this decision. In a certain sense, you can't fundamentally help a person who has decided to die. There are many patients who come in with that decision underlying everything. They are trying to die. Unless I can get them to try and change that decision, I find myself attacking a Hydra-headed monster. New problems will shoot out all the time.

I feel I have to get at the patient's fundamental decision. Whether to be productive or to be passive and be taken care of is a kind of fundamental decision. Notice that they're all interrelated, all very closely connected, and the depth of therapy will depend on how fundamental a decision one can get the patient to make, because the fundamental decisions underlie the day-to-day decisions. If I can get to the fundamental decisions, than a profound change takes place in the person in a short time.

One of the things I want to make clear is that I do not try to get the patient to necessarily make the decision, I just try to show him that he has made some kind of decision and that it is important to be aware of it. *My real goal is awareness, an awareness in terms of the choice he has made, the context in which he made the choice, and the payoffs.* What I'm always looking for is awareness, not necessarily change. But with something as destructive as a patient planning to commit suicide,

I would have to tell him that it makes me unhappy, that
I'm uneasy at the thought of his killing himself, that I'll
have to work on that.

When decisions are of a minor kind, it is often a waste
of time to give them too much attention. A young man
told me how he made decisions. He met a well-settled
person who had no problem making decisions, and
asked him, "How do you do it?" And the friend said,
"Well, whenever I have a decision to make, I consult
the *I Ching*, the Book of Changes. I toss a coin and I
make a decision." Since then the young man has been
using the *I Ching* to make all his decisions. So one can
toss a coin; it really doesn't matter. I have several rules
for those kinds of decisions. Pick the one that is higher
alphabetically, or the one that has the fewest letters, or
always pick the left vs. the right. These things just don't
matter, because if you can follow that kind of advice, it
indicates how unimportant these choices are.

Awareness is the most important thing, because some
of the most successful work patients have been able to
accomplish did not take place during the time they
were in therapy, when nothing seemed to happen except they recognized that they had choice. And they
left me with apparently nothing happening. Often I
met them months later and found that they were
changed people. They were the kinds of people who,
for one reason or another, had to do it for themselves.
They were able to do it alone, without me, but they had
the tool of awareness.

Decisions are not things that are just talked about;
they are practiced within the context of the therapy
itself. The first thing I ask a patient is what he wants to
work on. I ask him to make a choice. After he decides

on the problem he wants to present, the next decision I ask him to make is how long he wants to work on it. How many times a week does he want to come? How would he like me to treat him? I give him all these choices and, instead of talking about decision abstractly, try to make the problem the person has in the outside world the problem within the therapeutic situation and give him practice in decision-making.

One of the first people I applied this method to was a girl who was working as a call girl. She had read my book, and she came up to me at a lecture and said something nice like, "Are you the prick who's taken all the bread from the call girls?"

I said, "Right." And I added, "You must be one of them." She made an appointment, and I asked her, "How long do you want to see me?"

She said, "Oh, about a year and a half." I said, "What for? How about being finished by June?"

She said, "No, that isn't long enough." Then we argued back and forth and decided that she should be finished by January. In February she was married to a colleague of mine. It's a very good marriage; they're doing very well and they're very happy. They had a baby recently. She got practice making decisions all throughout the therapy—to lie down, sit up. Choices about everything. "Would you like to discuss dreams?" I constantly presented her with choices.

Every good therapist, no matter what his school, does this. Sometimes I say to somebody, "How long do you want to come?" He says, "I don't know, I don't care." Well, then you know what his decision is—not to make one. This is the decision I deal with.

I may say, "It seems to me that you decided at some

point in your life not to make any decisions. There must be a very good reason why you did that. Can you tell me the reasons?"

The payoff for this particular decision may be to avoid anxiety. It may also be a form of covert hostility, a way of getting even with the world. "I'm not going to tell you. You want me to, but I won't tell you."

When somebody has made a decision that he can't carry out, which is a problem most of us have, I ask him to be aware of what happened that he was not able to carry out the decision. Usually one has to constantly make the decision over and over. If, for example, one makes the decision to express negative feelings, he will constantly find himself in situations where habits from the past will prohibit him from expressing his negative feelings.

I saw a man and wife recently, and the man said, "Instead of planning on how to fix up our new house, my wife ran off and went swimming. Well, that was okay."

But it wasn't okay. He didn't feel it was okay. He was really furious about it, but he said that it was okay because that was his habit. Eventually he made the decision to express anger and annoyance when he experienced it.

I try to make the whole therapy situation a no-lose game. Because the patients have been losers for a long time. When someone doesn't carry out a decision, our tendency is to act like a coach, and say, "You can do it, try again, challenge your fear." Often when I do that, I don't get anyplace. But if instead I carefully investigate with him what prevented his carrying out his plans, we have a better chance of success.

Sometimes it may not be appropriate to make a decision. I was talking to a group recently, and a woman initiated a discussion by saying that she had a decision to make but felt she couldn't make it at this point. She wanted to make decisions about her future career. When she started telling me how difficult it was for her to make them, I said, "Probably at this point you're not ready. You need to wait a while to get yourself ready."

She said, "That helps a great deal."

Nobody has to make a decision when the therapist decides he should make it. So I would very strongly stress the idea that people be given their choices even about making the decision, even one which seems like a jim-dandy decision.

A lot of the maneuvers we engage in are designed to propitiate the internal judge who is watching us all the time. When we think of alibis for the rest of the world, that's not nearly as important as the alibi for the judge that's in our head. If we are able to make decisions about our life choices, then we are able to make other decisions; so we tell ourselves, when we have a difficult decision to make, that we can't make one, because then that proves that we're not guilty. Most of us have a constant wish to avoid responsibility.

When we work on a decision without being fully aware, we may still go through on a not-quite-aware level, asking ourselves, "What are the payoffs?" What are the payoffs of smoking? What's the payoff of not smoking? You weigh the alternatives and you *decide* where the better payoff is.

CHAPTER 6

DIRECT
DECISION THERAPY
AND
MARRIAGE PROBLEMS

SINCE so many more people today have made the choice to consider marriage a nonlegal, voluntary association, I will, in discussing marriage, include those people who are legally married along with those who are living together in a more or less permanent relationship.

I have had the opportunity for many years to work with couples—or more than couples, because in some cases I had a chance to work with *ménages à trois,* one man living with two women or one woman living with two men. In other cases I have had the opportunity of working with homosexual couples who came for marriage counseling.

One time I saw a man who was living off the earnings of his call-girl wife. Originally he came in and presented her problem, that she had a "work-block"—she did not want to go out and hustle and call johns in order to get more work. At that time he wanted me to see her about this work problem. I accepted, knowing what the results would be, for the more I "tried" to help her with her work problem, the more she decided that she was not going to be a call girl anymore.

Many of the people involved in so-called antisocial activities, or at least those not sanctioned by law and society, are so negative that any suggestion that they leave this sort of occupation, whether it be call girl or bookmaker or confidence man (or woman), merely reinforces their decision to remain in it. When she gave up being a call girl, they had serious financial problems and both she and her husband came for marital counseling.

One of the first things I try to do in a marriage situation is to observe the interaction between the partners. This is not easy, because often they want to play the divorce-court game, in which each presents his grievances against the other and expects the therapist to act as judge. In dealing with marital families and couples in the past few years, I have found it very useful to work with my wife, Ruth, because it seems more even when a couple treats a couple. We are looking forward to including my son, David, who is studying to be a clinical psychologist, into the treatment team so that we can have a whole family—husband, wife, and children—represented on the therapeutic side.

I tell couples that I am not planning to act as judge, that I am going to try to understand them rather than try to say who is "right" and who is "wrong." Sometimes this is very difficult, because, I admit, there are occasions when the problem that the husband or the wife present about their marriage may be a problem I have experienced myself, and I may tend to jump in heavily on one side, or overreact in the other direction. Anybody working with couples should be clear about his own choices in his own marriage or relationships.

When they can move away from the courtroom game and I can have the opportunity to watch their interaction with each other, it gives me insight into the kinds of choices and decisions the people have made and especially the decisions that are behind their present difficulty.

Many people enter marriage with unreal expectations. They may have experienced serious deprivation in their early lives, and they expect the marital partner to make up for this. It is very difficult for a mere human being to live up to such expectations.

Some people come to therapy bitter because the partner has not lived up to *unvoiced* demands that they are making. One very common demand of this kind goes somewhat as follows (I will use "he," but the same applies for both members of the team): "He should know what I want."

This is a very typical, but almost impossible demand. A couple comes in and the husband says he has tried to make the marriage a good one. His wife, however, is bitter. She is bitter because there are so many things he does not do. For example, she complains that he never comes and suggests that they go out.

I ask her whether she has asked him to take her out, whether she has told him that this is what she wants.

Her reply is, "Does he think I like staying home all the time? Doesn't he know that this is what I want?"

It comes out in the discussion that this is the first time she had made this request explicitly. When we discuss why she has not told him before, she says, "If he really loved me, he would be sensitive and understand that I have this great need."

There is a semantic problem. People see their wishes and desires as a great need. It is obviously a strong wish, but hardly a need, that she go out. She has *decided* that he does not love her because he has not been able to read her mind. He has *decided* that she is so irrational that there is nothing he can do that will satisfy her. He has, perhaps, made it difficult for her to communicate her wishes. The assumption I follow is that there are decisions on both parts which make the marriage difficult.

The belief that "he should know this if he loves me" is one of the major difficulties in communication. It is difficult for many people to accept the fact that their thoughts are not instantly communicated and that people have to communicate what may seem to them their most obvious wishes in order to have them met.

Another decision that many people have made leads them to say about the marriage, "I'm stuck. I have the children to think of. There is no way I can leave. It is a terrible, desperate situation and if things don't improve I will kill myself. I don't see any other way out." It is very important in such cases to explore the options, to show that there are possible decisions of either leaving or of rearranging the situation, opening paths of communication.

Another common problem arises when a person decides, "I deserve better." This does not mean that he necessarily believes himself to be such a wonderful person. Rather, the difficulty usually is that he at some time, perhaps long ago, made a decision that he was inadequate, but that now, for some mysterious reason he deserves a better fate than the one he has. Husbands feel that their wives should have been better-looking, more articulate, better homemakers. Wives feel that their husbands should be brighter, more successful, better lovers, more intelligent, and that *they* deserve better.

This is related to the early decision (actually it is a fantasy) about how marriage is going to solve their problems, and obviously they feel they deserve this. They are angry with the other partner for depriving them of what they feel are their just desserts.

In recent years, there has been an increasing problem over the question of faithfulness. The decision, unexamined by many husbands and wives, is that the other partner must be, should be, has to be, completely faithful—not only in deed but even in thought. This is not a brand new phenomenon, naturally; what is new is that many couples are engaged in exploring new options, and that the wife, as frequently as the husband, will opt for an open marriage in which neither partner is necessarily bound to the rules of faithfulness, and that either one has the right to have affairs and relationships, often purely sexual ones. This is not an easy thing to work out, and although many people feel that in principle it is a very nice idea, their emotions are still into another way of being.

A young and bright professional was explaining to me that he was going to live with his girlfriend, who was returning from an out-of-town university. While she was away, he had established a number of very important relationships with women whom he enjoyed, who he thought had taught him a lot and made him a fuller person. He said he would like to be able to continue some of these relationships but knew that when his girlfriend came back and he told her this, she might want the same privilege for herself. He felt that the thought of her being with another man was impossible for him to tolerate. He felt as though a knife were twisting in his guts at this idea.

He understood the irrationality and the injustice of his demand, and for that reason was at first unable to express it. His fantasy was that his girlfriend would come back, be completely and totally faithful, not even tempted by other men, but that he would continue his debonair experimenting with other women. Now, he said that he wanted to give up his jealousy, but what he did not recognize was his decision behind it.

After discussion, he realized that his decision was that he should be thought of as a nice person. How could he, as a nice person, indulge in other affairs and also if he was a nice person, have a girlfriend who would find him imperfect and be interested in other men? It was after he recognized this decision to be perfect, to be well thought of, that he recognized how this decision was interfering with his ability to function well in many relationships. Only then was he able to change that decision. Once he did, he could contemplate his relationship with his girlfriend in a much freer way. The intense jealousy dropped away, and he felt a greater willingness to commit himself to a full relationship with his girlfriend.

In dealing with a couple, then, the first problem is to recognize the old decisions that they are laboring under and that make life between them difficult. I ask the couple, after they have had the opportunity to express their anger and disappointment to each other, whether they are going to decide to keep the relationship together or whether they want to be separated. I find it helpful to focus directly on this primary problem. If they are not ready to make such a decision, we can explore other difficulties. But sooner or later the decision to stay together or separate has to be made. Very often couples come for counseling, not to figure out how to work together but to justify their already-formed decision to separate. It is necessary to bring this out into the open, so that they are able to make an enlightened decision eventually.

One of the problems that couples face in marital therapy is that frequently they feel ashamed and guilty about their decisions and their ways of working together. In working with such couples, Ruth and I have found it helpful to share some of our own problems to illustrate that even though we have had some thirty-five years of experience in marriage, even though we are relatively aware people as a result of our own therapy and the years we have spent working with other people, we still quarrel occasionally and frequently still make silly decisions.

This has a freeing effect and makes it easier for people to discuss their problems with us. Not always, though. One woman who came to see us about her daughter was very upset when she heard us yelling at each other and told us how disappointed she was because her own marriage had been "so perfect." She would not present any difficulties of her own marriage, but several months later, after we had terminated treatment because we moved from New York, she

called us to tell us that she was not living with her
"perfect" husband any longer.

One difficulty we sometimes encounter is the belief
that the mate is so wonderful that the other partner
cannot continue the relationship because he is ashamed
of being angry or annoyed with someone so perfect. It
frequently helps to make clear to such people that it is
impossible to live with a saint. One's own problems
make one feel inadequate and imperfect.

The old attitude of the anonymous therapist, who
told and shared nothing of himself in the relationship,
tended to make many patients feel even more inadequate when they were faced with this "perfect" therapist. One of the better and more fruitful methods of
psychotherapy is the recent trend for therapists to
share their own difficulties with their patients.

Another problem which occurs frequently with
couples is the unwillingness of each one to look at
things from the partner's point of view. In this case
we have often found it helpful for couples to exchange roles, to have the husband say lines usually
attributed to the wife, and for the wife to say lines
usually attributed to the husband. This is remarkably
difficult for some individuals, which indicates how little attention they have paid to their mates and how
exclusively engrossed they are in their "own thing,"
how rigid they have become in defending their own
positions.

If they can be helped to make a decision to look at the
marriage not only from their own point of view, but
from the point of view of their partner, a great step
forward has been taken. I hope, dear reader, you will

not take this as a suggestion meant for your mate and not for you.

In my own marriage, I made a decision which may seem absurdly simple but which has had important consequences for me and for Ruth. Since I have spoken in public and frequently traveled alone for many years, naturally I found myself, because of my desire for company, with other women. As a result of a crisis in our relationship a few years ago, I realized how much more pleasant, how much more attentive, how much more gallant and sensitive I was to these women whom I would see only a few times compared to the way I treated my wife, who through so many years of difficulty had been an understanding and helping person. So I came to a conscious decision to treat her as well as I would a woman I was not married to.

Now I think of paying her the same kinds of compliments I would pay to someone I was interested in establishing a relationship with, of taking her to good restaurants, buying her little gifts. In general, I decided to treat her as if she was a new mistress. The results have been so satisfactory and so excitingly fulfilling that sometimes I think of writing a book suggesting that a man have a few mistresses just to learn how to treat his wife. I also realize the importance of paying greater attention to my wife's wishes, and this in turn has led to a much more open relationship between us. Now we have greater freedom to discuss both our difficulties and—what is so rarely done in marriage—to discuss the satisfactions and pleasures we find in each other.

One of the things I have learned in my own marriage is that I often had difficulty in asking for what I wanted —to take a trip by myself, to buy an expensive piece of equipment—and was angry with Ruth when she didn't suggest it. Increasingly I have learned to ask for what I want. We find this a frequent problem in other marriages. When we can both tell a couple we are working with that we have decided to deal with such problems in this way, it has often helped them make a similar decision.

CHAPTER 7

DIRECT
DECISION THERAPY
AND
PSYCHOSES

ONE psychological problem that is often referred to as not being within the will of the person, not being a choice, is psychosis. In fact, it has frequently been defined as the loss of control, a situation in which a person has no choice. Yet to date, the most dramatic results I've had with Direct Decision Therapy have been in the treatment of psychotics. One of the first patients I treated this way was a girl I saw in a hospital in Europe, who came before a presentation I was giving to the staff. She started to act up as I was questioning her, and I said, "Hey, you don't have to talk like that. Cut it out!"

She looked up at me and said, "How did you know?"

I was modest, and said, "It takes one to know one," and then we got along very well, and discussed what she was doing in the hospital. Since I was demonstrating the technique, I asked her about the payoffs for being crazy. I should add that when I first saw her she was fat, wearing a pair of house slippers, and really looked like a deteriorated back-ward schizophrenic. She had been in the hospital about four years at that point, and she had previously been to quite a few psychiatrists, and had a long history of treatment, so I asked her, "What are the advantages to being crazy?"

She replied, "There are lots of advantages." She then listed the advantages: 1) she never had to worry about a job; 2) she didn't have to worry about dates—back home when she sat alone on Saturday nights, her mother would say, "Everyone's going out, why aren't you?"; 3) she could do and say anything she wanted. She would yell at her mother, because she said, "I'm crazy." She could do anything, and no one would do anything to stop her.

So I said, "Well, under these circumstances, what do you want to do?"

She said, "I'd like to leave the hospital."

I asked her, "What for? Look at all the tremendous payoffs you have."

She said, "Well, I'd like to live, to be part of life."

I saw her five more times. Once she told me how much she was suffering, and we went through an entire fantasy trip in which she saw her mother, and she was able to express some of the fury and anger she had at her mother. She told me how she would like to kill her mother, to destroy her, to cut her up into little pieces and fry her.

But at that first session she decided that she was going to get out of that hospital. She asked me, "How can I do it?"

I said, "It's easy. All you have to do is act sane. The

only difference between you and us [the staff of the hospital] is that you act crazy and we act sane. If you want to get out, act sane."

She was going out on a weekend pass with her family. She said, "I'm going to tell them that I'm going to be sane."

I said, "Do you know what will happen?"

She assured me, "They'll be happy."

So I told her, "Don't be so sure. In fact, now they will think you're really crazy."

And that's what happened. When she went home and told her family that she was going to be sane, her sister said, "Oh, no—she's getting worse, she spoke to that American and now she's really in a bad way." But this girl had enormous determination, and we worked at it very hard. At some points she was very discouraged. When she got out, she found that she had lost a lot of the social skills that most people develop out of experience. One time she went to a party and no one was paying any attention to her because the other women there were more attractive, so she started to tell everyone how sick she was. There were other times when she found life very difficult, and she sought out every person in that city whom I knew and told them all how I was torturing her. Even after I left Europe, she wrote me a letter saying, "I didn't know how difficult it was to be sane, you didn't warn me and if you ever come back here, I'm going to kick your ass all the way to the nearest mountain." That's a Scandinavian expression. But within a year she had lost weight, looked much prettier, and went hitchhiking around the country. She had changed so much that when, at a restaurant, she met one of the woman doctors who had treated her, the doctor was envious of the attention this former patient was getting because she was so attractive. Some time later, she met a man she liked and they were married, and she had a lovely baby. She told me that after the child was born she began to get sick again, but then she remembered my philosophy and said to herself, "You can either go crazy or you can be the kind of wife and mother that you really want to be." And she decided to become the wife and mother she really wanted to be.

I find that people who have been psychotic seem to recognize this idea of decision better than many people in the profession. Several months ago, I was invited to San Francisco to address a conference on the creative use of psychosis, the theory that "craziness is good for you." I described some of my cases, and some of the professionals there said I was crazy. But a lot of the crazies who had been through psychosis said, "Of course!" They could get up and say when they had decided to be crazy, and under what circumstances they had made that decision. They got up and said when they decided to go straight. Now, this is not as simple as it seems, because one of the problems is that when people make the decision to be crazy, it really takes over and becomes extremely difficult to reverse.

When I question patients who have had nervous breakdowns—psychotic breaks, whatever you want to call it—I ask them, "At the time of your breakdown, could you have made a choice?" And they usually remember some point at which they could have made a decision one way or the other.

For example, one woman was in Bermuda, waiting for her boyfriend at the airport, and when he arrived she found out that he'd been with another woman. This is the point at which she said to herself, "Shall I yell at him and tell him off or should I let myself go?" Well, she decided to let herself go, and became catatonic and had to be hospitalized. But she was confident, when I asked her, that she could just as well have decided the other way. I think many of us have had the same kind of experience before a hysterical fit. If any of you have been hysterical, you know that. Many people have had a feeling of having to decide to go crazy or to hold on, and at that point you can be very aware of that kind of choice. Now, one of the reasons that contributes to the choice of insanity is that very often people find themselves in a situation that seems completely untenable; there doesn't seem to be any way out. So they decide that the way out is to go crazy. Or, for example, they decide not to listen to anyone. I knew a young man who had been considered autistic as a child. The members of his family were always critical of him, demanding perfection from him, so he decided, "Well I'm not going to listen to them." He turned them off the way you turn off a hearing aid. And because he wasn't listening, he began to invent fantasies of all kinds. If you're not paying attention to the outside world, there is no way in which you can correct a fantasy; you don't have the correction of reality, and pretty soon you don't know the difference between fantasy and reality, you have no way to check it out. So when I say this is a choice, I don't mean that such people are malingering in any sense; they really experience themselves as being out of control, and they feel this as painful.

Sometimes they get a lot of rewards (payoffs) for this crazy decision. Of course, there are people who have some kind of organic problem that makes it much harder for them to choose the decision to be sane, which requires greater control. If I can make an analogy, it's like what spastics have to do. There are spastics, victims of cerebral palsy, who start at an early age and they look just the same, just as deteriorated as another spastic, but for some reason they decide that they are going to combat it and they are able to lead comparatively normal lives. They improve their ability to walk and improve their speech. This requires tremendous determination, and it is truly difficult. Similarly, while there may be predispositions, organic situations which create, temporarily, psychotic behavior, there is, if you decide, some possibility of changing and controlling that behavior.

Most of you have at one time or another taken drugs that induce psychotic-like behavior, the most common of which is alcohol. Yet you know that under certain conditions you're able to control yourself. You may be drunk and act crazy, but when some crisis occurs, you decide that this is no time to act drunk and you straighten out; when you are stopped by a cop, you can act very normal. For example, a woman came to see me while under the influence of mescaline. She was "freaking out," and she described a scene in which she was in a field and if she went over the fence there would be no return. I asked her what she wanted to do, and we worked on it, and I said that if she wanted to, she could decide to stay here and not go over the fence. She looked at me suspiciously and said, "How do you know? You've never taken the drug." Well, it happens that I had, and I told her that I had, and she decided she was going to stay here.

Some time later she wrote up her experience, saying that she felt many people who have psychotic breaks as a result of an hallucinogenic drug experience had permitted themselves to go over the "fence," whereas she stayed here, on this side of the fence. It seems to me that even though organic predispositions or conditions could cause this psychosis, there is still a large area of control.

I believe that the manic-depressives, who alternate between states of high mania and deep depression, have a rather more difficult time. When they are in a manic state, though, it's wonderful. A friend of mine once said that, if he could choose, he'd like to be manic because manics can work twenty hours a day and have a great time, can think up great, creative plans; they are just wonderful in the manic state. All that energy to do all those things seems so fantastic. If only they didn't have to be depressed afterward! We now have a drug, lithium, that tends to stabilize manic-depressives by cutting down on the manic state. But a lot of patients won't take it. Even though they know that depression will follow, they still won't take it because they don't want to give up any part of the manic state.

The dynamics of the manic-depressive state make a lot of sense to me. What happens is that once these people let themselves get into a manic state—and there may be physiological reasons for it, possibly a change in blood chemistry—they seem to have enormous energy. But when they have been in this state for a period of time (during this period they usually act like psychopaths; that is, there is no operating "superego," as the psychoanalysts call it, and there is no conscience; therefore they can expend this tremendous energy every which way) they begin to develop guilt, and the guilt gets them down and starts to punish them.

These people really punish themselves, and act in ways which are considered socially undesirable, and as a result they get depressed.

Working with manic-depressives, I've tried to warn them about this, and as I write this I remember a girl I explained this to, who would call me up in the middle of a state and say, "Oh, boy, superego's after me, but I'm not going to let him get me!" She felt it was a real fight, and she fought very hard. When she first came to see me, she was quite depressed, so depressed as to be like a real catatonic. One time she came in and couldn't talk, she was so depressed. I asked her, "How was your weekend?" and she said, "Great."

I asked, "What did you do?"

She said, "I went to a party and got drunk and had a good time."

I said, "Well, maybe that's your true self; alcohol brings out the true self." And then I added, "Why don't you want to be happy?"

She said, "If you're happy, people demand things of you." So in that case you could understand why she chose depression, because to choose happiness meant responsibilities, demands.

Another time I saw a woman in a hospital who was deeply depressed. She was a teacher, and she had come to this small town where her husband had been made principal of the school, and all the teachers were angry that an outside person had been brought in. She had to care for an invalid mother and retarded brother-in-law,

had to do all the work herself. She was very conscientious, a devoted person. She couldn't duck out on the
work. The only way she could escape was when she
sank into the depression. Then she could act as if she
had no choice. I explained to her that I understood
quite well why she was depressed, and I told her that
any time she wanted to get out of her situation, which
indeed was almost intolerable, all she had to do was
pretend to be depressed, she didn't really have to get
depressed. And she said, "That wouldn't be honest."

Shortly afterward, she decided to go home and alter
her situation in such a way as to remove some of her
responsibilities. It wasn't easy, but she decided that the
alternative was worse.

One of the problems that I have when I try to get
people to consciously take charge and choose depression when they want to and not choose it when they
don't is that they feel it isn't honest—or, worse, that
other people would catch on.

In dealing with people labeled psychotic, one of the
things I feel has been helpful to them is my complete
conviction, as I have mentioned before, that they can
change. This I take as a given: they don't have to be the
way they are. I try to communicate this to them in
everything I say and do. This is basic to my feeling, and
that in itself I think is therapeutic. Let me give an
example. There was a psychologist who went into a
school and supposedly tested the students, and then
picked out some of the students and said to their teachers, "Within the next year these students are going to
show great growth; everyone will be surprised at the

growth." The result was that not only did their school work improve but even their IQ's improved. I take the same attitude in working with people who are supposedly very disturbed or have serious problems. That is one very important thing—the attitude. In all my experience with people who were labeled psychotic, I could find very little difference between them and me. All my experiences have reinforced my conscious decision to assume that anybody can change if he has the time and the energy and the understanding.

In speaking to the psychotic, it is extremely important to do what I do right from the beginning—try to get into his head, try to see the world as he sees it. A woman came to see me. She came from a conservative, wealthy family and was married to a militant radical, a patient of mine. He was always trying to get her interested in politics, but she didn't get interested. One day he called me and said, "Would you please see my wife? She's freaking out."

So he brought her in, and I said, "What's the problem?"

She said, "Any minute a plane will come over carrying the atomic bomb that will wipe us all out."

Apparently she had decided, "O.K., you want me to start worrying about war and bombing—I'll *really* worry about it." It was a way of dealing with her anger at her husband's insistence that she get involved in antiwar politics. At that point I didn't feel that I should bring this to her attention—even if I had been as aware of it then as I am now. So what I did was join her where she was, to show her I understood.

Her husband said, "Tell her how silly that is."

But I said, "No, it isn't silly, because it is literally true that any plane that is up in the sky could be one from Russia (or from New Jersey!) trying to bomb the hell out of us!" So when a plane flew overhead, I said, "Come on, get in the closet!"

She said, "What do you want to go into the closet for?"

I answered, "That plane may have the atomic bomb."

By saying that I showed her that I had listened to her. One of the first things is to convince the psychotic that you understand. O.K., this was her obsessional fear. This was her fear of the plane, etc. The important thing here is that you must indicate to troubled people that you will listen to them *on their terms*. That doesn't mean I have to feel exactly the way they do, but at least I must try to show that I know where they're at. That's the essence. For example, a woman in a mental hospital whom I met while making rounds was standing with her hands folded, her eyes looking toward the sky, and I asked her what the problem was. She said, "I'm going to be crucified today."

One of the staff members said, "Come on, you know that isn't true—you've been saying that every day since you came here two years ago."

She acted as if she didn't hear him, because he hadn't heard her on her terms. She just repeated, "I'm going to be crucified today."

So I said, "Do you have any idea what time?"

She said, "At two o'clock."

So I said, "Have you prepared your statement?"

She asked, "Statement? What statement?"

I said, "Obviously, we are going to cover this on television and radio, and I would like you to make a statement. Why are you being crucified? Suppose we rehearse a little now, what you will tell the world?"

You see, I was trying to utilize where she was at and move her a little beyond that—get her involved in conversation, but around her idea.

She then told me that she was going to be crucified to take the sufferings of the woman in the next bed, who was suffering so much she couldn't stand it.

So I said, "I'm very glad to meet you, because I'm going to be crucified, too."

She said, "You? What for?"

I looked up at heaven and said, "You know who my Father is, You should know who I am."

She looked me over very carefully and said, "That's funny, you don't look like Jesus."

At this point we had a relationship. We had something going and we went on this way for a while with discussions of this kind, and she became quite animated and forgot to stare up at heaven. Then time was up and she was supposed to leave, and the psychiatrist who was in charge of her ward took her back to the ward. When the psychiatrist came back, she was giddy with laughter. She said, "Sometimes I wonder who is crazy, we or the patients. As we walked down the stairway, her hands were clasped and she was looking up at heaven and she came into the ward, went to her bed, turned around and looked at me, and winked."

For a moment, at least, the woman was out of her psychosis.

Before a therapist can do anything, he has to establish a relationship, and the way I try to establish this relationship is to get into the fantasy in which the patient is living. One of the things that we forget is the tremendous determination that the schizophrenic has to hold on to his fantasy.

People watching my attempts to join a patient will occasionally get angry at me and say, "How can you do this to such a patient?" One time I was speaking to a group, and every time I addressed one woman—who had been a judged schizophrenic some twenty years before and had been in therapy ever since—she would say, "I'm sorry, I didn't hear what you said."

The next time she said something to me, I said, "Oh, I'm sorry, I didn't hear you; my mind must have been somewhere else."

She repeated it, and I said, "I'm sorry. I must be blocking today."

The other members in the group became furious at me at this point. They said, "You're making fun of poor Annette. She has all this trouble, and you're making fun of her." And she said, "Leave him alone—don't you see, he really understands me. He is showing the way I am behaving, and it is good for me to know that."

When people speak in a disconnected way, as some schizophrenics do, it is often because they don't want to be reached; they utilize these barrages of meaningless words in an effort not to be reached. One of the things I do is try very carefully to listen and speak back in the same way, as close as I can to what they are doing.

When I did this with one patient, he said, "Well, finally, somebody here knows how to talk." The amazing thing is that if you listen very carefully, sometimes beyond and behind the gibberish there is a certain amount of communication and meaning, and if you can, for the moment, drop your preconceptions of what communication is supposed to be, you can understand.

It's like the first time you look at a Picasso. It looks like nothing. I remember once I was in the Museum of Modern Art, and a fellow was lecturing, describing different pictures. He came to a painting by Picasso, and somebody said, "What's so special about that? My six-year-old daughter could do that." The man lecturing turned around and, in mock seriousness, said, "You have a daughter who paints like Picasso? I'd like to meet her." But, of course, once you understand Picasso, then his paintings make a great deal of sense. There is satire in there; there is a wish to look at things in a different way.

If we could give ourselves the same freedom with schizophrenics, who frequently have just gone back to using the way very young children communicate—with allegories and pictures—utilizing the sound of the words to communicate rather than the exact meaning of the words, perhaps we could understand. If you show them that you have listened to them and understood (and one of the best ways of showing that understanding is repeating what they say), you have a good chance for communication.

One of the things difficult to understand is why people choose such an extreme solution to their problems as the decision to be crazy. One of the most important reasons, or one very frequent reason, for such a choice is rage, fury, anger. This generally comes out of early disappointment at the parental behavior of the people around them. They feel that they were short-changed. Now, when you are in that kind of situation, when there is no way out and you feel this enormous anger, then you can see that insanity or psychosis is a good way out.

One reason why some of these people decide to be

crazy is that they would rather be crazy than kill or commit suicide. They are afraid of killing, so they retreat into insanity, use it as a wall around them. It is also a very punitive wall.

If you are interested in getting even with your parents, one way to do this completely, and at the same time remain a "nice person," is to go crazy. Then it's no longer your fault; you're sick. While you're crazy, you have the marvelous opportunity to say all the things you don't dare say as a sane person. You can tell your mother she's a whore, you can tell your father he's always been trying to get you to bed, and any of the other kinds of things you hear psychotics say. Think of that kind of material and the things they say in terms of what they would have wanted to say but did not dare to. Once they are crazy, they can say all these things— it is acceptable because they are sick, disturbed, no longer in control. You must remember all these payoffs.

Now, sometimes they are in such a fury at the entire world that they won't talk to anybody. Part of their anger and our inability to reach them is this decision on their part not to talk to the world. In a sense, they are saying to everybody, "You're dead." They are killing the world by ignoring its existence.

The biggest problem is that the rest of the world, once a person starts to act crazy, tries to get him to act sane. The sane get frustrated at their inability to do this, because these people have made such a strong decision. Once they get frustrated, they begin to justify the psychotics' entire view of the world, because they get angry with them, they treat them with contempt, and yell and scream. We take the so-called psychotics out of society and put them in a separate place and label them different, no good, mentally incompetent. We give them all kinds of labels which justify to them the rest of their behavior. We enter a vicious circle.

Now, one of the things that happens is they become difficult to manage—they had been nice, compliant people before, and then they become unmanageable, and what is the hospital staff doing about that? One of the things they used to do was put them in restraint, put them in straitjackets, and then, when the restraint was not enough, they gave them shock therapy. The rationale for shock therapy was originally that someone made the mistaken observation that if one had epilepsy, he couldn't be schizophrenic. Therefore, you give schizophrenics an epileptic kind of attack with insulin shock, and that will wipe out the schizophrenia.

Well, this does not happen to be true; it has been discovered that epilepsy and schizophrenia are compatible diseases. Then the experts had to figure out another reason for it, and they decided that something goes wrong with the brain, and you shake the victim up and it gets going again for some mysterious reason. Later they figured out ways which were not so painful and abusive as insulin shock and they started to use electro-convulsive therapy and decreased the dosage and found different ways of making the patient unconscious at the beginning. But most of them don't like it, and because they don't like it, after they've had a series of shocks you get two possible results. It is rare that they remain exactly the same, and sometimes they get worse. Sometimes, actual brain damage occurs from the shock and suddenly there is a loss of memory, of recent events and sometimes of common words.

Then there are patients who decide, "This is too

much and a joke's a joke but I'm not going to do this anymore because if they keep shooting the juice to me this way . . ." The experience is something like a minor electrocution. So they give up their insanity.

Sometimes you extinguish the memory of the kinds of events that made them decide to be crazy in the first place, so that they no longer use that decision, and they stop. But when a year goes by and the memory returns, they go crazy again. Some people are given recurrent shocks, and get addicted. A famous American psychologist used to walk across the campus of the university he was teaching at and admit himself, now and then, for shock therapy—he suffered from manic-depressive psychosis. Recently he has been going to encounter groups instead. So he could be crazy without paying the consequences.

Today, of course, we have drugs, the so-called psychotropic drugs, a whole series of tranquilizing drugs and energizing drugs. You can think about all the drugs as being either mild sleeping pills (which is not literally true) or mild pep pills. The patients who are anxious are given a small amount of sleeping pill like drugs—not enough to put them to sleep, but enough to reduce the anxiety. If the patient is depressed, he is given a small dosage of pep pill like drugs, and it helps him out of the depression. But when you have somebody who is very disturbed, you have to give him such large dosages of the drugs that he is practically zonked out; he is no longer capable of communicating, of thinking in ordinary ways. You can just see the effort he has trying to speak.

There is a reality factor: We must recognize that once more we have large hospitals with very small staffs and the staff is frequently untrained or has very little training, and they are expected to deal with some very difficult people. Given that kind of situation, it is understandable why they prefer to use drugs, because at the least they are not going to do the harm that they might do in trying to do psychotherapy when they are inept at it.

Taking a realistic attitude, these are some of the reasons the drugs are utilized—it makes administration much easier. It is much easier to have a ward run nicely when everyone is zonked out. Those of you who have taught school have sometimes known what it is like to be in a classroom with thirty or forty children and wish you had a pill that would get them quiet.

There are a variety of psychoses. First, there is schizophrenia, or as some people prefer to call it, the schizophrenias, because there is such a wide variety of them. I think it's quite possible that here there may be, in some cases, a physiological inheritance, a predisposition. It's extremely hard to tell how much of it is due to this factor.

Some of the twin studies are impressive. In one study I'm familiar with that was conducted in Norway, the psychiatrist Einar Kringeln was able to get records of every twin born within a certain period of time. Then, either from hospital records or by testing them himself, he found out whether they were identical twins, or fraternal twins. Identical twins, since they come from one egg, have the same heredity, while fraternal twins are no more similar than any other siblings. Then he checked (in Norway they have records of every hospital admission) how many of these twins were ever committed to psychiatric hospitals with the diagnosis of schizo-

phrenia. He found that where one twin was schizophrenic, there was a much greater likelihood that an identical
twin would wind up in a mental hospital with schizophrenia than if he were just a fraternal twin. But only
a greater tendency was discovered; there is still a sizable percentage of identical twins of schizophrenics who
do not become schizophrenics.

The conclusion would be that there is a biological
inherited tendency to become schizophrenic. Conceiv-
ably, there is a greater sensitivity to various stimuli on
the part of the people who become schizophrenic. But
there are benign circumstances or choices that they
make. Rather than act schizophrenic, they use some
other way of dealing with the internal stresses than
these people experience when they try to deal with the
environment. It may be some tendency to think a little
differently from the rest of us, and because of that there
is more stress in the world for them.

The other major group of psychoses is the manic-
depressive psychoses, sometimes called the "affect psychoses." The manic-depressive person is not necessarily
one who is always either very elated or depressed—it
does not always go back and forth between these different states. There are manic-depressives who are almost
always manic; there are some who are almost always
depressive; and then there are the cyclical ones. Here,
too, some people believe that you can treat this with
chemistry, like lithium, an apparently inert drug that
doesn't change the mood in any way. If they take lithium often enough, however, it seems to cut down on
the swings of the cyclical manic-depressive. They no
longer have the very high elation or the low depression,
but you have a problem with this. Many of these people

just will not take the pill. It's the same problem you have with administering tranquilizers. In both cases you can see the question of choice, of decision.

In both the manic-depressive and the schizophrenic states, while we often explain their prevalence as inherited, sometimes the family really sets up this expectation. You will often hear a family say, "This kid is crazy, just like Uncle Morris," and pretty soon, the expectation is realized. In a sense, the person is rewarded when he behaves as he is expected to because then the family is happy—he is living up to their expectations. But even with this conditioning, he still has the power to make more decisions, one way or the other. He can say, "That's right, you say I'm like Uncle Morris, but I'm going to be crazier than Uncle Morris." Then he turns out really crazy. But there are a lot of people who were told, "You're going to be crazy, just like Uncle Morris," who then decide they are going to be saner than anyone else in the family. That's most of us who are out of hospitals! We decide on this opposite choice, given the same kind of conditioning.

You notice how anger can be used either way. Anger can be used to decide *not* to live up to the label, can be the motive for the decision not to give in and act crazy, or anger can be used to justify the decision to go crazy.

In the case of depression, we often speak of "retroflexive rage"—rage turned inward. What this means to me is that the depressed person is so angry at the world that he dare not express it, so he turns it on himself. That's not really true, because when he turns it on himself and acts very depressed, he is "getting" the world around him in the way he knows best. Because when he acts depressed, he is a pain in the ass to everyone around him, and they can't do anything. He has a great way of expressing his anger.

If anybody is having a good time, trust a depressed person to spoil the fun. You take him to a party and he'll look around and say, "I'm glad none of you have my problem—you can go out and enjoy yourself." Many mothers must get training in how to be depressed, so that when her kid feels good and wants to go out and enjoy himself, the mother says, "That's all right, dear. Don't think about me. You go out and have a good time. Don't worry about me." That ruins it effectively for everybody.

I was at someone's home the other day, and there was a party going on. This woman had set up a very nice party for her daughter. She cooked a lot of stuff, made a big cake, invited all her daughter's friends for a surprise party, and there they were. The kids came in and could have had a wonderful time, but the mother sat in the corner, looking on at them, and said, "I wish I could feel that good." She put a damper on the party because she had carefully arranged the whole party to show how she suffered. What better way of expressing hostility than to do it in such a way that nobody can pick on you? Those of you who want to express anger and still be nice people, don't forget depression!

Just to add to this mother's fun, I had a headache, and when she offered me a pill, I asked, "Will it make me sleepy?"

She said, "How would I know? I never sleep anyway."

The therapist, in dealing with depressed people has to train himself not to get involved in the way they want to get him involved—then he becomes completely helpless to the situation. If he gets as depressed as they are, that won't help. If he is willing to get *more* depressed than they are, that might be helpful, because then they'll probably try to get him out of his depression. I've done that with them on occasion. I've sat there and suffered very loudly and used their language, and I had one depressive who came in and spent a long time moaning about her fate, and when I kept sighing and saying, "What good would it do?" she really went to work to cheer me up. I didn't want to be cheered up by that time, I was enjoying my temporary self-induced misery.

Another thing I've asked depressives to do is enjoy their depression.

They say, "Enjoy it? You're crazy."

But I say, "Look, all you've got is your depression. You're stuck with it; you might as well enjoy it." I remember telling this to one fellow in a group and he told the whole group how he had got very depressed and he was going to try to fight it, but then he remembered what I said. He said, "I'll try what that son of a bitch said," and tried it and he was bathing in it; he had such a good time sponging himself with this depression that he burst out laughing. This is one of the dangers about enjoying depression.

Sometimes depression is due to not having been able to express mourning. We have a very uncivilized habit now of giving members of the family tranquilizers at funerals, so they can't experience their pain and grief. This can leave them mildly depressed for years to come.

Another example: a marriage breaks up and the children who remain with the mother are not permitted to mourn the loss of their father. This frequently leaves them depressed, too, because no one gave them the opportunity to carry through the mourning work. One of the valuable things that every religion I know about has is traditionalized mourning; giving people the chance to mourn provides a socially sanctioned way of dealing with the loss. The loss has to be experienced, it cannot be denied. If you can't express your feelings, you get stuck and you are depressed.

It is extremely important to determine which kind of depression the person is suffering from. I try to find out if there has been a loss—even the loss of a dog can be a great loss. If they haven't a chance to mourn, there can be trouble. It is useful to check this out at the beginning, not to think that depression is *always* rage turned inward.

The difference between the manic-depressive and the schizophrenic is that you can talk to the manic-depressive if he isn't too depressed. He doesn't use strange language, there is no thinking disorder, he doesn't act crazy in that way. In fact, he is either just very happy or very sad. He looks more elated or more depressed than anybody you've ever met. I should explain that when *I* act depressed or when I act manic or anything I do in order to reach and join the person where he's at—I'm not doing anything that isn't part of my repertoire, because nothing human is foreign to me. Certainly I know the pleasure of being schizophrenic or being manic or depressed. All these things are very good, and if you're with such people you should try to experience what it's like to be that way. You don't have to stay that way, and this is the biggest advantage you have. You can show them that they have the power to decide by demonstrating how you can be depressed or crazy—but you can also get out of it.

CHAPTER 8

IS THIS
HOSPITALIZATION
REALLY NECESSARY?

SINCE I am a psychologist, I have very often met people who, in casual conversation, seem pretty well put together and could function effectively on a social and even vocational level, but who have confided in me that they had spent time in a mental hospital or had intensive therapy for many years. It often seems to me that the big difference between them and those who haven't gone for therapy is that they decided that this was something they wanted to do, not that they were necessarily any different from others who made no effort in that direction.

Unfortunately, this is not a very popular attitude with many of my colleagues. In every hospital situation I've been in, and in most group supervision situations I've been in, it seems to me that a great deal of diagnostic one-upmanship goes on as each therapist tries to demonstrate his sensitivity, skill, and general competence by finding things wrong with the people he is treating.

Since I've had enough experience, it is not difficult for me to play this game. The only problem with it is that I am frequently very conscious that the people who are engaged in this game have at least as many problems as the people they are talking about.

For example, one of my friends is a bright, helpful person and a distinguished psychiatrist—but I have never heard him discuss any of his patients whom he did not immediately label as schizophrenic. He is so well known for this ability to detect schizophrenia in anyone who happens to come under his professional scrutiny that a woman I know became a psychiatrist as a result of listening to a demonstration of his when she was a medical student. Then and there she decided that she would specialize in psychiatry in order to prove to him that everybody wasn't schizophrenic.

When I have been able to help patients who have been diagnosed as schizophrenic to the point where they could obviously function very well, other professionals often say, "They must not have been schizophrenic, because they got better." The problem is not only that they call these people schizophrenic but that, in so labeling them, they place them outside the human pale and thereby excuse themselves in advance for any future failure to help such a patient.

There are many payoffs for taking this position. One that I have already mentioned is that the therapist who takes this view thereby takes credit for great diagnostic sensitivity. Then there are physicians, and psychologists too, who have built their reputations by telling everyone who comes to them how seriously disturbed he is. If you say to a patient, "You have very serious problems, but we'll work real hard and perhaps we can help you with them," there is always the opportunity to claim great clinical success.

Since I frequently join patients in their reality, I remember one who came to me and described how terribly disturbed she was. I agreed with her; I said, "It's true that your problems are far more serious than most of those of the people I see, but let's see what we can do."

When she felt better a few months later, even though I had not detected a great change, she could say, "You remember what serious problems I had when I first came to see you? You're truly wonderful."

For many practitioners, this is a distinct advantage: to convince the patient that he has serious problems so that they can profess great success. It is not uncommon, for example, to hear women talk about their childbirth as being extremely complicated and dangerous but that they were so fortunate in having a great obstetrician who pulled them through despite the difficulty of the situation. The problem is not so great if the therapist uses it in this way and accepts it as a challenge. Unfortunately, the problem becomes very serious when the therapist's expectation that there is not much that can be done is transmitted to the patient.

One of my most significant failures, and one from which I learned a great deal, was a woman who came to see me early in my career. Generally, I followed the rule of having the patient make his own appointment, but this time, because this patient was referred to be by my first supervisor, Dr. B., for whom I have strong positive feelings, I made the appointment even though it was the husband who called. He came to my office, which was then a part of my apartment, looked around

and wanted to know what was behind the door leading
from the waiting room. I explained that those were my
living quarters. He then wanted to know if I was married and if my wife was behind that door. When I assured him that she was, he relaxed and brought his wife
in for treatment. She was a charming, well-dressed
woman, and it is only now, with additional experience,
that I realize that she was a psychopath. I only saw her
for a few sessions and then she disappeared. Two years
later she came back; she had left her husband, got involved with a drug addict and a pimp who had turned
her on to drugs and persuaded her to become a prostitute. She was working as a prostitute and supporting
both of them. Because she was so involved with this
pimp and with the whole new milieu that she was living
in, it did not seem possible for me to treat her on an
outpatient basis. I asked her if she thought it was possible and if she had any suggestions. This was a time
before drug addicts had become the folk heroes that
they are today (heroes in the sense that there are now
so many special facilities for treating them, and there
is more rejoicing in the mental health heaven for one
cured drug addict than for almost any other kind of
case). At that time, such facilities were not available,
and we discussed her options, whether she thought she
could handle it by herself, and finally she said, "No,
there's only one thing for me to do. I have to hospitalize
myself and get out of this environment." I asked her if
she was sure that this was what she wanted to do, and
she was insistent that this was the only correct decision.
I then suggested that if she were to go into the hospital,
since she was bright and intelligent, she could probably
interest a staff psychiatrist in giving her treatment, and

told her that if she did go in she would have to use every one of her wiles to see that she was treated. When she entered the hospital, the first doctor who interviewed her called me and said, "We have this patient, Elizabeth, who says you have seen her, and agreed to her decision to hospitalize herself. We can't find anything wrong with her. Why do you think she should be hospitalized?"

So I asked, "Do you treat psychopaths?"

He answered, "No."

I realized that in order to have her hospitalized, she would have to have the diagnosis of schizophrenia, so I said, "Haven't you recognized the schizophrenia that is underlying the psychopathy?"

He said, "No, but we'll have to look into that."

A day later, he called to tell me that he had found the underlying schizophrenia. Obviously, you can find this in anybody when you look for it. She was then hospitalized and treated, and wrote me several times from the hospital, very kindly saying that thanks to the confidence that she had been able to develop with me, she was able to work successfully in the hospital situation.

I have often wondered why I failed so completely with her when she first came to see me with her husband. I think there is a very important lesson in that for me. One of the reasons that I later worked so hard to learn how to deal with problems like hers was the memory of that failure. After all, when she came to see me she had been a successful, effective person; she had worked in an advertising agency and was in charge of one of the copywriting sections. She was in a relationship. It was true that occasionally she had alcoholic binges during which she would run off with somebody, possibly on an impulse. But still she was functioning. When she described her problems to me, I kept trying to assure her that they were not so serious and that she need not feel so guilty about the things she did. This is standard operation which many therapists use all the time—as I obviously did at that time. But the more I "helped" her release herself from her very small but still functioning conscience, the worse she got. One of the things I realized is that all patients are not suffering from an overstrict conscience. Certainly that was not Elizabeth's problem. Not conscience but discomfort was what made her decide to straighten up; and since that time, I have learned that discomfort is as likely to motivate a decision as conscience.

Another example of how professionals are indoctrinated into seeing serious pathology was the time I was taking a course in the use and interpretation of the Rorschach test. The Rorschach is probably the instrument most frequently used by clinical psychologists, and some few psychiatrists, to diagnose personality. Throughout the course, we were expected to give as many tests as possible. I found it useful, not so much for personality diagnosis as for studying how people approach this test. I learned a great deal about the way people see the world, and from that I could deduce how they would deal with specific situations.

One of the added advantages was that I was taking this course on Rorschach at the time I was still working at the shoe factory. Sometimes I gave Rorschach tests to people who were applying for positions. I'm not sure that I ever learned to use the Rorschach to find out whether people would be good shoemakers, although there were some slight clues, but it did help me eliminate people who had very serious disturbances, because they would take one look at the card, turn to me and say, "Well, I guess you know I spent some time in a mental hospital." Apparently facing the Rorschach card convinced them that I was an expert. It is like the doctor's use of the stethoscope; once he puts it to your chest, you feel you are dealing with an expert.

One of the sad things about assessing factory people was the inability of many of them to give anything but the most stereotyped responses. There are some responses that are known as common, and generally people who are creative, a little different, or disturbed will give uncommon responses. However, from the people who worked for the factory, some of whom seemed fairly bright, all I ever got was a few common responses, all alike.

I remember one woman looking at the first card and saying, "That's a butterfly," the most common response to that card, and then looking up at me, she said, "Boy, have I got imagination. When I go, I really go!"

It may be that they were just being careful, as they should have been in dealing with a representative of management. However, in other respects I had a good enough relationship with them that they could speak about other things to me.

When I took some of these reports and presented them to my class, it was surprising how many aspects of pathology my teachers could find. One thing that aroused consternation in one of my instructors in Rorschach was a report in which I said, at the end, "Patient shows unmistakable signs of latent sanity." My instructor had never come across that before on any Rorschach report and asked me if I could explain the pathonomonic signs of sanity. Pathonomonic is a term used to characterize certain responses on the Rorschach which are given by people who show signs of very serious disturbances. Sanity was seen as a serious disturbance.

I feel that there has been much too much emphasis on labeling people sick, disturbed, or pathological rather than showing them they have the power of decision. That is not to say that some people don't seem kind of crazy. I generally don't hesitate to tell them so if they are acting so. The biggest problem is the punitive way this label is used.

A number of years ago, I saw a couple who wished to get married. Her parents, who came from an important Philadelphia Main Line family, were opposed to the marriage. First, their opposition was based on the fact that they knew from his own admission that the young man had formerly been homosexual. Second, they were concerned that he didn't earn much money. When I explained that I had considerable experience with homosexuals who had been able to make adequate heterosexual adaptations, it came out that the real objection to the young man was that he was Jewish.

The father of the bride-to-be, who was a professor at an important medical school in Pennsylvania, asked the girl to see a colleague of his, a psychiatrist. Now, at this time the girl was functioning better than she ever had in her life. She was working for the first time in many years, had gone back to school and was reasonably well put together. However, when she went to see her father's colleague, the psychiatrist, he told her that she needed immediate hospitalization.

Because her father had been authoritarian, she

tended to relate dependently to doctors in general. She asked me what I thought; was I sure that she didn't need hospitalization? I requested that she ask the psychiatrist to write me a letter explaining why he thought she did. In his answer, the psychiatrist made no comments about her, but suggested that probably, since he knew the father well and considered him a manic-depressive and believed that there were other manic-depressives in the family, she needed hospitalization.

When I wrote him and asked him what his success had been in hospitalizing manic-depressives, he replied, "Not very much." He was suggesting hospitalization for a condition which he didn't think the hospital could help, but somehow felt that she was tainted with the problems of her family. It is quite probably that his suggestion was made not because of the girl's condition but because he was acting out of concern for his colleague's anger that his daughter was planning such an unsuitable marriage.

When I started in practice as a psychologist, not knowing many psychiatrists, I didn't have any hospital connections so I had to work very hard to try to keep my patients out of the hospital. I think it is unfortunate when it is too easy for us to hospitalize a patient. There is considerable evidence that hospitalization is frequently destructive to the individual. It means he is withdrawn from society, he is branded as a lunatic, and he can't even run for Vice-President.

With the exception of the young woman I mentioned who had come back to me as a drug addict, when I thought that hospitalization might help her stay away from the environment she was living in so that she could kick the habit, I have never—in twenty years—

had any occasion to hospitalize anybody I saw. There have been two or three cases where patients, while away from me—on vacation, for instance—have hospitalized themselves. One can understand the need for hospitalization under certain circumstances. Sometimes the environment is so difficult and so obnoxious that the individual sees no other way out, or feels he has no other option; in those circumstances it is not difficult to understand why hospitalization could be a choice. But it has often seemed to me that there are other options that can be worked on that are more helpful.

Strangely enough, it is frequently the parents who object to a therapist's decision not to hospitalize a younger member of the family. I once saw a young man with his parents. He was obviously very disturbed. He babbled at great length, speaking a language that was almost un-understandable, begging me for tranquilizers.

Suddenly, I yelled at him in front of his parents, "Cut out this crazy stuff! You can behave yourself! Talk straight!"

The effect was miraculous, as it has been in other such cases. He smiled, laughed, relaxed and spoke fairly normally for the rest of the session. He had been in and out of hospitals since he was ten years old, and he was then twenty. When I spoke to the parents at the end of the session, they said, "This is remarkable, but don't you think he should be hospitalized anyway?"

I said, "I see no need to hospitalize him at this time. I am willing to work with him."

His mother then interjected, "But he can't be at home over the weekend. We're having a party and we don't want him around to spoil it." Obviously it interfered with this family's image of itself to have a crazy son. They preferred to have him out of the way. They refused to keep him at home, so together with him we found a place where he could stay and where he managed to make a pretty good adaptation.

One of the advantages that the beginning therapist has is that he doesn't know enough. Certainly when I started I was not as acute in picking up signs of what could be called serious pathology, so I worked very hard with people who probably would not have been accepted by other practitioners. One of the unfortunate aspects of greater experience is that I seem to get better and better equipped to play the diagnostic-sensitivity game. It has required a very real decision on my part to give up this ability and to look at people as having strength despite all the problems they are facing.

One of the problems I have now is that as I have begun to be successful and known in some areas for my work, I get fewer and fewer very disturbed patients and tend to have patients who are members of one of the mental health professions. The largest single group of consumers of psychotherapy are psychotherapists themselves, psychiatrists, psychologists, and social workers. At the present time, most of my patients are from the field.

One of the things that becomes clear to me the longer I work is how many times people seem to decide how to behave, and to choose their particular kind of disturbance. This did not become clear to me because of theoretical training or theoretical qualification. Every now and then I get questionnaires from different research projects, asking me about books or teachers who influenced me. But I have been influenced more than anything else by my patients; they have been my best teachers.

Once I was teaching at an institute connected with a treatment service, and I thought I would like to teach by demonstrating before the class. I wanted to treat somebody before the class so that they could watch how I handled the person and learn or not learn as the case might be. Since this was the very first time I had decided to try this method, I asked the treatment service to send me a patient. They were a little hesitant, but then the supervisor decided to send somebody who he felt couldn't be hurt because they had already planned to hospitalize her, thinking that she was not suitable for treatment at all.

When she came to the first session, she behaved quite disturbed. She screamed about her depression; she sobbed and she cried. The thing that was disturbing her particularly at that moment was that she and her husband had both gone to audition for a play (they were both actors) and her husband got a job but she didn't. She began to declaim about her feelings of rejection and depression and said that she was thinking seriously about committing suicide, because "How can you live in an atmosphere where there is so much rejection?"

I said, "What do you want?"

She said, "If I could only sleep, I might be able to get over it, but unfortunately I cannot sleep either."

I asked her why she couldn't sleep, and she said, "I found out from other people that when I go to sleep I leave my body. And when I leave my body, a dead person can come into my body. I don't dare fall asleep because I am afraid that a dead person will come into my body. I know a girl to whom that happened and she got terrible headaches." Now, that didn't seem to me like the worst consequence of having a dead person in your body, but I asked her more about it and she described leaving her body and observing it, and she had plans to go in for further astroprojection (as she called it).

She said, "You don't know how terrible it feels to be outside your body and look at it, you don't know the terrible things that go on." She described her life as one of being involved with all kinds of marginal people, people on drugs, people involved with far-out sex scenes. At the end of the session in which she had presented herself in this disturbed manner, I asked the class for their diagnosis, and the general consensus was that she was a paranoid schizophrenic. Certainly, from the way that she spoke, most hospital personnel would have diagnosed her similarly. At the next session, I suggested that we try hypnosis, since she had been talking a great deal about the occult, and one of the things about people who believe in the occult is that they enjoy hypnosis because they consider it an occult phenomenon. Actually, it is a phenomenon that can be explained in a number of other ways, but they like it. So I suggested to her that I hypnotize her. She had talked about her wish to take LSD, but had not yet taken it. So I asked, "How would you like to take a trip?"

She said, "Fine."

I hypnotized her and told her, "Imagine that you've taken LSD and you're on a trip. What do you see?"

She said, "Nothing."

I asked, "Nothing at all?"

She replied, "No—nothing."

I said, "All right, you're an actress. Think of yourself on stage in front of an audience."

She said, "Okay, I can do that."

She started to smile. I asked, "What are you doing?"

She said, "I'm smiling."

I asked her, "What is the audience doing?"

She replied, "Applauding."

So I said, as I have done with many people, "See if you can see some kind of a scene, see if you can see yourself in a play, in a performance, a play that has some meaning." But no matter how hard I tried with my variety of techniques that usually worked with even the least imaginative patients, she couldn't see anything except the audience applauding and herself smiling and bowing. So after about ten minutes I took her out of the trance and said, "You know, you are the most unusual case I ever saw in my life. Most people act sane on the outside and crazy on the inside. You're crazy as can be! You're one of the craziest people I've ever seen —on the outside. But inside you're completely sane!"

She looked at me and started to cry, not wildly, but sadly, and said, "So you know, huh?" Then she told me the story that follows:

You see, when I was fourteen, I decided I was going to be different. I knew I wasn't really very different, I was ordinary, but I tried all kinds of strange things to be different. I hung around with all the freaks, the ones who smoked pot, and I went to all kinds of funny parties and orgies and hung out with the most unusual people to be different. I know that at heart I'm just a very ordinary person and I didn't want anyone to know this. So I tried very hard to be different.

I tried to use that, because she had changed so radically. I tried to explain how different she was because she had been cured so quickly, since most of her friends spent a great deal of time in therapy. Couldn't she get pleasure out of being different this way? I said, "This is the most amazing thing. You're unique! You went from being a paranoid schizophrenic ready for hospitalization to a sane, well person. You discuss your problems quite well."

I thought that would give her another subject, so that when she went home she wouldn't have to talk to her crazy friends about leaving her body and suffering. She did have a different role: the magically cured patient. When we came to the third session, she was obviously in charge of herself, spoke calmly, answered questions from the class clearly and well. They tried very hard to prove that she was still crazy. They went after her in a variety of ways, and the more they did, the more disturbed some of the class members sounded and the more sane and well balanced the patient sounded. They asked her if she didn't think that it was peculiar that she had acted that way; they asked her about her depression and what would happen if she got rejected again; and her answer was splendid.

She said, "Well, I'd feel sorry about it and I'd even cry for a little while, but there's no sense in carrying on the way I did before. I was going on a whole psychotic trip, and that's unnecessary."

I've seen her a few times since then and she's seemed quite rational; I've never seen her in that disturbed way again. However, it is not a complete success story. Her husband, meanwhile, was seeing an analyst, and the analyst was telling him all kinds of things about his wife, and this was leading to a conflict. Unfortunately, when one member of a family goes into therapy, obviously he spends a lot of time talking about his mate, and many therapists become very strongly partisan to the one they are treating, and enemies of the one who is not their patient. She suffered from such a situation. In addition, her husband could come back every week from a session with new things to say at parties. All of his friends were in treatment of one kind or another, and he could go on and talk about the marvelous things that were happening in their analyses.

The story of her miraculous cure became old and she did not have anything else to add, so she decided to enter therapy, first marital therapy with her husband and then private therapy for herself. I spoke to her therapist at one time and he said that she had some mild neurotic problems, but he certainly never considered her schizophrenic.

Actors do present a special kind of problem. In some cases they identify so much with their last part that it is very difficult to tell where they leave off and the part begins. One of the problems that I have often thought of as I was treating actors and actresses is that many people who become very good actors are willing to take all of the problems that come with being an actor—not so much for the possibility of fleeting fame (but certainly this is involved) or money, but more than that, they wish to find an identity. So many of them fasten onto the identity of the role they are playing. Other actors always play themselves, doing different parts but remaining essentially themselves.

One of the finest actresses I have ever seen on the stage once came to see me because she had heard that

I utilized the simulated-LSD experience. She had been referred by a therapist on the West Coast who used LSD. She was intelligent, attractive, and obviously a gifted actress. In addition, she was married to one of the most distinguished members of the theatre. Because of her position in the theatre, she had been portrayed in a novel by someone who knew her well. In this novel she was described as cheerful, charming, gay, independent, debonaire, a warm and radiant person. In therapy, however, she presented herself as deeply depressed, tired of being regarded as only a body, as being prey for men to hunt with their sexual lusts, and she expressed a wish to die.

When we tried the simulated trance—LSD experience in hypnosis—all her trances fit the material she produced in her therapy image. She described a childhood of tremendous deprivation, filled with traumas; she described her life as full of emptiness, bitterness, and tragedy. She was so different from what was written about her in the novel. For a while I could not put the two together, and then suddenly I remembered the last part she had played; she had been playing this kind of unhappy character.

People don't have to be actors to take on such a role. A number of years ago, a woman patient described the bitterness of her life and told me that she had to take sleeping pills to be able to sleep at night and pep pills to wake up. She told me how horrible the daytime was and how she rushed for her sleeping pills to get some peace. It was strange for her to be speaking that way because until that time, she had seemed a rather emotionally flat person who did not describe anything unusual and seemed to be pretty much down to earth.

I could not understand the change, and I worked on it, trying to find something particularly traumatic in her youth that might have caused her to start speaking in this way. One time when I questioned her, she said, "You wanted me to feel, to express feelings. I feel now. What's so great about that? I feel that I'm being torn apart and I just can't wait for those two pills that I take at night."

Her words sounded familiar, but I must admit that it took me two weeks of hearing these phrases repeated over and over again until I remembered where I first heard them. They were used in the best-selling novel *Valley of the Dolls.* The next time she came in, I said, "When did you read *Valley of the Dolls?*"

She looked at me suspiciously and said, "What difference does that make?"

I said, "I just wondered."

So she said, "Oh, a few months ago."

So I asked, "And when did you start getting these symptoms?"

Her answer was, "Not right away."

Of course, it wasn't just this book that caused her symptoms. The interesting thing is *why* she decided to choose such symptoms. She was a very striking-looking woman, the kind who attracts attention wherever she goes. She had been married a few years and lived in a comfortable suburb, and her husband was making a comfortable salary. She had three pleasant children, the youngest of whom was just starting school, and she had been raised to believe that because she was so beautiful there would always be something marvelous and fantastic happening to her.

Unfortunately, it began to be more and more apparent to her that nothing very exciting like that would ever happen. So here she had her split-level home and her full-time maid, and the two cars—but her husband was not particularly interesting and was devoted to his work. One time, after a weekend marathon encounter session, she came home filled with a desire to get closer to him, and said to him, "I'm sorry I've been an awful wife to you. Let's see if we can't get along better and get closer than we've been."

His reply was simple: "You're crazy! You get nuttier all the time."

So of course she was upset and discouraged by her failure to get closer to her husband.

I'm not trying to suggest that all people who present problems deliberately decide to put on performances. Often after they start the performance, they forget that it is a performance, and it just takes over. However, sometimes I find it helpful to detach myself from the performance and appreciate it as a magnificent job of acting. There have been far greater performances in my office than I have ever seen in the theatre.

Patients are not the only ones getting into the act. Therapists have their parts, too. Some therapists like to play the part of the wise old owl who knows all the answers. Others like to play the part of dedicated co-sufferer. Others play the part of the grand interpreter. Others play the part of the super-sensitive therapist in the hopes that all their patients will announce that he is the most sensitive of all. There are many such parts.

A few years after I started practice, I was influenced in my role as therapist by two books: Lucy Freeman's *Fight Against Fears*, and Robert Lindner's *The Fifty-Minute Hour*. *Fight Against Fears* is Lucy Freeman's description of her own analysis. It is a touching, sensitive story. In the book, she depicts her analyst as kindly, warm, and friendly. So I picked up that role model. In *The Fifty-Minute Hour,* Lindner tells some fascinating stories in which the psychoanalyst is depicted as a super-sleuth, searching for the hidden mystery in the patient's background. The stories usually build up to a magnificent climax, when the psychoanalytic detective puts all the clues together and comes up with a magnificent dénouement. He told the story of one patient who suffered from compulsive eating, which lead her to become obese. He searches for the reasons for this compulsiveness until once she makes a slip and says, "Mike me a baby." The analyst recognizes that since Mike was her father's name, she got fat in order to act out the fantasy of having her father's baby. I also assumed this role of super-detective. I had read detective stories since I was quite young, and, as Sherlock Holmes was one of my first heroes, this was a role that I found very enjoyable.

When I played the warm, kindly, friendly analyst, I got very nice feedback, and patients told me how warm, kind, and friendly I was. When I played super-detective, they were impressed by my startling discoveries. There was only one problem. They didn't necessarily get any better from either method.

Here is, for example, one of my cases of detection. A very bright and charming patient, who was working as a part-time fortuneteller, once came to consult me about her phobia of injections. Unlike my model, Sherlock Holmes, she had a terrific fear of needles. She was one of several patients I have treated for this phobia. As

I listened to her associations, and put the clues together, I was able to prove beyond a shadow of a doubt —to myself—that it had all developed because of her aunt who had diabetes and that she used to watch her aunt inject herself with the syringe.

She had very ambivalent feelings toward her aunt. On one hand, she hated her, and on the other hand, she was homosexually attracted to her. So, here it was. The phobia was the fear of penetration by the aunt; she saw the aunt as a woman with a penis. Such a brilliant piece of detection! The only thing wrong was that she still had the problem, she still had the phobia. I was being friendly and kind, and therefore we had a very good relationship. Finally I was able to convince her to go to the doctor and challenge the phobia by having a booster shot for something or other. After she challenged the phobia, it went away. The detective work was interesting, but not helpful. The thing that really made the difference was her *decision* to challenge her fear.

One of the reasons I identified with this detective-story role was that I have tremendous curiosity. One of the things that has been neglected is what a powerful stimulant curiosity is. When I feel that I know everything about a case, it doesn't go so well. I remember once treating a patient who had been the heroine of a novel in which her life had been depicted exactly. For the first few sessions, everything went well. But after I read the novel and knew all about her life, the therapy did not seem to work so well. In contrast, once—as an experiment—I led a group in a clinic about whom I knew nothing except their names. I deliberately refused to read the first interviews, so I knew nothing about them. That group started off very excitingly and turned out quite well, because I had the advantage of my curiosity and their curiosities about each other. So now I do try to avoid preconceptions—of all kinds.

CHAPTER 9

DIRECT
DECISION THERAPY
AND
HOMOSEXUALITY

I NO longer define homosexuality as a problem *per se*. Homosexuality is only a problem when the person experiences it as a problem. I prefer to define homosexuality as a matter of choice. Only when it is experienced as compulsive, and the person would like to be able to do other things, is it a problem. I have had a large number of homosexuals come to me for treatment. Some of them came because they had all kinds of problems: they were depressed, they had problems keeping a job—the ordinary problems that everyone has. A large number of them (some fifteen patients) came in for treatment because they wanted to stop being homosexual. Within the last seven years all the homosexuals I saw who wanted to stop (with the exception of two cases) succeeded in kicking homosexuality and becoming actively heterosexual, if they stayed in treatment six months or longer. This was the case when the patient's goal was to stop being homosexual. If I tried to make it *my* goal, as I used to, my success wasn't so good. But if it was the person's goal, there was no great problem.

I have worked from two different models of homosexuality. The first model was that they were homosexuals because they were afraid of their heterosexual inclinations, had a phobia about heterosexuality. I found it possible to help them change. For example, I was conducting a group in which there was a man who wanted to stop being homosexual. He had been coming along well, but at one session he started to flirt with the men in the group. He said, "You're cute, what a lovely mustache." He hadn't behaved in this manner before.

I turned to him and said, "What woman in the group are you attracted to?"

He pointed across the room and said, "Her. That bitch came in here with her skirt hiked up around her thighs and I got very interested and excited."

That's why he had to flirt with the men. He was afraid of his heterosexual attraction, afraid of the vengeance of other males. Often when a homosexual is attracted to a woman, he will begin to act particularly homosexual. When you go to places where there are homosexuals and you are with a woman they find attractive, they will immediately inform you of their homosexuality to avoid facing hostility and anger.

They become blatantly homosexual in order to disguise their interest. This was one model that I used, but it is difficult and indirect.

Now, I work from the model that people make a homosexual choice (although this does not entirely exclude my first model). If someone wants to change, I tell him to change! For example, a man came in to see me who had been in therapy for eighteen years and had had a great deal of analytically, individually oriented therapy—private analysis, Gestalt, behavior modification, and lots of group therapy. But he was still a homosexual. He was doing all right in his life; some other things had improved, but not the homosexuality. So I asked, "You want to stop?"

He said, "That's right."

So I said, "Then stop."

He said, "How can I do that?"

I answered, "You've been analyzed and everything, you know all the reasons, no sense going on with that unless there are still too many advantages. Tell me the advantages. What's the payoff?"

"Well, one, if I'm gay and I go out with a man, I don't have to pay. We pay our own way. Two, if I'm gay, if I get lonely I just call up a guy and he comes right over —no hassle. Women! I understand there's always a hassle, you're never sure they'll go to bed with you, and you get into all kinds of problems convincing them. And a woman is too important to me. I'm very concerned that with a woman I will be impotent. With men, I don't care."

This is a very common response from homosexuals. The very importance of heterosexuality is frequently what drives them to the homosexual choice, because it is so important for them to be successful with a woman.

After we went through all these advantages, I said, "Under those circumstances, are you sure you want to change?"

He said, "I do want to change. I've decided that I would like to settle down. With guys, because that's the

way it is in our society, it's always painful. There's all
kinds of problems, and when I have boys on my mind
I find myself limp-wristed. Yes, I really want to
change."

So I asked, "When?"

"When I'm ready."

I said, "I thought you wanted to change now." And
we went through the whole thing. Finally he agreed
that if I would show him how, he was ready to change
now.

I told him, "Okay, you are to have no sexual outlets
except heterosexual sex. No masturbation, no boys that
you call up, no lying in the bathtub having fantasies, the
way you used to. No other outlet whatsoever."

He followed the decision. Within a few weeks he was
dating girls, and eventually he succeeded in having
intercourse with a girl. He had a regular girlfriend
when I last saw him, and has had no more homosexual
experiences. He appeared once at an encounter group
I was running. There was another homosexual there,
and my former patient said to him, "You know, you can
quit."

"How?"

And my patient said, "Oh, this guy here," pointing at
me. "He can get you to quit, if you really want to."

The homosexual said, "Well, what's so great about
that son of a bitch?" (He was in a state of what we call
positive transference!)

"Well, all the other therapists I saw didn't tell me to
stop—they analyzed me. This one told me I could stop,
so I stopped."

It may seem absurdly simple, but of course it's not.
You need a highly motivated individual and you need

to go through the payoffs both ways with him and you need to understand the context in which the original troublesome decision was made. In this case, his mother rejected him, and the only person he felt any closeness to was his father. His mother threw his father out of the bedroom, and he spent a number of his early years sleeping with his father. Now, that doesn't necessarily make him homosexual; I have known others in the same situation who did not become homosexual. In his case, the only time he felt warm and secure was when he was sleeping with his father, so you can understand why he might choose to find comfort with men. At the same time, he saw his mother as extremely judgmental, punitive, and inaccessible. You can understand why he would be afraid to approach women.

In another case, I treated a homosexual in a very different way. This patient wanted LSD therapy for his homosexuality. I wasn't doing LSD therapy, and I told him so. He asked me if I would hypnotize him and tell him he was getting LSD. I hypnotized him and told him he was taking LSD. Or, rather, he hypnotized himself; he was an amateur hypnotist. When he got through telling everything to relax (including his liver, his spleen, and his gall bladder—he relaxed things I never heard of anyone relaxing!), he said to me, "Okay, you take control now."

So I took control, which wasn't really my control, because he had given it to me. We went through the simulation of the LSD experience, during which he had a variety of fantasies. He started out very symbolic. The first fantasy was about a canoe going down some rapids, and he wanted to get into the canoe but was afraid to. (I think the sexual symbolism here is clear.) So I urged

him into it and said, "Come on, it's only your imagination, so get into the canoe, make the choice to risk it."

So he got in. I asked, "How is it?"

He said, "It's great." Here you see what sex represented to him—a dangerous situation. He saw it as a
canoe going down enormous rapids.

In his second fantasy he visualized a large cave that
he wanted to enter, but again he was afraid. I urged
him on. Well, once he got into it, he recognized the
cave as a vagina and thought it rather strange that it
had such vast proportions. He said, "Either I was very
small or my mother was enormous." This was his feeling at that time, the fear of being swallowed. A very
common fear among homosexuals is that if they get
involved with a woman they will be swallowed, completely absorbed and taken in.

After a few more sessions like that, he started to get
more and more realistic, and finally, in the hypnosis-
induced trance, he remembered and actually relived a
scene in which he was in bed with his young aunt and
she was approaching him sexually. I asked him how it
made him feel, and he said, "Disgusted." When I
pressed him further about how he felt, he said, "Actually, I am very excited by the idea and would like to
make love to her."

I said, "Well, it's only your imagination—it's not real
incest—so you can try it." In his imagination he made
love to his aunt and enjoyed it very much.

I only saw him four or five times, and then I left for
my vacation, during which time he wrote me some
lengthy letters and I commented on them and sent
them back to him. When I came back in September he
was making love to his wife seven times a day. He was

a man of fifty who had been a homosexual all his life up to that point. And to this day I don't know what I did for him. I wish I did, because I'd like to do it for myself.

I checked up on his activities. I had his wife come in, and asked her about him. She was very pleased—exhausted but pleased.

He had been married all this time, and on his honeymoon he had gone with some young man. He had been married for seventeen years without any kind of sexual expression with his wife. I saw him not too long ago, now about ten years later, and he has slowed down—to only four times a day. He still has other problems, and no one would ever nominate him for Mr. Mental Health, but his homosexual problem is solved. Really, it was a fantastic thing. Aside from the magical aspect of hypnosis in this "drug experience," all we did in the fantasy was show him that he had a choice. He chose to act heterosexual, to challenge the fear of heterosexual relations and overcome it.

I have treated a number of lesbians, and found a very similar situation. With lesbians there is less motivation to change than with male homosexuals, because in our society female homosexuality is not looked down upon. A female homosexual almost never gets arrested (unless she riots for her civil rights), almost never gets into trouble in any way. There are many women in very responsible positions for which no one would ever hire a male homosexual. Lesbianism is really quite acceptable, since society does not consider it particularly threatening. For this reason, lesbians have less motivation to change, and therefore it is much more difficult for them to switch.

Another problem with female homosexuals is that it

is sometimes an unrealistic choice to become hetero-sexual. What do you do if you're a woman of forty who has never been involved with men, and you are no longer attractive and you don't have the social skill with men that other women learn through many years of experience? Who are you going to be heterosexual with? Males don't have that problem in our society. That's one of the difficulties. If you want to change, there must be enough motivation, a reason for chang-ing. On occasion, women do.

To show you how people can make this choice, I would like to talk here about one of the most unusual cases I've ever had, which was resolved in a way I had nothing to do with. A young woman made an appoint-ment to see me, but when I opened the door to receive her, there was a truck-driver waiting for me. I said, "I thought I had an appointment with Miss So-and-So."

This hearty-looking fellow said, "I'm Miss So-and-So." She was dressed in male clothes, dungarees (this was ten years ago, and dungarees were not so common for women then), very sloppy, with short-cropped hair. She came in and told me about her life as a homosexual. She said she had no reason to change, no wish to change at all, but she had the problem that female homosexuals often have of falling in love with women who were unfaithful to her. She would get very unhappy, de-pressed, and suicidal. She also had the problem of drugs and of prostitution.

She was in New York with an aunt whom she liked very much, and the aunt was trying to help. However, she felt lonely in New York with this middle-class, very respectable aunt. The aunt called me and asked me if I knew of any gay bars where she could take her niece to meet some nice girls. I saw the girl for only a short time. We had a nice relationship, and then she met a woman and fell in love with her. This woman was going to Georgia, so my patient went with her. Two years later I got a call from her and she said, "I'm in town and I'd love to see you."

I said, "Fine, come in." At the appointed time, I dismissed the previous patient and went into the waiting room for her. She was not in sight. Instead, a very attractive, slim woman got up and said, "Don't you recognize me?" It was her!

I asked, "What the hell happened to you? Did you change your religion or something? How did it happen?" And she told me her story.

Her girlfriend, who was supposedly the more feminine one in the relationship, wanted to have a baby. The girlfriend, unfortunately, had had a hysterectomy and was no longer capable of conceiving. But my patient was. So she went out and got herself pregnant and entered the hospital under the girlfriend's name so that the baby would belong to her. She was giving her a baby, completely acting out the marital relationship. After the baby was born, she took one look at him and said, "Oh, no! Nobody is getting this baby."

She changed the whole situation and got the baby and then said to herself (although she had been one of the most committed lesbians I ever met), "My son is not going to have some miserable freak for a mother. He's going to have a real mother." So she let her hair grow, she chose new clothes, and even changed her occupation, from taxi driver to laundress. She made herself completely feminine. It was a very dramatic decision for, in this case, a good reason. In fact, this is often one of the main reasons why female homosexuals want to change; they want to have a child. Not that some of them don't have the child under other circumstances. In most states, however, the law does not permit adoption by a homosexual couple, so sometimes a lesbian enters a heterosexual marriage because of her great wish for a child.

The female homosexual is frequently afraid of competing with other women for a man. It's not that they don't like men; they do under certain circumstances. They like men so much that they pay them the supreme compliment of imitating them. You don't imitate somebody you don't really like, even though female homosexuals will talk about not liking men. For example, one of their fears is that no man can handle them. There is frequently such an attachment to the father, who is seen as very powerful, that they don't feel they can be dealt with by any other man.

A lesbian woman whom I was seeing individually came to a two-day marathon group I was conducting. She was too scared to get involved with anyone, but finally I got her to participate in some little game, and we started to talk more. I asked her some questions, and she said, "You bastard, you told me you wouldn't get me involved." And she punched me in the jaw. She was a gym teacher and was in pretty good shape. And just like in the comic strips, I saw stars. So I got angry and hit her back, and we got into a terrible fight. Fortunately I won, and pinned her to the floor.

As I pinned her to the floor, she looked up at at me and said, "I love you, Harold."

From that moment on, for the rest of the two days of the marathon, she took care of me like an adoring little girl. Apparently it really worked very well, because she then fell in love and went to live with a girl who looked just like me! (To her, at least.)

You find this fear of competing with women operating not only with lesbians but also among women who are not lesbians at all but who don't seem to be able to get married. They have difficulty getting boyfriends because they are so fearful of feminine competition. In some ways that can be more pervasive than a male's fear of his father. These things start out early in life. The little girl finds out that if she is competitive with Mother for Daddy, her mother is going to make her life a hell.

Among lesbians who dress attractively and are obviously feminine, there is frequently the wish for a new mother. They're still women, and they are often women who may have felt rejected by the mother and still yearn for close physical contact with a mother substitute, or else they have had so much contact that they crave it constantly. They're grown and Mother's out of the picture, and homosexuality is one means by which they can achieve this kind of contact.

Now, it is not necessarily true that in every lesbian couple there is one who clearly plays the role of the male and one who plays the role of the female. That's a common misconception. I have seen some few couples where it is dramatically so, but in many cases both partners are rather indeterminate, so you can't tell. But even when you see one very feminine-looking one and one very masculine-looking one, this is no indication of what goes on in the privacy of the bedroom. In fact, more often than not, the very feminine-looking one will be the aggressor sexually. This also happens with male homosexuals.

One of the problems we run into as a result of insisting on such notions as "latent homosexuality." Every heterosexual is a latent homosexual. We all have the capacity to be that way. So it's a meaningless term. As far as I'm concerned, the person is homosexual only if that's his preferred form of outlet. If he cannot have any other kind of relationship, then he is a homosexual. But anybody who occasionally tries the homosexual relationship is not necessarily homosexual. You certainly see this with women, because there's less stigma.

A very large number of women I know have had homosexual experiences and don't think of themselves as homosexuals, because it's so acceptable. It is quite acceptable for women from early girlhood through college age to sleep together, to hold each other; if a guy tried to get in bed with his roommate, he'd get killed. The acceptability of it makes it easy for many women to decide to engage in quasi-homosexual relationships which would cause men to be filled with fear.

The biggest problem that homosexuality plays in neurosis and psychosis is not the actual homosexuality but the fear of it, the constant need to avoid it. The problems people create for themselves because of this fear! One of the big advantages of the present movement away from such sharply defined sexual roles— male and female—as we used to have is that many men no longer feel terribly threatened if they do the dishes or change the diapers. If women's liberation were to become really successful and we no longer had such sharp sex-role differentiation, it would make being a man much easier (because he wouldn't have so many responsibilities and so many demands upon him) as well as making it easier to be a woman.

It would be easier just to be human, because one of the reasons for the escape into homosexuality, as well as the fear of it, is the insistence on the roles' being so different. It is a definitional problem. You can decide that anyone who has had one homosexual experience or even one fantasy or one dream is really homosexual, and that his heterosexual activity is really a flight from his homosexuality. That's one way of looking at it, if you are looking for patients to keep a long time. There are many who are adept at either situation. They're better off, perhaps, because they don't have to eliminate fifty per cent of the population from their sexual choices. Not only that but it proves that they are not compulsively heterosexual!

Homosexuality is a striking example of the function of decision in the sexual role one adopts. My experience has shown that homosexuals *can* if they so desire make a heterosexual choice.

CHAPTER 10

DIRECT
DECISION THERAPY AND
FRIGIDITY
AND IMPOTENCE

BECAUSE early in my career I wrote a book about call girls, I have had an unusually large number of patients who had every kind of sexual problem, and the role of decision-making seems to me particularly clear in dealing with these disturbances.

Many women have consulted me about frigidity. It is a problem that leads a great many women to therapy —which may be why so many psychoanalysts think there are so many frigid women around. But frigidity has to be defined specifically, because there are varying degrees. As far as I'm concerned, people should reserve the word "frigidity" for total sexual anesthesia.

For example, one woman, a college teacher, came to me because she wanted to have a child, and also was concerned about achieving tenure at the university where she taught. She believed that her inability to have a child was due to her anxiety about getting tenure. When we started to discuss her life and her attitudes, she told me that she had always found sex uninteresting, unexciting, and repulsive—something that her husband wanted to do and she wanted to get over with as soon as possible. She had never found kissing or hugging or any kind of physical contact with a man the least bit pleasurable. This is frigidity. She didn't feel bad about this, and the last thing in the world that she wanted was to get over this problem. All she wanted was to have a baby and get tenure. When she got that, she left, with no intention of discussing the rest of her problem. The mere fact that she was willing to deprive herself of an experience that so many people spend so much time worrying about, and seeking, indicated to me that there was a large element of choice in this matter. You cannot consider her really a victim of her past, because here she had the choice to do something about it. But she clearly specified that she had no such wish.

On the other hand, there are some women who find foreplay interesting, find hugging and kissing and romantic ideas highly pleasurable, but find any approach to the genital area repulsive. The largest number of woman patients I have seen who complain about frigidity do not belong to this group. Frequently they are women who come on in a very sexy way, very seductive, and most of them have had a lot of sexual experience. At first they often talk about enjoying sex very much, but then confess their problem, which is that they cannot have orgasm through intercourse, but only through extravaginal methods; that is, through oral or manual stimulation.

We have built a cult about female orgasm, and this

presents problems. Many women would be happy if the men they went to bed with just enjoyed themselves as best they could, but since we've made such a big issue of it women frequently have complained to me, "If only he didn't say, 'Did you come?' " It is very hard for many people in our achievement-oriented culture to let it go. We are so achievement oriented we go on six-day bicycle trips, we try to surf expertly, and we also have to have a competent score in lovemaking. This anxiety itself makes it difficult for many women to have orgasms through intercourse, because they experience such a demand to do so.

Very few women come for therapy who have actually chosen not to have an orgasm; they have made *other* decisions that prevent them from having an orgasm. For example, one decision that many women have made is, "I'm not going to give him the satisfaction." They are perfectly willing to cut off their nose, or another organ, to spite their face. Another decision some women have made is that they are fearful of letting go; they are self-conscious and busy watching themselves in performance, as if they were observing themselves in a mirror. Many women who consider themselves great sexpots fall within this class. They are so busy admiring how grand a job they're doing in evoking admiration from their partner that they are incapable of having an orgasm; they are concentrating too much.

The basic rule here is very simple. If most of these women could become convinced that they should just let it happen, rather than trying to make it happen, the problem would be solved in a very short time. I knew a woman once who could have about twenty orgasms per hour, and this could go on for at least three hours. At one time she had thought of herself as frigid because she never had an orgasm. She was busy trying out candidates for the job, but nothing ever worked until she gave up and said to herself, "Okay, so I can't have an orgasm; I like it anyway." Then she started to have orgasms and practically never stopped. You often have to go back and discover the previous decision.

One of the problems I often find in the frigid woman, as with impotent men, is great, unexpressed anger. If I can get these women to ventilate their anger, then they are able to have an orgasm. An interesting example is the woman who can be married for many years to a husband who is by all accounts a competent lover. (It does not require any great expertise to give a woman an orgasm; all it takes is a woman who is capable of having one. I expect that this comes as a shock to many male readers.) She has no orgasm with the husband. But then she goes out and has an affair because she is angry with him. Now she has orgasms without any trouble, because she doesn't have any hostility toward her partner in bed and does not need to express anger by withholding this great present.

When it's a problem of self-consciousness it becomes more difficult, because the woman is too busy watching herself. One woman who had this problem asked me to hypnotize her. So I hypnotized her and gave her a fantasy to use when she was having intercourse. The fantasy was that she was lying in a completely dark room. She was dressed in a black rubber wet-suit which had only one opening, and a light was shining down on that opening. She couldn't see what was going on, and the man who came into her couldn't see her either.

Well, she got so excited just listening to the fantasy during the session that I thought it might work, and I gave her the post-hypnotic suggestion that she would think of this every time she went to bed with someone. She made the decision to enjoy this sexual fantasy. She did, and she had a wonderful time.

Another problem that you sometimes find in women who don't have orgasms is their decision not to have fantasies. Not everyone needs fantasy, but some women do. When they decide not to have a fantasy, they frequently rob themselves of a potentially exciting source of stimulation. They think it's dishonest—how can you fantasize that you're in bed with Steve McQueen when actually you're with Joe Schlemiel? They don't think it's fair to do that. But it is one way of dealing with the problem.

One thing I do not believe to be a cause of frigidity, despite common belief to the contrary, is poor education. Many women say, "How can I have a fantasy when my family told me that sex was so terrible?" But it doesn't follow, because a lot of people who have been told that sex is horrible, and lived very deprived lives as a consequence, have no difficulty achieving orgasm once they changed their minds and *decided* that orgasm was what they wanted.

For example, nuns, who were certainly raised very strictly, when they leave the church, or sometimes even before they leave, manage, despite early indoctrination, to do very well in that department and have no problem with orgasm. Sometimes, in fact, their anger at being told all these stories can be channeled in the direction of sexual pleasure rather than in the direction of anti-pleasure. The worst education is not just specifically about sex, because that can be dealt with, but the general anti-pleasure orientation in many families, which is very hard to shake.

One study observed how police officers act hostilely to people dressed in the clothes and the hair-styles of the counter-culture. The police frequently fantasize, or have the opinion, that all these long-haired freaks are constantly involved in bizarre sexual activity. The police feel these people are pleasure-oriented, and this makes them angry. They feel it is a sin to be pleasure-oriented.

The difficulties that women have with the problem of frigidity are unfortunate, but men in our society feel much worse when they suffer from impotence. Impotence, again, takes several forms. Complete and total impotence is a man's inability to have an erection.

I learned the value of the negative approach when a patient came to see me with this problem. He claimed that he had never had an erection. He was both obsessive and negative. He was a chemistry professor, and I asked him how he had chosen this profession. He said, "I had a teacher once who told me the one thing I've got to remember is to never try teaching." So he became a professor of chemistry, rather than the research chemist he originally wanted to be.

Knowing that he was so highly negative and suggestible, I told him, when he started talking about his wish to be potent, that it would be a very dangerous thing; after all, an erect penis could be a lethal weapon. So he said to me, "Where did you get this Stekelian nonsense?"—referring to the psychoanalyst, Stekel. I then started to reread about eight volumes to try to find out what he meant. Eventually he told me that Stekel had said, "Remember, the patient is the enemy!"

I have to explain this negative approach in terms of

decision therapy. It sounds very different, as if it is trickery, but it is not. Many therapists of different orientations are using it. Knight Dunlap called it the theory of negative practice. People were encouraged to make the mistakes they usually made, such as reversing letters in typing. If you practice reversing letters, that gives you control over the situation. Similarly, Viktor Frankl calls it "paradoxical intention," and Hyman Spotnitz calls it "joining the resistance." Marie Colman Nelson calls it "paradigmatic psychotherapy."

In the shoe factory where I once worked there was an employee who always damaged the heels of the shoes she worked on. Her supervisor tried to teach her how not to do this. I asked her to practice damaging the heels on some discarded shoes, and I had a lot of trouble getting her to do that; she said she already knew how to damage them. But as she practiced, she was able to take control over the situation and choose not to damage the heels in the same way she had previously. That's what happens very often with negative practice.

My patient, the chemistry professor, had made a decision not to do anything a therapist told him, not to give anyone the satisfaction of helping him. He was willing to suffer the lack of sexual gratification in his life. The reason he had so decided was that his family had mistreated him, they had been cruel and harsh with him, but always said, "This is for your own good." They always convinced him that everything they did was for his benefit. So that anything that anyone in authority said, he wasn't going to do. When I said to him, "Don't have an erection for your own good," he had the choice whether to have one or not. He finally opted for the full life.

This is, of course, an extreme case. Most men suffering from impotence have only intermittent impotence. Sometimes they are reasonably potent and at other times they are impotent and unable to maintain an erection. Here, too, it is frequently a problem of hostility. If you can get a man who suffers from impotence to face his hostility and even express it, the impotence often disappears. In a sense, what he is doing is deciding to express his anger by withholding this gorgeous instrument of pleasure under his command. Of course, this is not often a conscious decision. Often such patients are so angry that they become fearful of the woman's revenge.

Fear and potency don't go well together, and it is evolutionarily necessary for self-protection to take precedence over the sexual impulse. When somebody suffers from fear and anxiety, his unexpressed hostility is often the cause, and often such men also have another way of expressing their hostility—by withholding. This is very characteristic of impotent men.

A lesser degree of impotence is that of the premature ejaculator. There are those men who ejaculate before entrance; the mere closeness of a woman gets them so excited that they cannot enter the vagina at all. But it is important, when someone complains of premature ejaculation, to ask him, "How long is premature?" (I once had a patient whose trouble was that he couldn't wait longer than forty-five minutes and his brother-in-law said he could wait at least two hours!) The average time is under ten minutes, according to reports of research on young men.

One of the ways in which the therapist can overcome premature ejaculation is to say to the patient, "If you

really want to change, don't try to satisfy the woman."
One of the most frequent causes of premature ejaculation is the man's decision that he must perform su-
perbly. The resultant anxiety frequently causes premature ejaculation. Now, this would seem to be opposing
what I said a while back about hostility, but actually it
is the same, because the wish to perform well is often
due to fear of retaliation. That's why you find, in the
gossip of uneducated males, a whole host of stories
about the terrible things that can happen to the male
organ when it's encased in the female organ. There is
a fantasy of the vagina dentata (it has teeth in it), and
some men become involved in inspecting it carefully to
see if it has teeth, to see if they're going to get caught.

Some men who have told these stories say they know
someone who got stuck just like a dog, and the two of
them had to be carried out in an ambulance. This is
based on the great lack of knowledge about the difference between the human male and the dog. In the dog
there is cartilege which extends itself during intercourse. Human beings are not built that way. I think
that the prevalence of this myth is due to a fear of
vengeful women, because most men in our society
were raised by females who punished them. This is why
so many men react so adversely to the idea of women's
liberation. They are enough afraid of women as it is,
and they fear that if women get together, then they'd
better take to the hills.

In premature ejaculation, the combination of fear
and hostility has to be dealt with. There are a number
of physical devices used to overcome this problem,
prosthetic devices that can be attached to the penis that
permit intercourse with a limp penis. There are also

anesthetic creams, actually intended for the relief of hemorrhoids, that will desensitize the penis. There is a little problem with this technique, however. It anesthetizes both partners, so that what you gain on the merry-go-rounds, you lose on the swings. One advantage to both these physical methods is that sometimes the anxiety syndrome is dissipated.

Again, before any of these methods should be suggested, it is very important to question the patient carefully, to find out whether he really wants to cure the impotence or premature ejaculation. It is also important to look at decisions he may have made which have prevented him from enjoying pleasurable intercourse without artificial devices.

Vaginismus is a condition of severe muscular spasm, a contraction, which can occur as a result of fear. Some women suffer this on their honeymoon, making intercourse impossible, but a great many myths arise because of this condition. (A few years ago a man told me about a poor woman who had a "crossbone," a supposedly structural defect preventing intercourse.) But vaginismus is due to fear. The more the man tries to help the woman overcome the fear, the greater the fear becomes. In one case I had, a couple had been married two years, and in another case five years, and there had never been vaginal penetration. In one of these cases the woman seemed rather strange, so I saw both her and her husband and I told the man, "You know it's really your fault, don't you?"

He said, "What do you mean, my fault?"

I said, "If you were a real man [and in the culture he came from this was extremely important] you'd have had her already."

The wife said, "Oh, don't say that," and became very protective. The more I attacked him, the more protective and sexually excited she became, and he finally said, "Yes, it's my fault."

When he had made the decision to accept the blame, she—making a decision of her own—said, "Let's go home." Then and there the problem of vaginismus stopped, and they had successful intercourse. Now, all these great feats are only the cases that work!

A woman with a similar problem came to me. Unfortunately, she had had so much therapy that she couldn't describe it to me in specific terms. All she could say was, "My husband and I are both children, incapable of a mature relationship." So I suggested that—like children—they play, but have no sex. So they played, and, of course, did have sex, and had it successfully. That's where negative suggestion can be very helpful.

Twenty years ago I often had female patients who complained about their husbands' sexual demands on them. Today the problem is frequently reversed. I see more and more women who complain that their husbands are not nearly as interested in sex as they are. Particularly in those cases where I have said to them, "Don't have sex," they decide to go home and fight like mad to fix me. On other occasions, they take my word for it.

One couple I knew didn't have sex for ten months, during which time they had the best time in their twenty years of marriage. They didn't fight nearly as much, they weren't angry with each other, and they were tender and kind to each other. Very often, because of the cultural demand, both men and women think they must have sex all the time, and they make impossible demands on themselves. There is no law that says a marriage must be based exclusively on sex. So if I can deal with them rationally, I say: "You don't have to have sex if you don't want to have sex." Unfortunately, if either the man or the woman has sex only in order to please the other, this generally leads to hostility. You get this especially with women. A lot of women make themselves frigid long before they get married or have a permanent relationship, when they think that they have to go to bed with any man they go out just with because he asks. "They feel so hurt if I don't go to bed with them."

Another thing that happens is that sometimes women prefer to go to bed with a man rather than get emotionally involved with him. That may sound like a contradiction, but it happens. A girl was telling me about this awful guy she went with, and he started with, "Aren't you going to let me up to your apartment?"

She said, "No, go home, good night."

He asked, "Why not?"

She told me, "Rather than talk to him I balled him, because it was easier than talking to him."

When people go to bed out of this kind of anger and annoyance, the results are likely to be disappointing, following a law which one of my patients calls "Greenwald's Law," which is: "Bad sex drives out good sex." That's bad sex, when you go to bed to propitiate somebody. It has nothing to do with sexual excitement or love, and obviously it's going to cause difficulty. Of course, there are those who feel very strongly about the relationship between sex and love, and that deserves another whole book. There are many who no longer require marriage and propagation as the only requirements for sex, but there are also many who believe that it is only proper when coupled with love. Unfortunately, at the same time there are many people who are quite capable of having great sexual pleasure only when there is no love present, because they have been educated that sex is something you do with bad people, not with those you love, like your mother or sister. So these people need the pleasure of illicit sex, such as prostitution, because that is what is exciting to them. It is difficult for them to combine love and sex.

Many analysts and psychotherapists complicate the problem by stating their own "moral" positions—that sex is only good if the people are in love, or whatever it is. Obviously, for some people this is the most rewarding kind of experience, but that doesn't mean that sex is necessarily bad without it; it's not. Steak is very good, but you can live with hamburger too. It is not sound practice for therapists to impose their own moral decisions on patients by calling them scientific facts. There is no scientific verification that sex with love as a form of release is any better than sex without love. Sex with love is a different kind of experience, but sex without love is not necessarily pathological, as some have tried to call it.

One of the reasons many therapists have problems with sexual disorders is that they advocate their personal moral attitudes, rather than helping people achieve their own goals. There is nothing wrong with having moral attitudes, but you must separate them from scientific attitudes and clinical attitudes. What I would now say to a person, when he is involved with something that I personally find repulsive, is that I state my position. I think that I owe that to my patient. I might explain, "I don't like what you're doing. I find the idea of your doing it with a hippopotamus repulsive, but that doesn't make you sick. It makes you adventurous!" That's the problem: we often confuse our morality with some kind of scientific premise. But the decision is the patient's—not anybody else's.

One of the basic principles I have in therapy is that if someone has tried one particular approach for a long time and it hasn't worked, it's time to change the approach. For a long time a man had been telling his wife she was too fat. Everyone had spoken to her—her mother, her mother-in-law, her sisters—but the criticism was having no effect. To take the pressure off her, I said, "It's not your fault, it's your husband's fault." Her husband understood what I was trying to do, which was to change the situation from one of conflict to one of decision—her decision. The important underlying point was not that you don't have to be a performer, but that you can enjoy yourself or not enjoy yourself, as you will.

There is too great a demand on people; the sexual aspect of life has been so played up that we transfer it to every situation. The man who is impotent feels completely hopeless and useless. Even if he became President of the United States, it wouldn't help him; he would still feel like a inadequate failure.

CHAPTER 11

DIRECT
DECISION THERAPY AND
VOYEURISM,
EXHIBITIONISM,
RAPE, AND FETISHISM

SOME people enter therapy, not by choice but because they are referred by the courts or by some other outside agency, or when they are afraid of getting into trouble, for example, voyeurs, exhibitionists, and rapists.

The voyeur is not unusual in our society. We have all kinds of institutions which are made to pander to voyeuristic wishes, such as the centerfold of *Playboy* magazine. Sometimes I think young people who see a nude woman for the first time look for a staple in her midriff. Then there are the burlesque shows, strip teasers and, increasingly, the nude shows. In some places these include live demonstrations of sex. When I was in Copenhagen, several faculty members of the University of Copenhagen took me to see one of these live shows. (Since I was an American, they were sure I would be interested.) There were demonstrations of a woman using a vibrator on herself (is the Industrial Revolution beginning to take over sex?), two women making love to each other, and a couple having inter- course. There are many suppliers of voyeurism in the movies, and all kinds of printed matter is sent through the mails in envelopes reading, "This is sexually ori- ented material. Do not open it if you will be offended." I get these regularly; I'm apparently on many of those mailing lists.

This kind of voyeurism doesn't cause any trouble. The voyeur who gets into trouble has to do it in an illicit way. I knew a young man, a graduate student of psy- chology, who would search for apartment houses where he thought women would be undressing or where he might be able to see intercourse. He would climb up on the fire escape to look in. He was caught several times, and that's one of the reasons he came for therapy.

Despite the availability of legal outlets to gratify voyeuristic wishes, the number of arrests of voyeurs hasn't diminished significantly. One reason is that these people believe they have to seek their gratification in a dangerous way, to add to their pleasure, climbing on the roof or fire escape with a pair of field glasses, devis- ing difficult ways of getting a view of women's locker rooms, like drilling holes in the walls. One fellow I knew always carried a drill with him because he never knew when he might need it to drill a hole to peek through. This kind of voyeur reveals an aggressive, hos- tile attitude; he has to look when the woman doesn't know she is being watched.

I have never heard of women getting arrested for voyeurism, and I think the women's magazine that recently published the nude picture of a male actor in its centerfold did so more as a joke than as an enticement for women. Women don't seem to find those magnificent specimens that men carry around as exciting as men seem to find the lack of such a specimen. Psychoanalysts have all kinds of explanations for this phenomenon. One is that men fear castration. Voyeurs want to look at the female, who doesn't have a penis, in order to reassure themselves that they are different. For some reason, this kind of reassurance makes them very excited.

Although this castration fear may be a factor in some cases, it seems more probable to me that these men were raised in an atmosphere in which mothers or sisters were seductive as far as dress was concerned, displaying themselves partially but not completely; or at least the man's interpretation is that the behavior of a parent or sibling was seductive. Until recently, most women kept themselves well covered, and there was tremendous curiosity generated about the female sex. Pathological voyeurism is an effort to fulfill that curiosity, and also an expression of anger that something is being hidden.

Voyeurs get really furious if their opportunity is interrupted. They find a house with a great view of the bedroom window, and they see a woman undressing slowly, and get more and more excited, and just at the moment when she is about to take off her underwear, "the bitch turns the light off." They are angry, and experience deprivation, a sense that something hostile has been done to them personally. I think the feeling of deprivation is why voyeurs decide to adopt this aggressive attitude. I will cover the treatment of voyeurism and exhibitionism together, because they are so similar.

The pathological exhibitionist engages in behavior which seems to be related to what is normal courting behavior in the animal kingdom. Many male animals preen themselves in front of the female as a way of exciting the female. They strut back and forth. Again, exhibitionism as a problem comes up only with men; very few women exhibit themselves for sexual reasons. Women frequently exhibit for financial reasons, like strip teasers or women in nude shows. Sometimes they will do this for kicks with a male companion. I knew one girl who used to go out to restaurants with her boyfriend, leaving off her panties; she would deliberately display herself, as if accidentally. They both got very excited about that. But this is not the kind of thing we usually mean when we talk about exhibitionism. Male exhibitionists usually display the male organ to women they do not know. Frequently they masturbate at the same time.

I have found two reasons for this behavior among the exhibitionists I've treated. It is important to distinguish between them. In one case, they know how excited it makes them to look at a nude female, and therefore believe that it would make a woman excited to look at their male organ, and so they display themselves. Many of these exhibitionists seem to prefer young children, and exhibit themselves in playgrounds.

Exhibitionists exhibit themselves in a variety of ways, but always it is important to them to get the attention of the woman. One man used to carry pebbles around with him and throw them at a window, so the woman would look out, and then he would display himself. In

another case, a man used to stand on the platform of a
subway station and, as the train pulled out, expose himself to the female passengers in the car. These were
men who received great sexual gratification from the
act. They found it possible to have an orgasm with very
little masturbation if they could display their erect organ to women.

I used to think that sexual excitement was the chief
reason, but I have come across several cases in which
the decision to exhibit oneself was based on hostility. I
saw a very brilliant man, an experimentalist in one of
the physical sciences, who had been arrested for exhibitionism several times but never in the small college
town near New York City in which he lived. He would
come into the city to go on his exhibitionistic binges,
because he was concerned about being recognized in
his own town. He was afraid of being arrested, and at
one therapy session, when I was trying to learn the
background of his behavior, we ran into a problem.

He had been going to psychoanalysts who strongly
believed in symptom substitution, and he felt that if he
ever gave up his exhibitionism, something much worse
would happen—he would probably become schizophrenic. So that was one of the difficulties I had to deal
with in working with him at all. I questioned him carefully as to the circumstances when he felt compelled to
exhibit himself.

He had gone on one of his binges shortly before his
first session with me. During that day, he had attended
a department meeting at the university with which he
was connected. He was up for promotion to the rank of
full professor from associate professor, but his department decided not to promote him. He left the meeting,

drove his car to the city, and exhibited himself to five different women that night. What he did was stand in front of a store window on a street that wasn't too crowded, knock at the window until one of the female clerks looked out, and then exhibited himself.

I asked him what feeling he wanted to cause in these women. He said he had made the decision to shock them. He had taken the hostility he had built up against the people in the department who had passed him over and expressed it by shocking women with his erect member. He was one of the first people I treated with Direct Decision Therapy, and this was the "payoff" for him; the shock of these women was his way of dealing with anger, plus a reassurance of his masculinity. He said that it made him feel more of a man, that he didn't feel so helpless as when he was at the departmental meeting and had to abide by the academic rules of courtesy and politeness. At that point he felt un-manned. His exhibitionism was a way of restoring his feelings of masculinity and of expressing his anger and hostility. Clearly this was the payoff.

He said he was angry at the whole establishment. He was a radical, angry at the hypocrisy and rigidity of society. Exhibiting himself was a gesture of defiance against this hypocritical society. I pointed out that, though he *believed* he was attacking the establishment, he was actually just playing their game. I told him that the establishment believes that all radicals are exhibi-tionists at heart anyway, and follow all kinds of strange sexual practices. I pointed out to him that he was really not fighting the establishment, but was giving them ammunition. At that point—and he used the key word himself—he said, "That's it. I've *decided.* No more exhi-

bitionism! Up against the wall, hypocrites. I'll fix you!"
And he stopped exhibiting himself, stopped cold.

Later, he told me that he still had some exhibitionistic impulses, so I said, "Look, you're married. Try it with
your wife." And he wrote me a long letter about the
exciting time he had exhibiting himself to his wife, and
how much freer he felt acting out sexual fantasies with
her, rather than having to run the risk of being arrested. He didn't think that the exhibitionism was
wrong, but he was afraid that, if he were arrested, the
different causes he was associated with would suffer.

He stuck with his decision until several years later,
when he left the country. He was in Germany, and he
didn't like the Germans anyway, so he thought he
would show them what he thought of them, but then
realized it wouldn't be useful to him, it would be too
dangerous. He controlled that impulse, and found a
substitute outlet—writing angry letters to the newspapers. His letters, which were vigorous and outspoken
became so popular that the local papers would practically feature them. Then he started writing letters to
professional journals in his field. He had become capable of assertive acts that were more direct that the
pseudo-assertion of exhibitionism.

With all these people, I have worked on the consequences of their behavior, because there is no sense
getting involved in moral discussions. If you try to in-
volve them in a moral discussion, that's not where
they're at.

"What do you think it does to a young girl when you
do that?"

"They love it."

You can't get very far with that. If you say, "Do you

want to risk the consequences?" then they see it more clearly. One man, who specialized in exhibiting himself to girls under the age of ten, did say he wanted to avoid the consequences; he didn't think the act itself was wrong.

He was sent to me for several sessions. He told me he had planned to present a lengthy brief at the trial in favor of exhibiting himself and playing with little girls. He was going to submit in evidence a letter that he had received from his daughter, because when she was a little girl he used to play with her and exhibit himself, and she did not disapprove. When I asked an attorney friend of mine what he thought of that legal tactic, he said, "They wouldn't sentence him; they'd hang him right in court."

With this man's kind of exhibitionism, the only things a therapist can deal with are the consequences of the behavior. The patient should be led to decide to give up the behavior in order to avoid the consequences, regardless of whether it is "right" or "wrong," and to find substitute gratification. This particular man found a young woman who was willing to shave her pubic hair; her childlike body excited and satisfied him.

The rapist is an extreme of the same kind of thing. There are many men, as I have pointed out in discussing impotence, who have decided they need to express their anger in order to be potent. When rapists are arrested, they often turn out to be people who have been known previously as gentle people, who have been quiet and isolated. These men frequently do not feel potent unless they can rape.

There is one way for women to avoid rape, which I learned from two different women who had managed, when assaulted, to avoid being raped. They happen to have been call girls, but the technique can be used by anyone. One of the girls was walking in a small town in upstate New York, and suddenly a fellow leaped from behind some hedges and threw her down on the sidewalk. It was a deserted street, late at night. She looked up at him and said, with rare presence of mind, "Not here, honey. Let's go someplace where we can be comfortable."

At that point, he got up and ran away. In another case, a man broke into a girl's home, grabbed her and threw her on the floor, and she said, "Why here? Let's go into the bedroom." He went away.

I had a patient who had a pathological fear of rape. I told her about this technique of avoiding rape. Some months later, she went drinking with a friend of her husband's, and when they got home, he took off her glasses and threw her on the floor and she said, "Why here? Let's go into the bedroom." Then he released her.

The indication here is that if the rapist cannot employ force and violence, he is not interested in sex. With some rapists I have worked with, we dwelt on the dangers they were courting, the consequences of their behavior. Unfortunately, that very danger (as with some exhibitionists and voyeurs) is part of the excitement. And some men who have a problem with potency can only be potent in anxiety-provoking situations. (One man couldn't have sex in the comfort of his bedroom, but on the front seat of a car or in a parking lot behind a restaurant, he was ready to go.) This extra spur of anxiety helps these men, and so it is with the rapist: the fear and danger seem to give them the stimulation they want.

Sometimes it is helpful to explore the reason they chose rape as the preferred way of achieving sexual excitement. Past incidents usually engender this kind of behavior. One rapist told me of fighting with girls when he was quite young, before he was capable of intercourse. He had found wrestling with them very exciting and pleasurable, so, when he was grown, he tried to repeat the experience with older women. Rapists, of course, pick all sorts of unusual objects for their attention. It's not unusual to find rapists who specialize in women over seventy or in crippled women. The wide variety of sexual choices is astounding.

Associated with voyeurism and exhibitionism is the growing popularity of group sex. I want to distinguish technically between mate-swapping and group sex. Mate-swapping is usually carried on in privacy. I knew a couple who were friendly with another couple, with whom they played bridge every week. After a while they got bored playing bridge with each other, so they substituted a mate-swapping session for the weekly bridge game. Each couple would retire to a separate bedroom. Eventually, one of the women and one of the men became enamored of each other, and the couples broke up and married their former bridge opponents.

Many people think group sex is new. Actually, it goes back to primitive times, when it was quite common in ritual fertility rites. Also, rather than being a sign of excessive sexuality, it is frequently a sign of deficient sexuality. Primitive tribes had to engage in such activities because, living on a marginal diet that did not produce an excess of energy, they did not find sex easy. In some animals, group sex seems to be instinctive. Herd animals such as sheep, seals, and cattle remain inactive until one couple starts the sexual act, and then the others follow suit. There is something about watching sexual intercourse that is exciting to many animals, apparently including the human animal. Group sex has been popular in different societies and even institutionalized in ritual. For example, once a year at a certain time of the moon, it has sometimes been a form of worship.

When I first started practice, I heard of very few examples of group sex, and I still remember how shocked I was the first time a female patient told me she was going to an orgy. As I mentioned earlier, I tried to talk her out of it. I didn't say that the thought of this nice woman doing this thing was abhorrent to me, which it was, but I told her she might get arrested or run the risk of getting a disease. Well, after all that introduction, she had a great time. She had to prove me wrong.

She came back and said, "You know, we've been working for a long time on my fear of homosexuality, but now I am no longer afraid—as a result of going to that orgy. I was at the orgy and some girl came up to play with me and I realized I didn't want it. All these years I was afraid, and now I'm not afraid." Her decision to go to the orgy had not only challenged me, but had, actually, challenged her own sexual anxiety.

Group sex takes different forms, depending on the participants. It used to be that group sex was the property of the avant-garde, the theatre people, jazz or rock musicians, or the underworld. Today it is a middle-class activity. A recent study shows that many proper and politically conservative middle-class people have decided to engage in group sex, and have organized sex clubs, and magazines and journals in which they advertise for the kind of partners desired. It seems that the general trend of sexual permissiveness is a phenomenon that has spread in the last five years. I have come across many people who have participated in these parties.

Some are highly organized. One that I know of may be the oldest continuing orgy, going on for at least twenty years. It is run by a well-known theatrical personality in New York City. Because he knows a lot of people who are theatrical producers, he gets a lot of costumes from plays. When the guests arrive, they sit down in the "conversation pit" and have a drink; there is polite, civilized talk as he carefully analyzes the personalities of the guests and then takes them into the robing room and gives them appropriate costumes. One girl said she was given a dress that would be called Chinese except that it was slit to the top of the buttocks and nothing was worn underneath.

There is a play by Genêt called *The Balcony,* which describes a similar scene. After the costuming, the participants play musical chairs. They don't use chairs, though. A whistle is blown when everyone is supposed to change partners.

Then there are less structured parties, with greater spontaneity. My informants tell me that among older Bohemian orgiasts there was no attempt at any kind of force or persuasion. If one wanted to participate, O.K. If not, O.K. Sex parties can run to quite considerable size. I asked one group sex regular the size of the largest orgy he had ever been to. He said, "About fifty people. But thirty of them were perverts; they only watched."

Exhibitionism and voyeurism are given social sanction within the confines of the orgy. Some people believe group sex is disguised homosexuality, and that the man who wants to participate sexually with several women and also be with one woman while he watches the woman he will be with next being made love to by another man, is really using these women as a bridge, a way of getting to the other man. This may be true in some cases, but I have found that many men don't believe that women have strong sexual desires. When they are themselves involved with women, they can't tell—maybe she's faking—but when they see a woman being made love to and responding, they are reassured that women really like sex.

It's a great surprise, like a story the humorist Sam Levenson tells about the boys on his block telling him how babies are made. He said, "Papa, maybe, but Mama, never!" Many men need reassurance that females, too, are interested in sex.

We live in an increasingly isolated society; people are more and more withdrawn. Married couples have decided to have fewer children, and family units don't function as they used to, as economic units as well as emotional units. In industry, people's jobs are more alienating. Group sex is a way of achieving instant intimacy. One goes to a party, and within fifteen minutes, one is in bed with everyone. There are people who say this leads to a greater intimacy than an encounter, and some have even tried to combine group therapy with group sex. I don't know what the results were. We don't have any documented evidence on the therapeutic results of group therapy with group sex; perhaps some graduate student will write a doctoral dissertation on the subject.

In the early days of psychoanalysis, there were many cases of a so-called deviation called fetishism. One fetishist, discussed in an earlier book of mine, *Active Psychotherapy,* liked corsets. The fetishist finds some object more exciting than a person. In England there are apparently a great many rubber fetishists—people who are turned on by wearing rubber garments. A well-known British writer went out with a woman I know and insisted that she wear a wet-suit whenever they made love, because the feel of rubber was very exciting to him. Fur is another fetish that is common. Many people are excited by furs, and one of the classic pornographic books is titled *Venus in Furs.* Other people get excited about a glove. Men will steal gloves from women they like in order to masturbate holding onto the gloves. More commonly fetishists use more intimate garments—panties or bras.

There are almost no female fetishists. One of the explanations some psychoanalysts give is that the fetish is a substitute penis; you don't have to worry about having a penis if you have the object. Another possible explanation is that women have been raised so differently until quite recently that they were more inhibited about sexual acting-out in general, so they didn't go into fetish sex as men did. Men need to be excited in order to perform sexually. Women don't. They do not have to go through so many self-stimulating acts as men do. But I think the simplest explanation is that it is a matter of conditioning.

I knew a man who was turned on by white boots; he didn't care what the girl looked like if she wore white boots. He would follow her for miles in a state of sexual excitation. We discussed this at great length, and he remembered that as a boy entering adolescence, he watched a woman across an alley who got undressed until she was completely nude, except for her white boots. So by association—like Pavlov's dogs, which salivated at hearing a bell because it was originally rung in association with food—this man "salivated" when he saw a woman with white boots. He would buy boots and put them around his apartment. He had white suede boots, white patent-leather boots, and, of course, it was difficult to explain them to visitors.

Conditioning is one cause of fetishism. Actual decision is another. Many fetishists have problems with interpersonal relationships, and it is much easier for them to get excited about an object than a person. You don't have to make conversation with a pair of white boots. Growing out of the original conditioning, fetishists then make a decision to stay with this object because they believe it is easier than dealing with a human being, with the dangers and difficulties that a human relationship presents.

I want to distinguish between a fetishist and someone who just likes boots a great deal. When a man asks his wife or girlfriend to wear white boots, that's just a preference. The difference between strong preference and fetishism is that the fetishist becomes so fixed on the object that he is incapable of sex except in the presence of such an object. If he wants to change and give up his compulsivity—if he gets tired of making it with a pair of white boots—he can be helped by realizing that he can convince the woman he likes to wear the object or have it close to her, and if there is enough commitment, they can carry it through together.

When a fetish is part of the body, it is not so impersonal as when it is an object, but again it is probably due to conditioning, a strong fixation on that level. The therapist has to explore with the person his reason for deciding to take this path and not another.

One of the biggest problems with all these sexual compulsions is that they are so gratifying. With a lot of other neurotic manifestations, there may be some form of payoff but no real gratification; in fact, the opposite happens: anxiety neuroses or obsessions only cause trouble. But sexual varieties are a source of pleasure. The voyeurs, the exhibitionists, the group-sex people all find their aberrations very exciting. So the therapist has to help the person find some external reason for making a decision to change. It used to be morality, but again, as we get more and more permissive, and the general attitude about sex becomes "As long as you're not hurting anyone, there's nothing wrong," what can I tell someone who happens to dig feathers? He'd say, "That's my thing, man. How can you put it down?"

Sexual preferences are choices, and it's difficult for a therapist to say one way is better than another. The problem is the compulsivity which makes it difficult for these people to have full relationships. Many people who are involved in fetishism or voyeurism do miss the human relationship, and it's too easy an out, like a drug.

When you dam up sexual energy and give it only one outlet, then you have a lot of energy behind it. It can really seem to the person as if the thing has taken over, because often he doesn't think of trying to escape it. When you get the person to give up the object, then it is easier for him to move in another direction.

Often a person burdened by these compulsions will say, "What can I do? I'm a victim of my history." The therapist has to point out that that is partially true, that there are factors which may have caused him to make this kind of choice. But it is still a choice, and in every case, the therapist will find that there were occasions when the patient felt his compulsion but didn't give in to it. For one reason or another, he decided not to. So it is very helpful to show such people that they have been able to make that choice at some time, and that they can continue to decide on that choice. It is also useful to show them other areas in which they have a great deal of control. I remember talking to a promiscuous woman who explained that she was promiscuous because she had no self-control, she would go to bed with anybody. She was a woman of forty, and very slim. I asked her, "How do you keep so slim?"

"Well," she replied, looking at my belly, "I control myself!" I could then show her that in some ways she had much better control than I did, so couldn't she decide to control herself from being compulsively promiscuous?

Some of the ardent women's liberation people will say to exhibitionists, "What do you think you've got there that's so great?" and then get into a political discussion about it. This rather discourages the exhibitionist, who is not there for political reasons. Another thing some of the women who get annoyed by men exposing themselves do is go around and deliberately stare at men's flies, to see how they react to this. Men find this behavior disturbing. In general, if a woman expresses no reaction at all to an exhibitionist, he is likely to give up and just go away.

There are some women who do get turned on by exposure of the male organ. One woman told me that she found it very exciting. She was sitting in a car once, right in the middle of downtown Manhattan, and a man came over and opened his raincoat, and started to play with himself. She said she was so fascinated that she couldn't get the car started. One fellow I knew exhibited himself in Central Park. The woman said, "You look like such a nice man. How can you do such a disgusting thing?"

He said, "You know, you're the first woman who ever spoke to me that way." So they became friends and had an affair. It is the only story of this kind I ever heard of, and to this day I'm not sure it wasn't just his fantasy— because many exhibitionists do have the fantasy that the woman takes one look at this magnificent treasure they hold between their legs and is immediately overcome with passion.

CHAPTER 12

DIRECT
DECISION THERAPY AND
SADISM, MASOCHISM,
TRANSVESTITISM
AND TRANSSEXUALISM

PHYSICAL sexual masochism and sadism do not come to a therapist's attention as often as psychic masochism and sadism, in which people enjoy torturing or being tortured psychologically. It is impossible to tell by looking at a person whether he might be attracted to sexual masochism or sadism. I knew one woman, a successful physician and psychiatrist, who worked as a top-level administrator. At a meeting she could be harsh and overbearing and tough, but actually she was a pathological masochist who could enjoy sex only if she were beaten.

She came to my office once with a black eye, and we talked about it, and I could see that she really had had a good time. I don't mean that she was beaten to the point of great pain, but she got a lot of sexual stimulation from the beating. Conversely, some passive, gentle-appearing men who may even seem effeminate are the very ones who have collections of canes, whips, and chains.

Now, a good deal of the sado-masochism that goes on in sex is symbolic. That is, a couple will tie each other up, but if one or the other really got upset, they would stop. But they dream about it, they get excited about it. For masochists, being tied down or threatened assuages guilt feelings. They are not responsible for their sexual behavior; they are not responsible because this strong, overbearing man "forced" them to do it.

Another pleasure for the masochist is a kind of skin eroticism, that is, stimulation of the skin. I think that what psychoanalysts have called fixation (like the oral or anal fixation) is really a specialized kind of excitation which starts out as a general feeling of contact pleasure. Many people, especially women, have described being sexually involved, as a purely tactile gratification. They enjoy being held, enjoy the stimulation to the skin. But some get a diminution of effect as this continues; they build up a tolerance. so they want more and more stimulation. Slapping or biting becomes necessary for stimulation. as this loses its novelty, they may proceed to sterner fare, anything from the very rough sex common among many people—*"un peu sauvage"* as the French call it—to severe beatings, flagellation. Some of the female masochists I know have complained that they can't find a man who is willing to beat them enough; they complain that there are not enough "real men" around, not realizing that a much more refined kind of sadism is exhibited when the masochist says, "Beat me," and the sadist says, "I won't."

I have known a great many masochists who received

pleasure by identifying with sadists. They would say, "Beat me," but identify with the beater, and the same thing might happen with the sadist identifying with the one getting beaten. Often when people express sexual sadism and sexual masochism in psychological ways, they are better off if they can convert it to more direct sex play, because unless there is something very sadly wrong wtih them, and they are completely out of control, or act as if they were, generally these are mild problems.

There is a French book, *The Story of O*, which gives a complete description of the female sexual masochist. Her explanation of her behavior, which I have seen corroborated in a great many female masochists, is that this is a way of demonstrating great love for a man. If you permit a man to humiliate you, to beat you, to send you out to make love to his best friend, you are demonstrating how devoted you are.

These are people who *decided* a long time ago that in order to win love, they must be completely compliant, and they are only too happy to find a situation in which they can be so compliant. Similarly, the sadist has decided to express his superiority. Freud said that women are basically masochistic. His explanation for this involved the so-called fact that since the end product of the sexual act, childbirth, is painful, women therefore learn to enjoy pain. The man, on the other hand, has to initiate the woman by breaking the hymen; therefore men have to learn how to enjoy giving pain. So Freud gave it a kind of biological determinism. But with social change and the advance of female liberation, there are many women who refuse to accept the masochistic role because they consider it not a biologically determined fact but rather a socially determined myth, a means whereby men maintain dominance over women. My own belief is that many men are afraid of women, and the way they overcome this fear is by demonstrating physical strength, and that many women act masochistically, not because they are afraid of men, but because they have learned that this is a way of dealing with masculine fears of women and of female power.

Because sexual roles have been so strongly differentiated, many people are not satisfied with the sexual role they were originally placed in. Many men have decided they don't want to be men, and many women have decided they don't want to be women. In the literature of psychoanalysis, there is a lot of talk about penis envy, which is supposed to be biologically determined rather than caused by the socially dominant position of the male in our culture. Freud did say that in a male-dominated society, obviously many women would prefer to be men, because males have more power and more freedom. This was particularly true in the Victorian period, when women had many fewer rights than they have today. It was quite understandable that some women would envy the male role, and therefore perhaps the organ that goes with it.

One thing that Freud overlooked was that there are almost as many men who suffer from vagina envy. I've known lots of men who think that women have it very easy; they don't have to work, don't have to worry about having erections to have sex. They are taken care of. All they have to do is get married and bask in security the rest of their lives, while the poor men have to go out and kill themselves to earn a living. You get both kinds of dissatisfaction, and therefore you get people who decide to change. They are not satisfied with their born sex role.

There are alternatives. One is to become a transvestite, dress up in the clothes of the opposite sex. In the past, women have often dressed in masculine clothes, and today, with the growth of what are called unisex clothes, they do so increasingly. So you have women who dress in men's clothing, and no one pays much attention, and if a man dresses in a pants suit, you can't really call it women's clothing. Male transvestites tend to go in for old-fashioned women's clothes—corsets and lace and high-buttoned shoes with high heels—the kind of clothes females dressed in when they were growing up. They have decided to recapture the period when they were first excited.

Transvestites are not necessarily homosexuals. Many transvestites dress in women's clothing in order to masturbate with heterosexual fantasies. Others like to dress up in feminine clothes when they are having sex with a woman. Otherwise, they act "normal" sexually.

I had a woman patient who had been a homosexual for many years. She finally decided to change and become heterosexual. She got married, and the first night her husband appeared in bed completely in drag. She suspected he had married her because they wore the same size dress.

Some male homosexuals like to dress in female clothes. this is very common in homosexual communities like Cherry Grove, Fire Island, off the coast of Long Island. There they have fairly elaborate theatrical shows, for which they get all dressed up in female clothes and act like female impersonators.

Some women who are homosexual, and some few who are not, decide to dress in rough, masculine clothes. The homosexual does not consider transvestitism to be a special problem, however; it's just one aspect of being homosexual. Especially the male ones who are referred to as homosexual "queens," who like to act and appear extremely effeminate. But the heterosexuals who are transvestites sometimes come to me for treatment because they think it's demeaning in some way, and they talk about it as being something they have a tremendous compulsion to do. One simple way in which I treated a heterosexual transvestite was as follows:

This man was one of the biggest, ugliest men I have ever met. He kept talking about how he had to dress up in women's clothes, so I said, "Okay, why don't you bring them to the office and dress up?" I had a full-length mirror in the closet of my office, and at the next session, after getting all dressed up, he took a look at himself in the mirror. He laughed out loud. All these years he had been doing it in privacy; it was only when I said "I want to see what you look like" that he decided to look at himself. Actually, he did a good job. He had a stubble of beard but covered it with pancake make-up, and he wore falsies and was quite attractive. If I had seen him on the street, I would have considered him an attractive woman. But once he had seen himself in the mirror as he was accustomed to seeing himself psychologically, he laughed and made the decision to get rid of the stuff, and never bothered with it after that.

To people who talk about a tremendous compulsion, I say, "Okay, if you enjoy it, there's no big deal, but if

you insist on it, you're probably trying at some level,
maybe not consciously, to con me." I think they believe
that there is a compulsion but it is something that I have
never found difficult to treat once they *decide to
change*. They really don't harm anyone; in fact, they
help clothing manufacturers. But sometimes they're
afraid that their wives or children will find out, so they
stop.

Professional female impersonators go to great
lengths to disguise themselves and have a variety of
ways of hiding their male parts, like covering them
with layers of sanitary napkins and then putting on
tight little panties so you can't detect their male equipment. They wear falsies and buy very expensive wigs,
and some even go in for electrolysis in order to remove
any sign of a beard. Some of the professional female
impersonators are not homosexual. There was a famous
actor at the turn of the century, Julian Eltinge, who
won fame by playing female roles, and even had a
theatre named for him in New York. It happened that
he had worked for Al Woods, whom I later worked for,
and the reason Woods hired him was that he thought
this "woman" he saw in a part was really great, and he
sent for her and it turned out to be Julian Eltinge. He
was, as far as I know, a normal male, but impersonating
women was his job, and he did it extraordinarily skill-
fully.

The question of choice is even more dramatic in
transsexuals. With advances in surgery, it has been possible to apparently transpose the sexes; someone who is
biologically born a male can become a female, and vice
versa.

It seems, at least in the cases I've seen, as if these transsexuals were fulfilling a parental wish, as is often true in other cases of strange behavior. It is still a choice that a person makes. Nobody forces them to change sex. (Some transsexuals deny that they had any choice. When I asked a group of them, "How did you make the decision to change?" they answered that they had no choice, that there was no way they could have continued living as they were.) I believe this is truly how they feel. Life in the sex they were born to was intolerable for them because usually the decision is made at a very early age. Sometimes, of course, the decision is also made where the individual is taught to regard himself as actually being of the opposite sex.

A man who becomes a "woman" is actually a castrated male after the surgery. The process begins with the administration of female hormones over an extended period. This causes most of the male body hair to disappear, and breasts to develop. The patient continues this treatment until he is ready for the actual operation, which takes place in Casablanca, Mexico, Denmark (the well-publicized operation on Christine Jorgensen was done there) or Johns Hopkins Hospital in Baltimore.

What happens is that the surgeons just chop off all the male parts and replace them with a plastic pouch, which creates a "vagina." Some surgeons have developed a refinement: Instead of chopping off the penis and testicles and throwing them away, they skin the penis and, after they construct a pouch, surgically turn it inside out, so there are nerve endings and the person can enjoy sexual pleasure after the operation.

My friend Dr. Leo Wolman, who is a gynecologist and has treated a number of transformed males, tells

some interesting stories about them. When the person
gets the operation that he has yearned for all his life, he
may be overeager to put his new equipment to work.
One person who had the operation in Casablanca was
told that he wasn't supposed to use the new sexual
organ for a while, to give it a chance to heal, but between the hospital and the airport he propositioned the
taxi driver and he had to be returned to the hospital. It
took him three trips to get to the airport.

Recently there have been attempts to transform
females into "males." This is a very difficult operation.
Consider the determination that is necessary to go
through with it, once the decision has been made.

The woman takes male hormones, which cause her to
develop a hairy appearance. I once had the opportunity
to see one of these women during the time she was
getting her shots, and I felt it was a terrible waste,
because she was a lovely, attractive woman, and she
was sprouting hair all over her body. Maybe for my own
reassurance, I asked the doctors what happens if they
stop the shots, and they told me that the hair would go
away. It seemed like such a shame to spoil this lovely
girl, but this was what she wanted. She had made the
decision to be a male.

After the shots, the next step is to remove the breasts.
Then comes the difficult part. In order to construct a
penis, the surgeons have to graft something on, and
what they do is graft skin from the abdomen to the arm,
and then from the arm it is grafted around cartilege
taken from the back and placed around the sewed-up
vagina, and then the skin is placed around the cartilege.
So that they end up with a "penis" that is more or less
erect all the time, which is scarcely normal for men.

There have been difficulties with these operations. In

one case, one of these "men" went horseback riding, and his penis fell off. In another case, it developed gangrene. Apparently, the operation is not yet perfected. However, I've seen a number of women who are eager to have the operation.

You can speculate on the reasons. I think some can be attributed to attitudes on the part of the parents. Very often a mother will say to her son that she had wanted a daughter.

In one such case the woman stated when she saw her former son, now her daughter, "I laughed and exclaimed, 'How wonderful, welcome home.'" It seems to me that her son, now a woman, had made this drastic decision, not simply to please himself, but, more basically, to become the person his mother had always wanted. And the mother was, indeed, pleased.

This is not always the case. Very often the mothers are disturbed by public opinion. When I was speaking to some transsexuals I talked with one who looked like a very attractive black woman. It was the kind of situation where I didn't know who was who, biologically— what they had started out as, and I asked this woman, "What did your mother say when you first made the change?" And she answered, "My mother said to me, 'If you come around here, everyone will know. They know I had a son—what are they going to think when I have a daughter?' And my sister said, 'Stay away. How am I going to explain to my kids that their uncle is now their aunt?'"

There are a few cases of actual chromosomal disharmony, where a person may be biologically more female than male even though he has male organs, but these cases are rare. Most of the transsexuals I know about did not have any chromosomal difference, or any other discoverable physical difference. Their "need" to change seems to have been entirely psychological. While we might some day find physical causality, I feel that the psychological motivation shows how powerful the decisions we make are, and I marvel that these people are willing to go through such pain and trouble because of their decision.

Recently, some places have permitted change of birth certificates and official change of sex, so that people who have these operations can be officially recognized in their new sex. This is very important to many transsexuals, who feel it is an important civil right to choose your sex.

One time I was in a French restaurant and saw a very striking blonde at least six feet tall and her "girl" friend. I was talking to them, and then they said, "Excuse us," and went to the powder room. When they came back, and I suddenly realized from their conversation, that they were both men, I asked one of them, "Do you find it embarrassing to go to the ladies room?" and she/he said, "No." This magnificent blonde and her friend were still working as men during the day. They had not yet had the operation, but were taking female hormone shots to test their decision. Recently I inquired what had happened to them, and learned that the blonde, who during the day was a psychiatrist, had fallen in love with a woman just about a month before he was due to leave for the operation, and called the whole thing off. Apparently this compulsion which is talked about isn't always that great.

CHAPTER 13

DIRECT
DECISION THERAPY
AND
SUICIDE

A PERSON who commits suicide is someone who has made a decision to do so, and this is evidenced by the great preparation that many people make for suicide. Suicide requires a decision and the implementation of a plan. People will go to great trouble to get a gun, or whatever other device they plan to use as a weapon to kill themselves. Sometimes they have to collect a lot of drugs. I've known people who wanted to commit suicide and didn't want any one doctor to feel responsible, so they got prescriptions for sleeping pills from three or four doctors and combined them to commit suicide.

In most cases, then, suicide is not only a decision, but a decision which has been given considerable thought. What is hard to understand is how often people who are planning to commit suicide will bathe, shave, change to clean underwear, get dressed up. There is a strange incapability on the part of many of us really to consider ourselves dead. In a way, many suicides think not of being dead but of the effect their act will have. They see themselves dead; they see everyone mourning. They have decided that everyone will be sorry when they're dead. Again, a payoff.

Suicide, like some depressions, is frequently an expression of rage turned inward that the suicide either dares not express openly, or he feels that this is the most effective way of expressing it. I knew a woman who was married to a drug addict, and she begged him to stop taking drugs. When he wouldn't, she said to me, "I'm going to take heroin and give myself an overdose and die. I'm going to show him." Obviously, there was great anger there, a wish for revenge of a very strange kind, and yet even in avenging herself she did not express direct, outward aggression but turned it on herself. When she decided to express her anger directly, she gave up her suicidal plans.

Suicide is a good example of how aggression against someone else works when you turn it on yourself. If you punish the other person with your suffering, the extreme of that suffering is suicide. It is the most common reason people commit suicide, the one most therapists emphasize, but it would be incorrect to treat all suicidal impulses as being due to this, because there are other possibilities. One possibility is that somebody feels very guilty. He feels that what he has done is so bad that he deserves capital punishment.

A patient telephoned me one time, her voice quavering, and said, "Doc, I don't want you to feel guilty. I want you to know that you did everything you could. I was just not worth saving, and I have the pills here and

I'm going to take them and jump out the window. Either way, I'm making sure. I thought I'd call you up and say good-bye."

So I said, "If you don't cut it out, I'm going to come over and break all your God-damn teeth and stuff them down your throat!"

She laughed, and said, "I knew I could depend on you."

She felt so guilty about her intention to commit self-murder that when I offered to beat her up, I took care of her guilt for the moment.

Hers was not an idle threat. It may seem that way, but she had attempted suicide before she came to therapy and was in a coma for three days; she was fully capable of suicide.

Many suicidal people say they just want to end it all. Another very common cause for suicide is disappointment in love, very much as in mourning. One of the most frequent reasons for committing suicide is that a man's or woman's loved one leaves, especially if he leaves for someone else. The abandoned ones still have too much "love" to avenge themselves directly. They do not want to live, but they want to get even. Suicide is one way to get even, to make the other person sorry. Sometimes it is real loss—but then they would be willing to commit suicide quietly.

Too often they want to commit suicide in such a way as to make it clear who was responsible. They are suffering not a loss of love but a loss of control or power. They wanted to control the other person, and they couldn't. You find this with psychopaths who do not seem capable of love, but they get involved in the control aspect of a relationship and find that somebody they thought they had completely under their control is ready to walk away. Then they get suicidal.

I treated a man for a while who was planning to leave his wife. He came to therapy to get absolution, to prove that even his doctor said that it was all right for him to leave her. His wife was about to have a child, so he waited until the baby was born, and then he went directly from the maternity ward to his girlfriend's house and told the girlfriend's mother he loved her daugher so much that he had left his wife with the newborn baby. The mother was very impressed by his "honesty."

Well, it would not have mattered; he was involved in a power struggle with somebody else. He thought that a girl he had met in one of my groups had a big crush on me, and for that reason it was important for him to get her. Whoever he might be involved with, he would be involved in a power struggle. This time it was with the therapist. He was willing to take that chance.

Shortly after the baby was born, the wife decided that her husband was getting impossible. She came to see me, and I asked her, "What do you need him for? He's mistreating you, and there's very little chance that he'll change in the immediate future. Why don't you just leave him?" She left him; he broke down, he cried, he was suicidal, so she took him back. Two weeks after that, he started running around again. His wife decided to put up with him as other people had done all his life. Very often you have those who need to control someone else—who have a great need for control, themselves.

It is important, in dealing with suicidal persons, to show that you can't be threatened. But this is not the same as challenging them, because if you challenge a person to commit suicide, he may well do it. If somebody comes in and says, "I feel terrible. I feel like killing myself," you can't join him by saying, "Why don't you do it?" Because he just might do it. He sees it as a challenge, as if you do not believe him. So the first thing I try to do with a suicide threat is to be calm about it. Seriously and interestedly, I discuss with him why he is considering such a decision, explaining my philosophical position, which is that people have as much right to end their lives as to continue them. Since I have changed to that position, I've had no suicide attempts from my patients. Before that, when I really thought that the decision to commit suicide was insane, there were attempts, but, fortunately, none of them was successful. Once I said "It is up to you and your choice," there were no more attempts.

I believe that once the threat of suicide can no longer be used as a weapon, the impulse no longer promises a payoff.

People constantly try to distinguish between the person who makes a gesture at suicide and the one who really attempts suicide. This is not a valid difference, because very often the person who makes a gesture makes a mistake, and turns out dead—and it is very hard to change the decision at that point! Sometimes a suicide gesture is a cry for help. Every suicide threat must be taken seriously. It may start out as a demonstrative gesture; but then the would-be suicide has to keep attracting attention, and each time escalate the threat to continue to get attention.

I believe a great many deaths are suicides that we do not recognize as such. A large percentage of traffic fatalities are really disguised suicides. I have known people who planned to commit suicide that way—drive off a bridge, hit a telephone pole, hit (God help all drivers!) an oncoming car. One patient of mine drove her car full speed into the wall of her garage. By some miracle, she was not killed.

When one is confronted by a suicide gesture, the first thing is to assess the situation calmly, but to show interest, concern. It is helpful not to be frightened. I remember a striking thing that happened in a psychology class I was taking, when the teacher was discussing suicide. The class got quiet and uneasy, and he turned around and said, "Are you people worried about suicide?"

Someone said, "Oh, yes."

He asked, "Why does it worry you?"

The student said, "It would have a very bad effect on my practice." This was a very devoted person—filled with the milk of human kindness.

The instructor said, "Oh, no, not necessarily. As a matter of fact, I once had a patient who committed suicide. He left a note saying that I was his psychiatrist, and that he was in treatment with me. The only thing that happened was that a lot of other people who wanted to commit suicide came to me, hoping I would drive them in the same direction."

That is a very important story to remember, because one of the things that many patients fear is that the therapist is not concerned about them. One way they think they can get the therapist to be concerned is to threaten suicide. They think that therapists are vulnerable to these threats. If you indicate that their suicide would increase your practice and your fame, they might give up the suicide attempt if they are using it as a ploy against you. You cannot use any of these devices in a general way, but only if you understand what the suicide is about.

Other people seem to want to use suicide because they are just tired, weary unto death. They are slowly running down, and they want to end the turmoil. Well, I don't know, that's not entirely a bad thing if you feel tired and bored with the world. It is possible that, by working with such patients, a therapist can help them regain their interest. Exhaustion and boredom may cloak a very serious depression. Boredom is sometimes a product of not wanting to experience any feelings, and is a kind of mild depression. One of the feelings that these people do not want to experience is rage. But I can understand situations in which suicide might make sense—the terminally sick, for instance, who know that the illness will go on and on, and not only will it go on and on and mean suffering for them, but it will exhaust all the family finances and cause a financial catastrophe.

Under such circumstances, a decision to commit suicide certainly seems rational and understandable. But there are many people planning to commit suicide who will say, "My family will be much better off without me," when they are not talking about such a realistic situation. What they mean is, "I'm a bad person, I'm a drag," and they intend to punish some oppressor for making them see themselves in that light.

There is one kind of suicide I really dread because it is so difficult to deal with him, unless you get him to make a firm pact with you that he will not kill himself —and that is the impulsive suicide.

A woman I know was walking along the West Side of Manhattan. She walked down to the Hudson River, looked at the water, and said, "I think I'm going to jump in." Until that moment, she had had no thought of committing suicide, but, purely on impulse, she jumped in. Fortunately, she was fished out. Another woman felt pretty good; and then realized that in the last eight days she had slept with eight different men and had not experienced any guilt about it. She was standing on a subway platform and said to herself, "I'm going to jump in front of that train." She started to move toward the edge when someone pushed her away —not to save her but because she was in his way—and knocked her on her can. She said, "Son of a bitch, I'm not going to kill myself when there are people like that around!"

Anyone who contemplates suicide should carefully explore all other alternatives. There are always alternatives, if you look hard enough. For example, Sweden has a very high suicide rate, while Norway, whose people have a similar background, has a very low one. I've found that Norwegians, when they get into situations from which others might seek escape through suicide, ship out as merchant seamen or fishermen, giving themselves surcease from the stresses of their present life and a chance to explore other alternatives. A similar decision would make sense for many people. Don't jump. Ship out and shape up.

CHAPTER 14

DIRECT DECISION THERAPY IN CONNECTION WITH HYPNOSIS

IN MY practice, I have found that hypnosis can play an extremely important role in decision-making. That may strike many people as unlikely, since hypnosis seems to imply the absence of will, but I think I can make my method clear if I recount how I got started using it.

Several years ago, a writer friend came to me with a suggestion for a project requiring the use of hypnosis. While the project never materialized, I did become interested in hypnosis and took an intensive course in the subject at a hypnosis seminar at one of New York's major hospitals.

It was only after I had begun to use hypnosis in my therapy that I remembered something which in my early years as a psychoanalyst I had forgotten; I had, as a college student, become interested in hypnosis. Just by hearing about it I had figured out how to do it, and

I had occasionally hypnotized people at parties as a kind of parlor stunt. Later on I had became ashamed of this activity, and when patients requested hypnosis, I gave them all the reasons, taken from orthodox psychoanalysis, why it was not appropriate.

These reasons included the supposed fact that hypnosis eliminated resistance and that it was important for the analysis to interpret the resistance. As I became involved with hypnosis and began to use it, I discovered that, rather than eliminating resistance, it merely clarified it.

For example, I remember once hypnotizing a girl who complained about her drinking and wanted me to help her stop. Following her expressed wish, I hypnotized her and told her that she would not be interested in drinking any more. Later that same evening, she called me and said, "Hey, Doc, it didn't work. I'm drunk."

Obviously then, hypnosis does not eliminate resistance but, as in this case, merely highlights it. One reason I use hypnosis is that, at a talk and in some papers, I had suggested that a patient frequently knows the correct way to be treated if you will only listen to him. When one of my patients requested hypnosis, even though I had had some training in it, I still refused. She quoted my own words to me, and I agreed to hypnotize her.

At the time, she had many severe problems, including the compulsive use of marijuana. When I hypnotized her, she went into a rather deep trance and presented material which she had not presented before, and at the end of our session, when I awakened her, she pointed out with enthusiasm the value of hypnosis to her. She said, "Did you see how my shoulders, which I usually keep up to fight the world, had relaxed?" And then she added something which was to be of great importance to me in further treatment, "You know, it's great. Just like smoking pot!"

Thereafter, with several patients who wanted to quit using marijuana, I hypnotized them and taught them to hypnotize themselves so that they could get by without the use of the weed. Somehow or other, word of this got around and an expert on marijuana, who had written three books on the subject, came to see me to see whether or not I could actually simulate the effect of marijuana with hypnosis. I hypnotized him and suggested that he was smoking marijuana, gave him all the instructions that the typical marijuana user follows— "You are breathing deeply, mixing it with air"—and told him that it was good, strong grass.

After the session, when I instructed him to come out of the trance, he looked up at me and, as often happens with people who wish to deny the fact of their hypnosis, said, "Sorry, I wasn't hypnotized at all." Of course, I did not argue with him—there is no point to that—but said, "I'm sorry; you can leave now," at which point he said, "I can't; I'm too high."

Some time later, a woman came to see me who was a heroin addict. I knew better than to try to hypnotize her and suggest that she would not be interested in heroin; a number of experiments had proved that this method of treating addiction does not work. So instead, after having her carefully describe how she gave herself a fix, I hypnotized her and proceeded to suggest that she was giving herself a fix and would feel high.

When she awoke, she felt very good, and even

though she was suffering from deprivation, not having had a fix that day, she said that she felt just as good as if she had had one. Therefore, I hypnotized her again and told her that whenever she wanted to give herself a fix, she would say to herself the number 263, put her finger at her arm the same as she would her "spike," the hypodermic needle, and would get high.

Incidentally, when she first came to me I was surprised that she wanted to see me; she insisted that I was the only therapist in New York City she would go to, and it was only after several weeks of work that I understood the reason—her source of heroin supply was around the corner from my office. However, in a short time, she learned how to visualize the suggestion or, as she called it, the mental fix, quite well.

Before she was completely cured of the habit, one of her friends asked her to take a fix. As is usual in such circumstances, when she refused, her friends taunted her, told her that she was chicken or too stingy, that they would pay for it. So, she went along. This time, even though her habit was about two "nickel bags"— that is, two glassine envelopes of heroin at five dollars apiece—she decided to save money, used only half a bag, and gave herself the mental fix. Several hours later, she woke from an overdose reaction.

It is possible that she had received pure heroin that time and that the other times it was cut much more, but her friends, who were accustomed to the same heroin she was, did not suffer from overdose reactions at all. So obviously, hypnosis had an effect; the suggestion had an effect stronger than that of just heroin. In fact, so successful did she become at giving herself mental fixes that she was able to kick the habit without any special discomfort and informed me later on that addicts were offering her ten dollars for the magic number.

Of course, the difference between this woman and other addicts is that she had come to the decision to kick her habit. Hypnosis was only the instrument to help her implement the decision. So I'm not suggesting that hypnosis is the cure for the heroin problems plaguing the nation. I have seen only six heroin addicts. Three of them were helped to kick the habit; the other three "kicked" me.

It was about this time that a man came to see me who wanted me to treat him with LSD because he had read a book on LSD. After that book appeared, I got a number of calls from people who wanted LSD therapy, which at that time was available legally. I explained that I was not a physician and was in no position to give them LSD, and referred them to a physician who was then using it; most of them went on to this doctor. But two or three, including a gentleman I'll call Patrick, insisted on coming to see me anyway.

Patrick had taken LSD a few times and found it useful. He believed that with the use of LSD, I could cure his homosexuality. I, therefore, agreed to hypnotize him and tell him that he was taking LSD, and then guide him on an experience similar to the psychedelic experience of a hallucinogenic drug, LSD. Our work was quite successful, the barrier to his decision was removed, and now, ten years later, he is a confirmed heterosexual.

In another case, a woman who was suffering from frigidity asked for the LSD experience. I used hypnosis, and during the course of it, because she was an extraordinarily creative person, she presented a whole series of brilliant pictures indicating the relationship of her anger at her mother to her inability to enjoy sex. She had decided not to identify with the femininity of her mother. For some time I continued to use the simulated LSD experience with a number of patients who were able, under that rubric, to present material of a kind that was usually not produced in ordinary therapy.

When I spoke at a meeting of the Association for Humanistic Psychology and alluded to this technique, there was considerable interest in it. That evening, I was invited to a party. Practically all of the people at the party had heard me speak at the convention, and, as the evening progressed, a number of them asked me whether I would hypnotize them. Earlier that day I had spoken for the first time at an American convention on Direct Decision Therapy. I had emphasized the question of choice. Now I had a good opportunity to experiment with the combination of hypnosis and Direct Decision Therapy.

Twenty of us gathered in the bedroom, and instead of using the usual authoritative techniques of hypnosis, I changed my spiel completely and told them something like the following:

> If any of you would like to be hypnotized—but only if you wish—you can close your eyes and relax. I will count from one to twenty. At the end of that count, if you wish, you can go deep, deep into it. If, on the other hand, at any time during the course of my counting you decide that you do not want to be hypnotized, just open your eyes and watch. You do not have to be hypnotized unless you really want to.

The result was astounding. Of the twenty people there, nineteen appeared to go into a trance. One decided that she did not want to and, as I had suggested, observed the others.

When they were in the trance, I said,

> If you would like to experience a psychedelic sensation, you can tell yourself that you are taking LSD or Mescaline or any drug that you would like which will produce this kind of experience. While in this experience, you will see fascinating pictures which will tell you something about yourself. I will now give you five minutes, at the end of which time, when you are ready, you can come out of it and open your eyes.

At the end of this time, when people began to open their eyes and sit up, we started to talk about their experiences. Many of them were exciting and very moving, to them and to me, as they described their insights and what they had learned about themselves from this brief experience.

But one of the young men present, who told me that he had taken about fifty trips with the use of LSD, was very angry at me and told me, "That was the worst trip I've ever taken. It was a real bummer." It became obvious to me that this had been his choice. He had wanted me to give him "real" LSD and when I did not, he decided that it was a bad trip.

This again made clear to me how much even experiences like the drug experience or the hypnosis experience are still subject to the will and choice and decision-making powers of the individual.

Since then, I have had occasion to use this technique, but I always make it completely permissive; I never insist that anyone try hypnosis. It has also made it much easier for me to do hypnosis and, I think, establish a better relationship with the person who has requested it. I have also, with the collaboration of the patients, used it for other problems like weight control, most dramatically with people who claimed they had never been able to lose weight, no matter what they did. With the help of hypnosis, again making it completely permissive, several people have reported that they were able to reach goals of weight loss that they had previously never been able to achieve.

One of the things this had made me realize is that the ability of a subject to become hypnotized has very little relationship to the skill of the hypnotist but depends primarily on the subject's choice. Those who have deeply decided to let themselves be hypnotized are the ones who can be. To me, this clarifies the mystery of why some people can and others cannot become hypnotized. Since I began to understand that, I have myself been able on at least one occasion, when I was with someone in whom I had complete trust, to allow myself to be hypnotized. This has also helped me avoid the greatest danger of hypnosis. Frequently people have asked me whether or not hypnosis is dangerous. My conclusion is that hypnosis is dangerous, but only to the hypnotist. I have known too many people, both professionals and nonprofessionals, who learned the comparatively simple technique of hypnosis and began to imagine themselves as having magical powers, when all they were really doing was acting in collaboration with the individual who wished to be hypnotized.

Therefore, my position is never to make a decision to hypnotize anybody but to give them the opportunity to become hypnotized if they wish. My experiences have led me to see very clearly that hypnosis is a clear demonstration of the power of decision, and the patient utilizes the hypnotist in the way he wishes. There are some people who need hypnosis because perhaps they made a decision to believe in magic. It helps them deal with the problem that so many people have carrying through decisions about a new way of being. Mainly they do not wish to take the responsibility for all the past unhappiness they have caused themselves, and so they can say, "It was not me. I couldn't have done this myself. The hypnosis helped me to carry it through."

I see no harm in helping people avoid responsibility for the mistakes and unfortunate experiences of the past by using hypnosis, even though I believe that ultimately, as I have pointed out a number of times, people make the decisions they make because in the context of their lives, it seemed that these decisions were the only possible ones for them at that time.

Hypnosis has also made possible to develop a relationship that is more collaborative than many in normal therapy. In order to be able to hypnotize somebody, or rather to assist him in becoming hypnotized, the therapist should be constantly aware of the wishes of the patient. For that reason, some writers have pointed out that in hypnosis it is not always the hypnotist who is maneuvering the subject; it is just as much the subject who is maneuvering the hypnotist.

I do not believe that it is either one of them, but rather it is a collaborative relationship in which both agree to participate in helping bring about the specific state. It has been difficult to convince some of my hypnotist colleagues, who do not wish to be robbed of the aura of magic that they feel surrounds their practice.

CHAPTER 15

HOW DIRECT
DECISION THERAPY IS
RELATED
TO OTHER THERAPIES

WHEN I speak publicly about Direct Decision Therapy somebody often comes up and says, "Isn't that just like Reality Therapy?" (which I do not happen to know very much about) or, "Isn't what you're saying exactly like behavior modification?" Frequently people say, "Isn't this R.E.T?" (Rational-Emotive Therapy). About a year ago I spoke on Long Island to a group of people who were predominantly psychoanalytically oriented. Some of them were highly experienced psychoanalysts, and they felt that DDT was basically psychoanalysis by a slightly different name.

I happen to agree with all these people. They are all correct. Because I believe that what I am talking about, good therapists of all schools have in one way or another always known.

Let us examine some of the schools. Take psychoanalysis. It seems to me that what Freud wanted—and he said so—was to replace the neurosis with the "capacity to choose." That was his goal in treatment. The way he did it was to make people aware of the things that were driving them, or that they thought were driving them, so that they had greater freedom of choice. In a number of his papers he speaks of the fact that even after you get someone to deal with his resistance, he still has to live by what Freud called the reality principle; that is, he still has to make it in reality. This means to choose.

Freud may not always have expressed it this directly, but since then a number of psychoanalysts have made the issue even clearer. For example, Leo Rangell, a famous Los Angeles psychoanalyst, states in an article in the *International Journal of Psychoanalysis:*

> A large part of psychoanalysis deals either perspectively or retrospectively with the major decisions of life, such as marriage, career, and where and how one has chosen to live. . . . Even when these choices have been made prior to the start of analysis as is typically the case with adult patients, the explorations of their deep unconscious roots occupies a large part of psychoanalytic work and such major decisions always remain open to question, analysis and change is indicated.

While Rangell considers the problems of decision to be unconscious, I have found again and again that when I stay very closely with the question of decision and choices, it is much easier to make it conscious than if I just let things flow on in the tradition of free-association analysis.

In another paper, "The Decision-Making Functions of the Ego," Rangell states: "Such decision-making is indeed a necessary preliminary activity . . . before defense or other actions can be electively instituted." In other words, one chooses one's defenses. After saying that, he then says, "It is not possible to do more than allude to the clinical aspects of this subject, due to its widespread relevance."

To me, this is an amazing statement, and I do not know why he chooses not to give more than passing acknowledgment to a subject which he says is of such widespread relevance. He goes on to say, "Problems of choice and decision-making play a frontal role in all of human behavior and course their way through all neuroses and other psychopathology. . . ." Many psychoanalysts will not look at the decision process, perhaps because it is so relevant. It is difficult for many of us to zero in on a relevant subject. It is easy to drift as aimlessly in therapy as in all other hard work.

When I have occasion to see people for classic psychoanalysis, most often psychologists or psychiatrists who want to be psychoanalysts, I now find it much easier to keep track of what is going on by studying what the patient is choosing to talk about in free association. In studying what people choose to talk about and the sequence in which they talk about it, I get to understand the kind of life decisions they have made—how they have chosen to lead their lives. Psychoanalysis happens to be a lengthy and difficult way of doing this, but it is certainly one way.

The earliest heretic in the psychoanalytic camp, Adler, disagreed with Freud on certain subjects, one of them being the question of intentionality of choice-making. Freud tried to model psychoanalysis after nineteenth-century physics, along the lines of cause and effect. As he went on to learn more about people, it seems to me he saw much more place for choice in the individual. In the beginning he did not have the theory of Id, Ego, and Superego; this came later on. So as he went on, he moved from the simple cause-and-effect relationship to discussing and studying what the individual himself was doing in situations.

Adler had insisted earlier that people's behavior was intentional, that it was goal-directed, that they were not simply acting as a result of certain causes but that they were acting in certain ways to get certain results. Adler had considerable effect on the development of many schools of thought, like those of Harry Stack Sullivan, Karen Horney, Albert Ellis, and Erich Fromm, and even on traditional psychoanalysis, with its present emphasis on Ego-Psychology, which sounds very similar to what Adler was talking about. (Ego-Psychology holds that the Ego's behavior is intentional, is interested in the consequences of its actions. Today, there is no longer a great difference, and some people move back and forth between the two schools).

Another Freudian offshoot is Transactional Analysis, in which Eric Berne, instead of talking about Id, Ego, and Superego, speaks of Child, Adult, and Parent. He says they are different, but I think it is mostly a difference in nomenclature and is certainly written more understandably. This is one of the reasons Transactional Analysis is so popular.

Berne makes the point that we are what we are because of the early decisions we have made. Many of the transactional analysts spend a lot of time dealing with decision. They speak of making decisions and new decisions. For example, in *I'm O.K., You're O.K.*, a recent book on Transactional Analysis, Thomas A. Harris says the following:

> The goal of TA is to enable a person to have freedom of
> choice. The freedom to change at will, to change the re-
> sponses to recurring and new stimuli. Restoration of the
> freedom to change is the goal of treatment.

He then goes on to explain how to do it, but the basic
thing is that he deals with the freedom to change, having people become aware and recognize that they can
change. The transactional analyst helps his patient
know when his Child is speaking, when his Adult is
speaking, or when his Parent is speaking. By doing this,
the Adult acquires the freedom to exercise decisions
and make choices, because he knows which is the Parent, Adult, and Child, just as the well-psychoanalyzed
patient would know which are his Id, Ego, or Superego
forces; therefore, he is able to make a rational choice.
For my part, I find it more economical to deal directly
with decision-making.

In recent years, there have been further modifica-
tions in psychoanalysis. Alan Wheelis, a San Francisco
psychoanalyst, states in a brilliant paper, entitled "How
People Change," from his book *The Desert:*

> Personality change follows changes in behavior. Since
> we are what we do, if we want to change what we are, we
> must begin by changing what we do. We must undertake
> a new mode of action. Change will occur only if such
> action is maintained over a long period of time. Should an
> honest man wish to become a thief, the necessary action
> is obvious. He must steal, not just once or occasionally, but
> frequently, consistently, taking pains that the business of
> planning and executing thefts replace other activities
> which in implication might oppose the predatory life.

You see how similar this is to what I described in the
treatment of homosexuals. I say that *if* you want to

change, to stop being a homosexual, you have to act like a heterosexual. You decide to stop being with the boys, stop masturbating, stop using any sexual outlets but heterosexual ones.

At the end of the paper he says:

> If, however, the greater awareness is of options unnoticed, of choices denied, of other ways to live, then freedom will be increased, and with it, greater responsibility for what we have been, are, and will become.

Another descendant of psychoanalysis is Erich Fromm, the author of *The Art of Loving*, who I think was influenced by Adler, because Adler stressed (and Freud in the early days did not) the social matrix in which the individual is operating. Fromm says:

> Man has choices. He can devote his life to hoarding or producing; loving or hating; to being or having. Whatever he chooses, he builds a structure, his character, in which certain orientations are dominant, and others necessarily follow.

Fromm, like Sartre, sees that character is the result of the choices we make. What you do when you are dealing with someone's character is to study those choices, and in that way you can understand his character.

Although Carl Rogers, perhaps the outstanding voice of what has been called humanistic psychology, has often been looked upon as practicing a point of view antagonistic to psychoanalysis, he states in his book *Humanistic Conception of Man* that he was very much influenced by the views of the psychoanalysts Freud, Adler, and especially Rank. In discussing man and what man is about, Rogers declares:

My experiences in psychotherapy have led me to have great confidence in the individual for making and implementing sound choices as he becomes more open to his experiences.

Another point Rogers makes:

In choosing what course of action to take in any situation, many people rely upon guiding principles, upon a code of action laid down by some group or institution, upon the judgment of others, upon the way they behaved in some past, similar situation. When I observe the client whose experiences in living have taught me so much, I find that increasingly, such individuals are able to trust the total organismic reaction to a new situation because they discover to an ever increasing degree that when they are open to experiences doing what feels right proves to be a competent and trustworthy guide to behavior that is truly satisfying.

This reminds me very much of a story Theodor Reik once told me about Freud. It is an important story because it indicates that one is capable of making choices on an intuitive, free basis. Reik met Freud in the street one day just at the time Reik was trying to decide whether to get a Ph.D. in psychology or to go to medical school and become a psychiatrist. He asked Freud this very important question: "What should I do?"

Freud replied, "Anything that important, don't think about, do what you feel like doing."

There are times when what you feel like doing may be right. You need experience and practice in permitting yourself to make choices. There are times when trusting your feelings, if you are aware of them, can be a useful way of making a decision.

Okay, so much for the uncovering, feeling therapists. How about the others?

Gestalt therapy is amazing in the impact it has had in the past few years. I knew Fritz Perls for a number of years in New York, when he led a comparatively small group. I believe that if Perls had remained in New York, he would have been just one of a great many psychiatrists, but fortunately he came to California, which is in constant search of gurus, and was hailed as a guru, which had not happened in New York. He had some very good technical things that helped, and many people who were too lazy to study any kind of therapeutic process with any great understanding were able, because of Perl's great technical inventiveness, to pick up a few gimmicks and declare themselves therapists.

I know some Gestaltists who went for one weekend someplace where they heard somebody who had worked with somebody who had worked with somebody who had worked with somebody who had worked with Perls, and therefore they decided their knowledge of some few gimmicks made them therapists. Actually, Perls himself was highly trained, with a knowledge not only of psychoanalysis, but also of existential philosophy and of psychodrama.

What he did so well was combine certain psychodramatic techniques with many psychoanalytic insights. Very often, instead of making an interpretation, which may or may not have an impact, Perls would instead get his patients to act something out. Many of the things he had them act out were actually dramatizations of choices. One of the techniques he used a great deal was the "empty chair" technique, which happens to be taken from Moreno, the father of psychodrama. For example, when a person is torn between the wish to be passive and the wish to be aggressive, Perls might have him sit in one chair and speak as the aggressive part of himself to the passive part of himself. Then he would change chairs and have the passive side talk to the aggressor. In this way, a person could experience both ways of being, and make a choice. Perls felt that in this way he could integrate these different attitudes, but actually very often the people would experience the two modes of being in the world and then choose which one they wanted.

Basically, many of these techniques, like the ones used in encounter groups, come down to two choices. The therapist says to the patient either, "Do what you are doing," or, "Do what you are not doing." If a person complains of being depressed, the Gestaltist might tell him to be more depressed, to experience his depression, or "*be* your depression." That is, have him be what he is. The opposite might be, "Now go around and tell everyone how you hate them." This might be the other side of the depression. When told to do what they are already doing, many people can, for the first time, make the choice not to do it. They cannot make the choice not to do it as long as you tell them to do what they are not doing.

A very common Gestalt or encounter technique, is to ask a person to say "No." You thereby ask him to take responsibility for the "No," to recognize that he is making a choice when he says "No," instead of its just happening. Once people can recognize that they are able to make one choice, they are able to make another kind of choice. This is why it is so important in all the schools to have people see that they choose to do what they are doing. I am not saying that there is always unlimited choice, but there is choice within certain limitations.

Another theory which I feel is related to psychoanalysis, although its author also considers himself an antagonist of analysis, is the Rational-Emotive Therapy of Albert Ellis, whose ideas have a strong resemblance to Adler's and Karen Horney's. The basis of Ellis's theory is that most people have chosen (and he would use the word "chosen," I believe) to make impossible demands on themselves; then, because they cannot fulfill these demands, they consider themselves useless and worthless.

Ellis believes that people make irrational choices. I, on the other hand, believe that if we fully understand the context of their lives, every choice they make seems like a completely rational one. Sometimes they do not have the proper data—as they would not, obviously, when they are three years old. Sometimes they have not thought of other options. But to them it is really not an irrational choice.

I find that Rational-Emotive therapy is a very useful technique in getting where you want to get. If, for example, somebody feels very depressed, before utilizing Rational-Emotive Therapy, which Ellis believes is closer to Behavior Modification than to the Psychoanalytic model, I would ask him first, does he want to get rid of the depression? I will not help him get rid of it unless he wants to, because he has the right to be depressed if he wants to. People have a right to make this choice, and sometimes there are many values to being depressed. Somebody once said to me, "Look, I'm a poor man. All I've got is my troubles, and you're trying to take them away from me."

But if somebody wants to get rid of his depression, and if you know that he is depressed because of a lot of things he is saying to himself, there is a way of helping him get rid of it. That is, help him challenge the nonsense he is telling himself. For example, a person may get depressed because he is rejected. This is common. When you ask him why he is depressed, he will say, "Everybody rejects me. I asked a girl to a dance and she rejected me." Ellis would say, "That's not what depressed you. What depressed you is what you told yourself about that. You said, 'Look how worthless I am, look what shit I am [a favorite word of Ellis, and you cannot practice RET unless you can pronounce "shit" convincingly], look how worthless I am! Even this ugly girl—the only reason I asked her is because I do not feel worthy of anyone else—even she rejected me. You see how useless and unimportant I am.' "

Ellis concentrates on the actual thinking process which translates into the things you are saying to yourself. This is a useful way of dealing with the problem after the person has made the choice. But first, he has to make the choice. One of the most important things is to listen to the person and help him do what he wants to do, not necessarily what the therapist would like him to do.

Moving beyond Ellis and all the others, I want to say that one of the biggest problems we have is the new demands therapists make on people—that they live up to their potential, that they "self-actualize." Why the hell does anybody have to live up to his potential unless he wants to? Yet that is a demand that therapists make on their patients. We say, "You're not living up to your potential. I'm going to make you live up to your potential." Maybe the patient does not want to. Maybe his potential is to be a murderer; you want him to live up to that? So again, it seems to be beyond the therapist's authority to decide what the patient should be, where he should be at, how he should live. No. Our job is to help him do what he wants to do. If you do not like what they want to do, excuse yourself and recommend another therapist who will be able to help them do what they want to do.

Sometimes you may not succeed with a patient, and that may be the most helpful thing you can do for him. In general, it is important (and most experienced therapists would agree) that you try to help people do what they want to. When you go beyond that, you are not playing the role of therapist, but you are, in a sense, taking a moralistic point of view when you decide that you know better than the patient what is good for him.

I am interested in having people become more aware of their choices, so that if somebody wanted to be *more* disturbed than he is (I have never had anyone request that yet), the therapist should be interested in helping them get that way.

One school of thought which seems quite divergent from my point of view is behavior modification. In behavior modification, basically what you try to do is arrange situations in such a way that the desired behavior is effected and rewarded and the nondesired behavior gets a negative reward. In other words, say in treating obesity, you would reward abstention in some way and use some aversive stimulus to eating. One way that has been suggested for treating obesity by behavior modification principles is to tell the patient that he can eat as much as he wants if he does it in the dark, in the toilet. That is an aversive stimulus to most people. Some behavior modifiers have wired electric-shock machines to the refrigerator and the patient gives himself a shock every time he goes to get something to eat. Unfortunately, some people get so addicted to the shock, they eat in order to get it.

Similarly, the therapist has to figure out what is a reward for that person. This is similar to decision therapy, because what I am trying to do is find out what are the consequences, the payoffs, the rewards for the behavior. So that there is a basic agreement that behavior is goal-oriented and that behavior which is rewarded tends to persist and that behavior which is not rewarded tends to be abandoned.

I never use any behavior-modification techniques until the patient and I have first explored the payoffs for the present behavior. I had a dramatic failure which taught me that. A woman asked for treatment for her airplane phobia. I used a technique that is different from the usual one. I asked her to imagine all the terrible things she could think of that could happen—all the catastrophes that would take place if she went flying. She closed her eyes and imagined wheels falling off in take-off, her plane smashing into another plane, the plane catching fire and herself trapped in it—a whole series of unpleasant things like this. The theory behind this is that if you ask a person to keep imagining the most feared things, these terrors lose their capacity to inspire fear. So we went through all that, and at the end of a twenty-five-minute session, she said, "Okay, I'm flying tomorrow." She called up and got a plane ticket!

I saw her a few weeks later, and asked, "How was the flight?"

She told me, "I didn't fly."

I asked, "What happened?"

She said, "I canceled. I couldn't do it."

Then I asked her the question that I should have asked in the first place. "What are the payoffs for not flying, of having this phobia?" The payoffs were quite significant in her case. Both she and her husband were physicians and were extremely busy people. She had very little time to spend with her husband and if she flew it would take only an hour or two and they would not have very much time to talk. If they traveled by train, then they had a long time—two full days—to be together. So that in her case it would have been absurd for her, with her wish for the longer companionship of her husband, to give up this fear.

I have found that in asking about the payoff, discussing that, and then getting the person to decide whether he wants to get rid of his phobia (or other troubles that behavior modification is often used for), I have a much better chance, and a higher percentage of success with the use of behavior modification techniques.

CHAPTER 16

HOW YOU CAN MAKE THIS BOOK PAY OFF FOR YOU

WHEN you finish this book, you can decide to put it away or you can decide to use it for your own further development. Since the goal of therapy is to help a person eventually become his own therapist, I cannot agree with many of my colleagues who look with disdain on self-help books. Certainly I have known many people who have found things they read in books, ranging from the Bible to the collected writings of Sigmund Freud, extremely useful to them in dealing with the problem of living. Secretly, most of our reading is a search for self-understanding or help. Aristotle pointed this out about the Greek tragedies. The greatest literature is that which most completely illuminates the human condition and thereby points the way to living with it.

While I hope that you have already found much of what I've written helpful, I would like to summarize my ideas in a way that others have found useful for themselves.

1) *State your problem as clearly and completely as you can.* Since this is for yourself alone, you can be as open as you wish. You may find it helpful, if you like to be systematic, to write the problems out. It need not be an acute problem or a crisis situation—just something you would like to deal with when you get around to it. This might be the right time; if not, try it when you do have the time and place.

2) *Examine your past decisions which helped create the problem;* the behavior you don't like; the attitude that causes you unhappiness or the inability to get as much satisfaction and pleasure as you would like and believe you can achieve.

3) *List the payoffs for the past decisions which are behind the problem.* They may be actual positive gains or the avoidance of anxiety. But in either case, they are still payoffs.

4) *Answer this question: What was the context in which you made the original decision?* What were the payoffs then and now? (This one is optional, but may be quite helpful.)

5) *Examine alternatives to your past decisions.* It is almost impossible to believe that you have no alternatives.

6) *Choose your alternative and decide to put it into practice.*

Do not confuse a wish with a decision. If you say, "I would like to lose weight," this is very different from a decision to lose weight and to pay the dues—the anxiety, the deprivation, the annoyance of dieting. Also, if you decide to lose weight, remember that this is not a one-time decision. Every time you sit down to eat, every time someone offers you anything to eat, you have to decide all over again whether you want to eat what you know will add to your weight or whether you want to be slim, attractive, and healthy. If you decide for the latter, you might substitute two glasses of cool, pure, refreshing water for the French-fried potatoes or the pie à la mode.

7) *Support yourself in carrying out the new decision.*

Since most of us are quite capable of making good decisions but frequently have difficulty in carrying them out, this is probably the most crucial part of the process—that is, successfully carrying out a decision we have made. It requires a further decision to do just that —to implement our decisions. It also requires the realization that just because we occasionally slip and do not carry it out under certain circumstances, all is not lost. Since most of us are not infallible, we must be able to accept an occasional fall from grace and pick ourselves up and continue on with the decision. Too often, because we fail once in carrying out a decision, we give up completely. This is unnecessary. We can always start again, if we want to.

Also remember, if you do not carry out a decision, but fail with awareness, you may be able to understand things about yourself, your behavior, your attitudes, that you could not before. Any time you choose not to carry out a decision, you may find it helpful to figure out what other decision you are following that is different from the one you thought you had chosen.

By all means, reward yourself liberally for carrying out a decision. For example, since I had to add this chapter after the rest of the book was finished and ready for the printer, I promised myself that I would buy a new suit as soon as I had done it.

Direct action is not the only kind of decision you can

make. You can also decide to alter your mood or your general way of being in the world. If you are convinced that you are a sufferer, you can either choose to continue suffering because of the many payoffs it brings you, or you can choose to *act* cheerful and soon you will probably find you *are* cheerful. As you already know, you may have been sitting home alone, depressed, unhappy, lonely. Suddenly the bell rings and a friend drops in. You do not want to burden your friend with your depression, so you *act* cheerful and pretty soon you *are* cheerful. If all else fails, you can always decide to enjoy your suffering. Remember, you do not have to give up suffering forever. That may be too frightening. But you can *choose* when to suffer and when to be cheerful.

Of course, I do not pretend that this is a cure-all and that everybody who reads this book will immediately become Mr. or Ms. Mental Health. You may need professional help in dealing with some of your problems or in achieving a larger part of your potential. You may find that considering the above seven steps will help you focus more productively on your therapy. In my experience with Decision Therapy, I have found that those who had already been exposed to its principles were able to progress more effectively not only with me, but with other therapists, as well as with many different theoretical persuasions. After a recent workshop, at which I presented the seven steps, many of the people there reported later how they were able to put them to use either by themselves or in collaboration with a therapist.

Decision Therapy, for me, is more than a technical stratagem: It has become a way of life. In my personal relations with myself and others, I have found it a rewarding way of looking at the world; in trying to understand people I meet, in terms of their own reality; in giving them choices, rather than telling them what to do.

Certainly it has had rich rewards in my marriage. Instead of telling Ruth what to do because I believe I know the solution to any problem I may perceive, I try to understand her decisions from her point of view and to explore options rather than come up with answers.

So often, problems faced in the interaction between parents and children are caused by so many parents insisting on their decision rather than exploring options with their sons and daughters. To demand is often to end communication and to make the possibility of mutual understanding and cooperation almost impossible. You may still decide that you want things done your way, but at least you can, if you want to, help your children grow into self-sufficient, creative people by giving them the opportunity to discuss alternatives and by giving them practice in making decisions.

One of the most unfortunate aspects of our entire educational system is how rarely students have the chance to make any choices after nursery school. It is an ironic commentary on our school system that most three-year-olds can make more choices about how to spend their time than graduate students, who often do not have a single elective subject once they embark on a doctoral program. How much more frequently we need to know how to make decisions than how to perform long division, and how much more time is spent on the latter!

One thing is becoming increasingly clear. You cannot

force anyone to learn. He has to decide he wants the information. Once he so decides, it is incredible how much he can learn, with or without schools.

Decision Therapy is, for me, an illuminating way of viewing history, past and present. The behavior of political leaders and even nations can be better comprehended when we stay with the decision process and the payoff for different options. In management, in economics, in military councils, decision-making and its consequences have been carefully studied. It is time to apply it to personal and public life.

I believe that groups that are oppressed are those with the least ability to make decisions about their own lives. Minority groups (women, the poor, and children) all too often are people who have very few options open to them. As they increase the number of opportunities for living by their own decisions rather than the arbitrary dictates of the state, of the community, or of their economic condition, they increase not only their choices but their very humanity. Man is first and foremost a decision-making being.

The kind of society I want to live in is the one which gives its members the greatest number of options and the maximum opportunity to participate in the decision-making process.

"THE BEST DECISION I EVER MADE"

HERE are ten case histories of Decision Therapy in operation.

Decisionmaker: Anne A., 30-year-old housewife. Married three years to a successful, busy attorney.

Problem: Bored and unhappy with her circumscribed life of shopping, cooking, cleaning house, and playing bridge.

Decision: To get out and become involved in life outside the home.

Consequence: Went back to graduate school for an M.A. degree and describes this as "one of the most exciting and enriching experiences" of her life. Now plans to go on for Ph.D. in sociology.

Decisionmaker: Bill B., 68-year-old retired master carpenter. Married thirty-five years.

Problem: Depressed, little enjoyment in living.

Decision: To enjoy life, have fun.

Consequence: Started to have sex regularly with his wife for the first time in six years. Went on camping trips, bought plot in the woods, and started to build a country home. Embarked on extensive reading program and frequently attends theatre, concerts and dance recitals.

Decisionmaker: Charlotte C., 29-year-old unmarried librarian.

Problem: Felt isolated and alone; attracted to women and fearful of becoming a lesbian.

Decision: To stop thinking about women.

Consequence: Within six months, she started to have heterosexual fantasies. Within one year, she started to date men. Two years later she established a permanent relationship with a man her age.

Decisionmaker: Dan D., 45-year-old physician. Married to his second wife for one year.

Problem: Got along badly with new wife. Felt she would never do what he knew was best, which led to many quarrels and bitterness.

Decision: To stop trying to control his wife, and to approach her instead as follows: "We have a problem. How do you think we can solve it?"

Consequence: Marriage improved almost immediately. Six months later, they rarely quarreled and were closer than they had ever been before.

Decisionmaker: Ernst E., 32-year-old executive working in his family's business.

Problem: Bored with business. Felt inadequate, constantly worried whether he could make it on his own if he had to.

Decision: To leave family business and start his own company.

Consequence: Failed in his first independent business venture. Made a new decision that business was not for him and instead enrolled in a school of social work. Became executive in a social work agency and feels he has found exciting, challenging professional life.

Decisionmaker: Sonia S., 28-year-old teacher living at home with parents.

Problem: Only went out with parents. Found herself arguing frequently with them over minor details. Envious of other women who lived independent lives.

Decision: To move out of parental home and get her own apartment.

Consequence: Suffered from loneliness for several months, then became active in religious and political organizations. Developed circle of friends with similar interests. Visits parents at least once a week and finds them interesting companions. Is going out regularly with a man. Object: matrimony.

Decisionmaker: George G., a 38-year-old successful executive. Married with four children.

Problem: Severe migraine headaches two or three times weekly for 20 years. No apparent physical cause. Went to see an eminent neurologist. Got into heavy political argument with him.

Decision: "I'm not going to have any more headaches and have to go to an idiot like this."

Consequence: Headaches tapered off, then stopped. Three years later, he states he is still headache-free.

Decisionmaker: Helen H., aged 50, married 30 years to a professional man, three children.

Problem: Discovered husband had been having an affair for five years with a 25-year-old nurse. Felt abandoned and despairing.

Decision: That she could leave her husband and did not need him for her existence. However, she decided to stay and try to work out the marriage with freedom for each to have other relationships if they so desired.

Consequence: Three years later, Helen and her husband agree that their marriage is now at a better level than it ever had been in the previous thirty years.

Decisionmaker: Irene I., aged 34, accountant, married to a businessman 20 years her senior.

Problem: Constant feeling that her husband was interested only in business and kept her around as a "convenience." Frequently surly and disgruntled.

Decision: To act cheerful, and to "kill him with kindness."

Consequence: He pays more attention to her. Even when he doesn't, she now feels convinced that she is a person in her own right; so while she enjoys his attentions when they are available, she has decided not to suffer and to carry on with her own interests when he is busy.

Decisionmaker: Jack J., 36-year-old school principal. Married, with two children.

Problem: Great difficulty in completing written reports. Frequent conflicts with teachers and students as well as with his wife and children.

Decision: Decided to stop trying to do everything *perfectly,* and work as best he could instead. Also decided to stop demanding perfection from others.

Consequence: His work slowly improved. He found he could cut in half the time it formerly took him to complete any project. Things at school improved when he made fewer demands on teachers and students. They also improved at home because he made fewer perfectionist demands on his wife and children.

INDEX